INNOVATIONS IN LITERACY PROFESSIONAL LEARNING

Also from the Editors

Empowering Struggling Readers:
Practices for the Middle Grades
Leigh A. Hall, Leslie D. Burns,
and Elizabeth Carr Edwards

Multicultural and Multilingual Literacy
and Language: Contexts and Practices
Edited by Fenice B. Boyd, Cynthia H. Brock,
and Mary S. Rozendal

Talk That Teaches: Using Strategic Talk
to Help Students Achieve the Common Core
Jeanne R. Paratore and Dana A. Robertson

Innovations in Literacy Professional Learning

Strengthening Equity, Access, and Sustainability

edited by

Dana A. Robertson
Leigh A. Hall
Cynthia H. Brock

THE GUILFORD PRESS
New York London

Copyright © 2023 The Guilford Press
A Division of Guilford Publications, Inc.
370 Seventh Avenue, Suite 1200, New York, NY 10001
www.guilford.com

All rights reserved

No part of this book may be reproduced, translated, stored in a retrieval system, or transmitted, in any form or by any means, electronic, mechanical, photocopying, microfilming, recording, or otherwise, without written permission from the publisher.

Printed in the United States of America

This book is printed on acid-free paper.

Last digit is print number: 9 8 7 6 5 4 3 2 1

Library of Congress Cataloging-in-Publication Data is available from the publisher.

ISBN 978-1-4625-5129-3 (paperback)
ISBN 978-1-4625-5130-9 (hardcover)

About the Editors

Dana A. Robertson, EdD, is Associate Professor of Reading and Literacy in the School of Education at Virginia Tech. He is a former elementary classroom teacher, literacy specialist, and literacy coach, and conducts research focused on classroom discourse, reading and writing challenges, and literacy professional learning and whole-school literacy improvement. Prior to coming to Virginia Tech, Dr. Robertson was Executive Director of the Literacy Research Center and Clinic at the University of Wyoming. He was named an Emerging Scholar by the Reading Hall of Fame, is a frequent presenter at national and international conferences, was a collaborating author on the International Literacy Association's *Standards for the Preparation of Literacy Professionals* (2017), and serves as a board member-at-large for the International Literacy Association. His work has appeared in many journals and books of educational practice and research.

Leigh A. Hall, PhD, is Director of Research at Merlyn Mind in Fort Collins, Colorado, where she focuses on understanding and improving K–12 educators' experiences with AI technology in their classrooms. Previously, she was a Professor at the University of Wyoming, where she held the Wyoming Excellence in Higher Education Endowed Chair in Literacy Education. During her time in Wyoming, she focused on how teachers can work with diverse learners to improve their literacy instruction, and the role that technology can play in enhancing and supporting that instruction. Dr. Hall is a recipient of the Outstanding Dissertation Award from the International Literacy Association and the Early Career Achievement Award and Edward B. Fry Book Award from the Literacy

Research Association. She has published in leading journals of literacy research and practice.

Cynthia H. Brock, PhD, is Professor at the University of Wyoming, where she holds the Wyoming Excellence in Higher Education Endowed Chair in Literacy Education. Her scholarly research agenda centers on the study of opportunities for learning. Dr. Brock explores the literacy learning opportunities of elementary children from diverse cultural, linguistic, and economic backgrounds; she also explores ways to work with pre- and inservice teachers and administrators to foster children's literacy learning opportunities. She has conducted qualitative research in cross-cultural contexts, including in the United States, Australia, England, Fiji, Thailand, Laos, Spain, Chile, and Costa Rica.

Contributors

Heather H. Aiken, PhD, Frank Porter Graham Child Development Institute, The University of North Carolina at Chapel Hill, Chapel Hill, North Carolina

Steven J. Amendum, PhD, School of Education, University of Delaware, Newark, Delaware

Leslie M. Babinski, PhD, Center for Child and Family Policy, Sanford School of Public Policy, Duke University, Durham, North Carolina

Alexis Barney, MS, NBCT, Tongue River Elementary School, Ranchester, Wyoming

Rita M. Bean, PhD, School of Education (Emerita), University of Pittsburgh, Pittsburgh, Pennsylvania

Mary Bratsch-Hines, PhD, Lastinger Center, University of Florida, Gainesville, Florida

Cynthia H. Brock, PhD, Department of Elementary and Early Childhood Education, University of Wyoming, Laramie, Wyoming

Noelle Clark, MS, NBCT, Evansville Elementary School, Casper, Wyoming

Gayle Cribb, MA, Department of Literacy, WestEd, San Francisco, California

Cynthia Greenleaf, PhD, Department of Reading Apprenticeship/Literacy, WestEd, San Francisco, California

Leigh A. Hall, PhD, Merlyn Mind, Fort Collins, Colorado

Pauline Harris, EdD, Early Childhood Education Research, Education Futures, University of South Australia, Adelaide, Australia

Robert Herrera, PhD, Superintendent (retired), Farmington (Michigan) public schools, and Western Michigan University, Kalamazoo, Michigan

Jacy Ippolito, EdD, School of Education, Salem State University, Salem, Massachusetts

Mira-Lisa Katz, PhD, Department of Learning and Technology, WestEd, San Francisco, California

Rachel Knecht, BA, doctoral student, College of Education and Human Development, University of Nevada, Reno, Reno, Nevada

Deidre M. Le Fevre, PhD, Faculty of Education and Social Work, University of Auckland, Auckland, New Zealand

Sarah M. Lupo, PhD, Department of Middle, Secondary, and Math Education, James Madison University, Harrisonburg, Virginia

Jeff Makelky, MA, Principal, Big Piney High School, Big Piney, Wyoming

Lauren Breckenridge Padesky, PhD, Indiana Institute on Disability and Community, Indiana University Bloomington, Bloomington, Indiana

Susan V. Piazza, EdD, Department of Teaching, Learning, and Educational Studies, Western Michigan University, Kalamazoo, Michigan

Jennifer Sharples Reichenberg, PhD, Department of Elementary Education, Literacy, and Educational Leadership, State University of New York, Buffalo State College, Buffalo, New York

Dana A. Robertson, EdD, School of Education, Virginia Tech, Blacksburg, Virginia

Kristine Sacha, MA, Akron Public Schools, Akron, Ohio

Erin E. Silcox, MA, Department of Curriculum and Instruction, University of Wyoming, Laramie, Wyoming

Mary Stump, MA, Department of Reading Apprenticeship, WestEd, San Francisco, California

Sarah Summy, EdD, Department of Special Education and Literacy Studies, Western Michigan University, Kalamazoo, Michigan

Dianna R. Townsend, EdD, Department of Literacy Studies, University of Nevada, Reno, Reno, Nevada

Contents

This book's companion website (*www.guilford.com/robertson-materials*) provides links to videos created by the authors about their chapter topics. The videos can also be accessed via QR codes at the beginning of each chapter.

INTRODUCTION

Innovation, Equity, and Sustainability in Literacy Professional Learning

Dana A. Robertson and Cynthia H. Brock

Historically, teacher professional development involved short-term staff development workshops or initiatives provided to school districts. These workshops were often evaluated by teachers' satisfaction with content and a report on what teachers learned. That is, evaluation typically asked teachers whether they perceived the workshops to be worthwhile. As well, these professional development offerings were often disconnected from teachers' classroom contexts and lacked sufficient duration to achieve meaningful changes to instruction or student achievement (Martin et al., 2014).

Over the past several decades, many larger-scale reform efforts have moved rapidly across educational contexts to improve teachers' literacy instructional practices and, ultimately, increase student learning (Woulfin & Rigby, 2017). Tied to accountability measures, these efforts included ongoing job-embedded professional development in which teachers were often mandated to participate. For example, No Child Left Behind (2002) used literacy coaches to promote excellence and equity for all students, yet the imposed training and prescribed curricula that went along with the coaching often translated into teaching improvement being about compliance to improve test scores (Hargreaves, 2014). This focus on prescribed curriculum and test scores had two unintended consequences. First, teachers were often not afforded the respect they deserved as professionals, who are central in promoting student learning. Second, the overemphasis on raising test scores led to an increasingly narrow curriculum to teach tested skills, especially for students from underserved communities (Hargreaves, 2014).

More recently, the American Recovery and Reinvestment Act (2009), with its Race to the Top initiative, called again for job-embedded professional development built on coaching and collaboration among educators. The Race to the Top initiative was focused on developing more rigorous learning standards and better assessments, while also supporting teachers and school leaders to become more effective and providing increased emphasis on turning around the lowest-performing schools. With this accountability-focused reform, however, the competitive stance of linking achievement levels to funding opportunities as schools "raced to the top" again led to inequities in high-quality learning opportunities being accessible to different communities across the country (McNeil, 2010; Ravitch, 2013). As McNeil (2010) wrote, "the Race to the Top program, declaring that a reliance on competitive funding and hand-picking winners means the majority of low-income and minority kids, who may reside in the losing states, will not benefit from additional federal funds" (n.p.).

These mandated professional development reforms, while being longer in duration and providing greater opportunities for ongoing support and coaching than previous staff developments, still did not address the contextualized needs of teachers or their students across the diverse landscape of schools (Martin et al., 2014). National and state assessments continue to show that a large number of students across grades fall below proficiency expectations for reading. From 1992 to 2019, reading results from the National Assessment of Educational Progress (NAEP) increased by only 4 points for fourth graders and 3 points for eighth graders. Further, the percentages of students at or above proficiency levels actually dropped between 2017 and 2019; the disaggregated results for students from underserved populations are even less promising (National Center for Education Statistics, 2019). These findings suggest that professional development innovations that value test scores over teachers or that call for imposed trainings, prescribed curricula, more rigorous learning standards, and increased testing as drivers of the professional learning (PL) have been largely inconsequential in providing ongoing, equitable access to high-quality teaching and learning opportunities for *all* teachers and students that sustainably improve literacy learning (Ravitch, 2013).

So, what are teachers and school leaders to do? This edited volume of literacy PL experiences is framed around the idea that meeting the challenge of implementing high-quality literacy instruction and meaningfully improving students' literacy learning requires teachers' PL opportunities that begin with teachers over test scores. Such PL builds capacity and cultures of learning in educational contexts through centering teachers' reflexive growth-in-practice (Archer, 2012; Lieberman & Miller, 2014), both individually and collectively, while also positioning social networks and collaborations that serve to provide equitable and sustained access to continued teacher growth. Such experiences not only foreground high-quality literacy instructional practices, but they also address ways that (1) teachers learn those innovative practices and (2) teacher learning can be enacted in classrooms to become part of the teacher's instructional repertoire (Dillon et al., 2011).

What Are the Essential Ingredients of PL?

Scholarship over the last 20 years has identified essential features that must be included in PL initiatives to meaningfully change teachers' instructional practices in ways that positively improve student learning (Darling-Hammond et al., 2009; Dillon et al., 2011; Gersten et al., 2010; Yoon et al., 2007).

1. Professional development should foster both teachers' content knowledge and their pedagogical content knowledge in ways that inform understanding of subject matter.
2. Professional development activities and content should be situated in and aligned with teachers' curricular and learning goals, as well as those of the school and district.
3. Professional development should prompt teachers to actively engage with academic content, pedagogy, and to collect and evaluate evidence of student learning over the long term (often 20+ hours; e.g., Desimone & Stuckey, 2014; Yoon et al., 2007).
4. Professional development should establish structures that promote teacher collaboration in their learning through productive and interactive learning communities and networks among educators.

Still, incorporating these features has not proven to be a surefire checklist for improved outcomes. The large-scale studies used to establish the aforementioned evidence-based practices, especially those with randomized populations, generally examine the average effects of a particular intervention (Bryk, 2015). These research findings are important for telling us, as members of an educational field, that particular professional development interventions are "likely" to work for the populations on which they are normed. However, they are not designed to tell us what it will take to make interventions work for varied subgroups of students and teachers across differing school contexts (Kaplan et al., 2020). Moreover, knowing "that" something is likely to work does not help us to understand "how" and "why" it may (or may not) work. The "how" and "why" matter when considering the equitable and sustainable implementation of innovative practices in unique contexts.

Building on these ideas of teachers actively engaging and collaborating in long-term opportunities, the term *professional learning* has gained in popularity over *professional development* to highlight the importance of teachers and their learning processes (Lieberman & Miller, 2014; Swan Dagen & Bean, 2014). As Lieberman and Miller (2014) write, teachers get "better at their craft by engaging in 'steady work' that is inclusive, broad based, and grounded in the day-to-day realities of school life" (p. 8). This "growth-in-practice model" (p. 8) further delineates focal points that set PL apart from other prescribed training or development initiatives. These focal points include:

- An ongoing inquiry-focused approach that promotes meaningful engagement with content and colleagues in reflective and critical ways.
- Knowledge creation through these inquiries rather than transmission of prescribed curriculum.
- A network or partnership of both inside teacher expertise and outside expertise.
- A focus on specific vexing problems teachers encounter with their students that also values teachers' experiences and knowledge (Lieberman & Miller, 2014).

Transformation of instruction that promotes student literacy learning occurs as teachers and school leaders go deep into what it means for students to develop literacy competencies and the types of instructional practices that foster such competencies. As this description of PL suggests, improving teachers' knowledge and practice so that they can deliver high-quality teaching responsive to students' differentiated literacy needs, as well as their broader educational and social-emotional needs, matters (Darling-Hammond et al., 2020).

If We Know So Much, What Gets in the Way of Meaningful and Sustained PL?

Whereas there are many examples of evidence for the potential of PL to increase teachers' knowledge, change literacy practices, and improve students' learning, there are also many examples of reports that such outcomes are not realized (Dillon et al., 2011; Timperley et al., 2007; Yoon et al., 2007). For example, although professional learning communities (PLCs) have taken hold in schools as one approach to situated and collaborative PL (Vescio et al., 2008), educators and organizations have struggled to enact these collaborative approaches in sustainable, efficient, and effective ways that meaningfully foster student learning (Bryk, 2015). Relatedly, literacy coaching has shown positive effects on teacher learning and student outcomes (Biancarosa et al., 2010; Sailors & Price, 2015), yet it has been difficult to bring instructional coaching in general to scale to realize equitable and sustainable gains (Kraft et al., 2018). Again, there are numerous examples of only mixed outcomes (Sailors et al., 2017).

Considering Teacher Quality

Research evidence in education and economics over the past several decades makes clear that improving teachers' knowledge and instruction in ways that facilitate high-quality, responsive teaching is the most important contributor to students' learning. Put simply, schools with effective teachers produce better learning situations for students (Dillon et al., 2011; Hargreaves, 2014; Taylor et al., 2003). Yet, engaging in PL opportunities that have meaningfully improved teachers' knowledge and instruction has not always been fruitful. McChesney and Aldridge (2021) describe three teacher-level acceptance and implementation barriers that reflect contextual influences above and beyond the design and enactment of PL opportunities: cognitive access, contextual fit, and teacher agency.

Teachers must have *cognitive access* to the new content. PL affects teachers differently depending on their previous knowledge and experiences (Desimone & Stuckey, 2014). Teachers and their students bring diverse social, linguistic, and cultural values to the classroom, and schools are steeped in institutionalized histories of how to "do school." Therefore, when considering the design and structure of PL, PL opportunities must be uniquely tailored and co-constructed with teachers across a range of different backgrounds, knowledge bases, and pedagogical expertise. PL occurs *with* teachers, not *to* them. Further, new practices and content are often met with implementation dips—those temporary struggles with enactment as teachers try out new ideas and adapt their implementation. As Sarason (1982) aptly wrote more than 40 years ago: "Any attempt to change regularities in the classroom places the teacher in an unlearning and learning process, a fact that has obvious implications for the time perspective of those seeking change" (p. 286).

Teachers must also see the *contextual fit* to the new content. Strong buy-in by teachers facilitates their chances of sustaining new instructional practices. At the same time, though, teachers need to see the value in these new practices for themselves and their students to invest the effort into meaningful PL (Desimone & Stuckey, 2014). Important questions must be addressed. For example, how do new literacy content and instructional practices cohere with teachers' needs in their classrooms, as well as their school and district curriculum and values? How does the PL help teachers address the specific needs (academically, emotionally, socially, linguistically, culturally, and more) of their students?

Teachers must have *agency* in the PL process. Teachers are the most important agents directly shaping the learning conditions for their students (Desimone & Stuckey, 2014; Li & Ruppar, 2021). Yet when teachers have real, context-based dilemmas, the stakes are high for them to take risks, be committed, and take ownership of new instructional innovations. PL opportunities should prepare teachers to respond to these dilemmas in their everyday contexts strategically, which requires that they have a depth of knowledge and long-term commitment to innovate and inquire to cultivate more inclusive learning opportunities for all students. Thus, improving teacher quality includes attention to cognitive access, contextual fit, and agency (McChesney & Aldridge, 2021). Moreover, improving teacher quality is an issue of equity in our schools (Hanushek, 2016).

Considering Networks and Communities

Whereas individual teachers matter greatly, the social capital of the school matters more (Hargreaves, 2014; Leanna & Pil, 2006). Strong collective social capital—the trust, collaboration, and collective agency of teachers working toward common goals—is more important in predicting sustained student achievement than the work of individual teachers alone (Leana & Pil, 2006). Further, strong social capital raises the individual human capital of teachers (Bridwell-Mitchell, 2015; Robertson et al., 2019), together conceptualized as the school's *professional capital* (Hargreaves, 2014), which means that PL is dependent not only on what happens in individual classrooms, but rather on the broader context of the school and beyond (Dillon et al., 2011).

As Hargreaves (2014) writes, high-quality schools across the globe "invest in, accumulate, and circulate the professional capital of their teachers in order to generate strong returns in teaching and learning" (p. xii). Schools have addressed the need for increased collaboration and reflection in two ways: through (1) PLCs—ongoing groups of teachers who meet regularly for the purpose of increasing their own knowledge and that of their students (Lieberman & Miller, 2014; Vescio et al., 2008); and (2) coaching collaborations (Swan-Dagen & Bean, 2014). These small social networks connect educators within a school or district and provide space for them to talk honestly, inquire critically, increase their knowledge and instructional repertoire, and assume mutual responsibility for literacy teaching and learning and the success and learning of their students.

Whereas the idea of collaboration is critical to teachers' broader impact, meaningful opportunities for teachers to engage in reflective conversations around important dilemmas and questions in their classrooms remain rare (Hunt, 2016; Servage, 2006/2007). Many times, PLCs are enacted in schools to solely serve the interests of externally imposed mandates rather than distributing teaching expertise horizontally through the school (Kennedy, 2014). Similarly, coaching initiatives can be used to support teacher autonomy and foster professional decision making about the instructional approaches students need or as a powerful means of socializing teachers toward conformity to teach particular programs or practices with fidelity (Robertson et al., 2020).

Moreover, not all teachers in all school contexts have equitable access to the same resources and PL opportunities. High-quality, ongoing learning opportunities co-constructed in person can be resource-prohibitive (Snell et al., 2019). Resources, such as funding, technology, or the amount and types of personnel a school can employ, are almost always tied to the economic status of the community in which the district is located. In addition, these resources are often temporary or targeted toward particular groups of students or narrow educational goals (Hargreaves, 2014). These scenarios leave resources uneven in their application within and across schools, leading to inequities for teachers and their students and communities.

Opportunities afforded by digital technologies, which have grown exponentially over the last decade, help bridge these inequities. Digital tools can connect teachers through social networks (e.g., other teachers, coaches, community members, and other external experts) within a building and beyond, giving them flexible access to collaboration with colleagues and instructional practices that are not readily available in their immediate context (Leighton et al., 2018; Main & Slater, 2022; Snell et al., 2019). Further, digital tools also provide a "footprint" to anchor teachers in sustaining practice over time through video-recorded instruction and websites that catalogue instructional resources and can be revisited for deeper exploration (van der Linden et al., 2021).

As previously described, agency, both individually and collectively, is consequential in accepting, implementing, and sustaining instructional innovations and PL (Li & Ruppar, 2021; McChesney & Aldridge, 2021). To realize the potential for teachers to exercise individual and collective agency, PL networks and collaborations within schools and across schools in districts need to balance three mechanisms that can foster or stall professional growth (Bridwell-Mitchell, 2015). Bridwell-Mitchell explains that:

1. Teachers and school leaders need to balance opportunities for *innovation and socialization*. PL structures should provide ample opportunity for teachers to explore innovations, while also bringing them together to exert supportive socialization pressure to generate, share, and use innovative instructional practices.

2. A balance of *cohesion and diversity of thought* must be involved in collaborative interactions. Bridwell-Mitchell found that teacher learning was associated with social interactions that occur within and across communities with a high level of cohesion and also a "tipping proportion" (p. 153) of interactions that express diverse attitudes and approaches. Teachers are less likely to grow in an ongoing fashion when they all hold the same attitudes and share the same approaches to problems of practice.

3. There needs to be a balance in *divergence and convergence* that characterizes teachers' shared understandings. That is, they need to come together about goals and approaches, while also encouraging critical questions and new ways of thinking. As teachers and school leaders are collaboratively innovating and circulating diverse ideas within a cohesive approach, it is the merging of understanding that brings individuals into the collective. Moreover, it is the multiple perspectives they can bring to their conversations that prompt them to question practices and consider new approaches.

PL as Innovative, Equitable, and Sustainable

PL is a journey, not a single event, and it is based on the complex interactions of teachers and school leaders within schools within districts within communities and onward and onward (Opfer & Pedder, 2011). Teachers need *cognitive access*, *contextual fit*, and *agency* to engage with and take up new knowledge and practices in ways that meaningfully address their classroom dilemmas. Teachers and schools need a collective agency that balances *innovation and socialization*, *cohesion and diversity of thought*, and *convergence and divergence of understanding* so that the school (and community) collective grows in its understanding of literacy development, teaching, and learning, and develops the capacity for continuous improvement. In these reciprocal interactions to co-construct understandings of teaching, teachers are not undermined by teacher-proof curricular materials, predetermined "best practices" that are strictly adhered to, or professional preparation that is blindly followed in an attempt to guarantee fidelity. Rather, teachers are seen as "professionals, innovators, and leaders in the complexity of classroom teaching" (Hoffman et al., 2016, p. 23), and they are trusted to use their knowledge to stand up for their professional convictions about what is best for their students (Paris & Lung, 2008).

For PL to be innovative, equitable, ***and*** sustainable, we argue for an approach that focuses on teachers' reflexive "growth-in-practice" in and through social networks and collaborations (Archer, 2012; Lieberman & Miller, 2014). This approach must be:

- *Innovative* in that the PL not only provides new instructional approaches, but also leverages collaborations, new modes, and tools to access this knowledge in ways that build teachers' adaptive expertise to make decisions and implement instructional practices in ways that advance the literacy learning needs of all students.

- *Equitable* in that the PL focuses on *all* students and *all* teachers in responsive and differentiated ways, valuing and privileging their unique identities, experiences, and funds of knowledge (Gay, 2013; Moll et al., 1992). It is customizable to how people have access to the PL (i.e., digitally, in person, hybrid) and to how individuals are supported in their work to understand the new approaches within their current realities.

- *Sustainable* in that the PL develops teachers' decision-making powers in ways that allow them to adapt and transfer new instructional approaches to more students, and empower them to build professional capital through their sharing and inquiring in their social networks. Innovations that help teachers solve their instructional dilemmas become part of their teaching toolkit with long-term commitment. Cultures of continuous PL improvement occur when learning processes and structures are (1) valued by educators and administrators, (2) are accessible, and (3) create opportunities for teachers to be viewed and treated as professionals.

Overview of the Book

Although teaching as a profession is not new, the context wherein teaching occurs continues to be layered with greater and greater knowledge demands. Whereas there is a general understanding of the features of effective PL, enacting these features in ways that meaningfully shift literacy teaching and learning is more elusive. This book does not intend to provide silver bullet solutions to vexing and complex problems of practice. Rather, the contributing authors provide snapshots of ways that schools, educators, communities, and researchers have grappled with the complexities of helping teachers develop innovative, equitable, and sustained expertise to foster student literacy learning.

In this edited volume, we present chapters that illustrate how literacy-focused PL collaborators have employed innovative ways, whether through digital technologies or other means, to understand and enact high-quality PL opportunities. Chapter authors explore how the unique PL contexts in which they work align to key principles of effective PL. They also illustrate innovative ways their approaches create access to high-quality teacher learning that ensures equity and sustainability with respect to the enactment of PL and its intended outcomes. The chapters in Part I focus on PL as reflexive growth-in-practice. The chapters in Part II foreground PL in/through/with social networks and communities.

Part I: Professional Learning as Reflexive Growth-in-Practice

The six chapters in the first section of this edited volume all have in common the notion that high-quality professional learning is best enacted through reflexive growth-in-practice. Drawing on the work of Archer (2012), we define *reflexivity* as the exercise of considering ourselves in relation to our social contexts, and vice versa, considering our social contexts in relation to ourselves. In fact, Archer (2012) argues that it is incumbent on individuals in social groups (including, but not limited to, classrooms, schools, and districts) to engage in such reflexivity if social groups are to function meaningfully and effectively. By *growth-in-practice*, we mean that thoughtful reflexivity in our day-to-day work in classrooms, schools, districts, and beyond, can improve our teaching and, subsequently, our students' learning (Lieberman & Miller, 2014).

Chapters 1 and 2 focus on context-embedded professional learning initiatives developed to address the unique needs of specific contexts. In Chapter 1, Le Fevre writes about a 5-year research and professional learning in literacy development project designed to develop the capability of professional learning facilitators of literacy in elementary and high schools across New Zealand. Le Fevre's professional learning work is situated in scholarship on adaptive expertise, which she describes as a way of working in complex environments that focus on developing deep conceptual knowledge and skills while simultaneously attending to the role of emotion and developing an evaluative inquiry stance. Chapter 2 portrays a much smaller context—that of one high school in the rural western United States—whereby Brock and her colleagues collaborated with the administrators and teachers at the high school to co-construct a unique, innovative hybrid approach to professional learning. This collaborative professional learning project was aimed at addressing a concern at the school—how to improve the students' engagement with informational text.

The next two chapters in this section explore how two different models designed to foster literacy learning were reflexively enacted in two unique contexts. In Chapter 3, Greenleaf and her colleagues write about the Reading Apprenticeship Model, which immerses teachers in experiential learning through literacy inquiry and practices that they integrate into their subject-area teaching. Following the professional learning journey of one high school history teacher, Gayle, in a small district in northern California, Greenleaf and her colleagues illustrate how Gayle enacted Reading Apprenticeship, participated in the project's inquiry networks, and led schoolwide literacy reform. In Chapter 4, Lupo and her colleagues explore the vexing problem of helping all high school students read complex texts in English classrooms. Using the Quad Text Set (QTS) framework, the authors shared how one high school English teacher, Hannah, in an urban high school with a multilingual population of students who speak 47 different languages, used the Quad Text Set framework to support her secondary students' comprehension in culturally sustaining ways. Hannah's story serves as an example of how designing and using QTSs across secondary content areas can afford teachers the opportunity to build that essential professional knowledge around reading comprehension and prompt important reflections and pedagogical planning related to culturally sustaining pedagogy (Alim & Paris, 2017).

The final two chapters in this section focus on reflexive practices around literacy coaching. In Chapter 5, Amendum and his colleagues describe the Targeted Reading Instruction (TRI) coaching model, which can be used to simultaneously help build classroom teachers' knowledge and capacity to change pedagogy. Amendum and his colleagues' work demonstrates how the TRI coaching model has demonstrated efficacy for both teachers and students across a variety of contexts, including urban, suburban, and rural Title I schools. This chapter also describes the enactment of a literacy coaching model. In Chapter 6, Reichenberg uses the story of Patrick, a teacher of English learners in an urban high school, to illustrate the efficacy of a powerful seven-step reflective coaching framework, PD-CASE-R. This model can be used to promote teachers' agency context-informed decision making as instructors.

Part II: Professional Learning in/through/with Social Networks and Communities

The chapters in the second section of this edited volume foreground the role of social networks and communities in co-constructing PL opportunities in classrooms, schools, and/or districts. Chapters 7 and 8 focus on face-to-face networked communities across schools; Chapter 9 provides an example of a hybrid (part online and part face-to-face) community in one school/university partnership; and the final two chapters in this section, Chapters 10 and 11, describe virtual networked learning communities.

In Chapter 7, Harris describes a unique, networked, face-to-face PL initiative enacted in four hubs across the state of South Australia. Harris's collaborative PL initiative was designed to support young Aboriginal children as readers. In Chapter 8, which is about another face-to-face, innovative, community-based, PL initiative—this time situated in Michigan—Piazza and her colleagues describe an 18-month PL partnership between a Midwestern university and three rural schools. The authors' in-depth description of their design-based research project provides a window into ways that PL collaboratives may increase equity and literacy learning in underserved communities.

In Chapter 9, relying heavily on Eagle Elementary School's existing digital infrastructure, Padesky and colleagues describe how they used digital tools to bridge face-to-face coaching divides between university-based literacy coaches and elementary educators. The school where coauthors Alexis and Noelle work is about 150 miles from the university where coauthors Lauren and Dana worked. In Chapter 10, also focused on literacy coaching and based on a study of elementary virtual coaching in Florida, Massachusetts, Ohio, and Pennsylvania, Ippolito and colleagues discuss the promises and challenges of virtual coaching for creating equitable PL experiences and outcomes for teachers. Shifting from virtual coaching to online professional learning in the form of micro-courses, in Chapter 11, Hall describes the benefits and complexities of the online professional experience she developed for middle and high school teachers to improve their knowledge of literacy instruction.

Finally, in the Epilogue, Hall looks back across the entire book, synthesizes key themes that cut across the chapters, and discusses possible next steps for us, as a field, as we promote and engage in the work of ongoing literacy PL.

At the beginning of each chapter, a QR code gives readers access to a short video from the authors related to their chapter topics. These videos can also be accessed through this book's companion website at *www.guilford.com/robertson-materials.*

REFERENCES

Alim, H. A., & Paris, D. (2017). What is culturally sustaining pedagogy and why does it matter? In D. Paris & H. S. Alim (Eds.), *Culturally sustaining pedagogies: Teaching and learning for justice in a changing world* (pp. 1–20). Teachers College Press.

American Recovery and Reinvestment Act of 2009, P.L. 111-5,42 U. S. C. § 15801 (2009).

Archer, M. (2012). *The reflexive imperative in late modernity.* Cambridge University Press.

Biancarosa, G., Bryk, A., & Dexter, E. (2010). Assessing the value-added effects of literacy collaborative professional development on student achievement. *Elementary School Journal, 111*, 7–34.

Bridwell-Mitchell, E. N. (2015). Theorizing teacher agency and reform: How institutionalized instructional practices change and persist. *Sociology of Education, 88*(2), 140–159.

Bryk, A. S. (2015). 2014 AERA Distinguished Lecture: Accelerating how we learn to improve. *Educational Researcher, 44*(9), 467–477.

Darling-Hammond, L., Flook, L., Cook-Harvey, C., Barron, B., & Osher, D. (2020). Implications for educational practice of the science of learning and development. *Applied Developmental Science, 24*, 97–140.

Darling-Hammond, L., Wei, R., Andree, A., Richardson, N., & Orphanos, S. (2009). *Professional learning in the learning profession: A status report on teacher development in the United States and abroad*. National Staff Development Council.

Desimone, L. M., & Stuckey, D. (2014). Sustaining teacher professional development. In L. E. Martin, S. Kragler, D. J. Quatroche, & K. L. Bauserman (Eds.), *Handbook of professional development in education: Successful models and practices, PreK–2* (pp. 467–482). Guilford Press.

Dillon, D. R., O'Brien, D. G., Sato, M., & Kelly, C. M. (2011). Professional development and teacher education for reading instruction. In M. L. Kamil, P. D. Pearson, E. B. Moje, & P. P. Afflerbach (Eds.), *Handbook of reading research* (Vol. 4, pp. 627–660). Routledge.

Gay, G. (2013). Teaching to and through cultural diversity. *Curriculum Inquiry, 43*(1), 48–70.

Gersten, R., Dimino, J., Jayanthi, M., Kim, J. S., & Santoro, L. E. (2010). Teacher study group: Impact of the professional development model on reading instruction and student outcomes in first-grade classrooms. *American Educational Research Journal, 47*(3), 694–739.

Hanushek, E. A. (2016). What matters for student achievement. *Education Next, 16*(2), 22–30. Retrieved from *www.educationnext.org/what-matters-for-student-achievement.*

Hargreaves, A. (2014). Forward: Six sources of change in professional development. In L. E. Martin, S. Kragler, D. J. Quatroche, & K. L Bauserman (Eds.), *Handbook of professional development in education: Successful models and practices, PreK–12* (pp. x–xix). Guilford Press.

Hoffman, J. V., Martinez, R. A., & Danielson, K. (2016). Emerging reading and the social practice turn in literacy: Still becoming a nation of readers. *Journal of Education, 196*, 19–26.

Hunt, C. S. (2016). Getting to the heart of the matter: Discursive negotiations of emotions within literacy coaching interactions. *Teaching and Teacher Education, 60*, 331–343.

Kaplan, A., Cromley, J., Perez, T., Dai, T., Mara, K., & Balsai, M. (2020). The role of context in educational RCT findings: A call to redefine "evidence-based practice." *Educational Researcher, 49*, 285–288.

Kennedy, A. (2014). Understanding continuing professional development: The need for theory to impact on policy and practice. *Professional Development in Education, 40*, 688–697.

Kraft, M. A., Blazar, D., & Hogan, D. (2018). The effect of teacher coaching on instruction and achievement: A meta-analysis of the causal evidence. *Review of Educational Research, 88*, 1–42.

Leanna, C., & Pil, F. K. (2006). Social capital and organizational performance. *Organization Science, 17*(3), 353–366.

Leighton, C. M., Ford-Connors, E., Robertson, D. A., Wyatt, J., Wagner, C. J., Proctor, C. P., & Paratore, J. R. (2018). "Let's FaceTime tonight:" Using digital tools to enhance coaching. *The Reading Teacher, 72*, 39–49.

Li, L., & Ruppar, A. (2021). Conceptualizing teacher agency for inclusive education: A systematic and international review. *Teacher Education and Special Education, 44*(1), 42–59.

Lieberman, A., & Miller, L. (2014). Teachers as professionals: Evolving definitions of staff development. In L. E. Martin, S. Kragler, D. J. Quatroche, & K. L Bauserman (Eds.), *Handbook of professional development in education: Successful models and practices, PreK–12* (pp. 3–21). Guilford Press.

Main, S., & Slater, E. (2022). Online continuous professional learning: A model for improving reading outcomes in regional and remote schools? *Journal of Teacher Education, 73*(2), 1–14.

Martin, L. E., Kragler, S., Quatroche, D. J., & Bauserman, K. L. (2014). *Handbook of professional development in education: Successful models and practices, PreK–12*. Guilford Press.

McChesney, K., & Aldridge, J. M. (2021). What gets in the way? A new conceptual model for the trajectory from teacher professional development to impact. *Professional Development in Education, 47*, 834–852.

McNeil, M. (2010, July 26). Civil rights groups call for new federal education agenda. *Education Week*. Retrieved from *www.edweek.org/education/civil-rights-groups-call-for-new-federal-education-agenda/2010/07*.

Moll, L. C., Amanti, C., Neff, D., & Gonzalez, N. (1992). Funds of knowledge for teaching: Using a qualitative approach to connect homes and classrooms. *Theory Into Practice, 21*(2), 132–141.

National Center for Education Statistics. (2019). The nation's report card: Reading. Institute of Education Sciences, U.S. Department of Education. Retrieved from *www.nationsreportcard.gov/reading?grade=4*.

No Child Left Behind Act of 2001, P.L. 107-110, 20 U.S.C. § 6319 (2002).

Opfer, V. D., & Pedder, D. (2011). Conceptualizing teacher professional learning. *Review of Educational Research, 81*(3), 376–407.

Paris, C., & Lung, P. (2008). Agency and child-centered practices in novice teachers: Autonomy, efficacy, intentionality, and reflectivity. *Journal of Early Childhood Teacher Education, 29*, 253–268.

Ravitch, D. (2013, February 26). Why I oppose Common Core standards: Ravitch. *The Answer Sheet,* February 26, 2013. Retrieved February 2013 from *www.washingtonpost.com/blogs/answer-sheet/wp/2013/02/26/why-i-oppose-common-core-standards-ravitch*.

Robertson, D. A., Padesky, L., & Brock, C. H. (2019). Cultivating student agency through teacher professional development. *Theory Into Practice, 59*, 192–201.

Robertson, D. A., Padesky, L. B., Ford-Connors, E., & Paratore, J. R. (2020). What does it mean to say coaching is relational? *Journal of Literacy Research, 52*, 55–78.

Sailors, M., Minton, S., & Villarreal, L. (2017). The role of literacy coaching in improving comprehension instruction. In S. E. Israel (Ed.), *Handbook of research on reading comprehension* (2nd ed., pp. 601–625). Guilford Press.

Sailors, M., & Price, L. (2015). Support for the Improvement of Practices through Intensive Coaching (SPIC): A model of coaching for improving reading instruction and reading achievement. *Teaching and Teacher Education, 45,* 115–127.

Sarason, S. B. (1982). *The culture of the school and the problem of change* (2nd ed.). Allyn & Bacon.

Servage, L. (2006/2007). Making space for critical reflection in professional learning communities. *Education Canada, 47*(1), 14–17.

Snell, E. K., Hindman, A. E., & Wasik, B. A. (2019). A review of research on technology-mediated language and literacy professional development models. *Journal of Early Childhood Teacher Education, 40,* 205–220.

Swan-Dagen, A., & Bean, R. M. (2014). High-quality research-based professional development: An essential for enhancing high-quality teaching. In L. E. Martin, S. Kragler, D. J. Quatroche, & K. L Bauserman (Eds.), *Handbook of professional development in education: Successful models and practices, PreK–12* (pp. 42–63). Guilford Press.

Taylor, B. M., Pearson, P. D., Peterson, D. S., & Rodriguez, M. C. (2003). Reading growth in high-poverty classrooms: The influence of teacher practices that encourage cognitive engagement in literacy learning. *The Elementary School Journal, 104,* 3–28.

Timperley, H., Wilson, A., Barrar, H., & Fung, I. (2007). *Teacher professional learning and development: Best evidence synthesis iteration.* New Zealand Ministry of Education.

van der Linden, S., van der Meij, J., & McKenney, S. (2021). Teacher video coaching, from design features to student impacts: A systematic literature review. *Review of Educational Research.* [Epub ahead of print]

Vescio, V., Ross, D., & Adams, A. (2008). A review of research on the impact of professional learning communities on teaching practice and student learning. *Teaching and Teacher Education, 24,* 80–91.

Woulfin, S. L., & Rigby, J. G. (2017). Coaching for coherence: How instructional coaches lead change in the evaluation era. *Educational Researcher, 46,* 323–328.

Yoon, K. S., Duncan, T., Lee, S. W. Y., Scarloss, B., & Shapley, K. L. (2007). *Reviewing the evidence on how teacher professional development affects student achievement.* U.S. Department of Education, Institute of Education Sciences, National Center for Educational Evaluation and Regional Assistance.

PART I

PROFESSIONAL LEARNING AS REFLEXIVE GROWTH-IN-PRACTICE

CHAPTER 1

Developing Adaptive Expertise to Support Effective Professional Learning

Deidre M. Le Fevre

Watch a related video from the author at this link.

Creating literacy-focused professional learning (PL) that is sustainable, has a positive impact on learning for all students, and addresses issues of equity continues to be challenging work. Providing access and engaging teachers in effective PL is complex, and no straightforward prescriptions have proved to be effective across contexts to date. For too long there has been a tendency to try to create templates for programs that might have a broad reach without considering the unique challenges of specific contexts and learning needs (Bryk et al., 2015).

Although no program has been shown to be universally effective in enabling all students to learn, many programs and strategies have proven to be effective in specific contexts. In addition, approaches to PL built on underlying theories of literacy learning and teaching and underlying principles of PL can promote change for improvement. This chapter focuses on one such underlying PL principle—the development of adaptive expertise.

Adaptive expertise is a way of being and working that enables people to create new and innovative solutions to both existing and emerging problems (Hatano & Inagaki, 1986) by drawing on deep conceptual knowledge, being driven by an inquiry stance, and focusing on improvement (Le Fevre et al., 2020). This chapter explores what adaptive expertise is, why it matters, and how you can support the development of adaptive expertise within literacy-focused PL. The concepts of adaptive expertise discussed have been developed from a PL initiative in Aotearoa, New Zealand. The research was undertaken by a group of colleagues at the University of Auckland (Le Fevre et al., 2020). The 5-year study of PL in literacy development involved school leaders and PL facilitators of literacy in elementary and high schools across New Zealand. We sought to understand what makes the facilitation of PL for leading literacy teaching improvement effective. Effectiveness was measured in improved student achievement outcomes in literacy and the promotion of culturally and linguistically responsive and sustaining pedagogies and practices for students. Findings were defined relative to concepts of adaptive expertise.

Effective PL

What makes PL effective? In the past, the tendency was to measure effectiveness in relation to teacher satisfaction, that is, whether or not teachers found the PL worthwhile, what they learned, and if they enjoyed it. However, we now understand that for PL to be viewed as effective, it needs to promote teacher learning that creates change for improvement in ways that have a positive impact on valued outcomes for all students. The improvement of valued student outcomes should be at the center of PL, and these results may be varied and include, for example, improved student competencies in everyday literacy, enhanced student well-being, increased student engagement in a literacy curriculum that is culturally responsive and sustaining, or higher scores in reading comprehension assessments. Effective PL results in change that improves varied (but valued) student outcomes.

Processes of engaging in PL also matter. In the past, one-off workshops that were delivered to a group of teachers outside the context of their students and teaching were typical models for delivery. Yet, it is now understood that opportunities for ongoing PL situated close to the students and teacher practices that empower them to inquire and evaluate change and improvement represent a more powerful model of engagement (Timperley, 2020). While PL was once primarily seen as the domain of external professional developers, it is now understood that people in a range of roles, including teacher leaders, can support PL situated within and across schools (Timperley et al., 2020).

Sustainable improvement happens when processes are in place to ensure ongoing improvement. This does not mean, however, that the change is *the same* across contexts, for what works in some places will not work in others, and the idea that there is a universal *best practice* that is generalizable across contexts is flawed (Bryk et al., 2015). In the past, researchers and practitioners have attempted to implement uniform and consistent change initiatives across different contexts with the assumption that the same outcomes will be achieved. Unsurprisingly, this approach has not tended to be effective. The problem lies in the fact that "there seems to be endless optimism . . . that somehow we can make things better by 'implementing' something called 'best practices' 'at scale,'" which demonstrates "an irresponsibly simplistic and schematic view of human learning and development" (Elmore, 2016, pp. 530–531). Human learning and development are far from simplistic, and understanding the complex nature of learning, educational change, and improvement can promote the design, implementation, and evaluation of effective literacy PL opportunities.

Creating Effective PL Is Complex Work

Creating effective and powerful literacy education is a complex endeavor. Students bring diverse social, linguistic, and cultural values and experiences to the classroom. Teaching and learning are complicated, nuanced, and sometimes unpredictable processes with uncertain and changeable outcomes, and schools are organizations with numerous parts and interactions between these parts (Mason, 2008). Teachers face multiple and varied challenges on a daily basis as they introduce new curricula, try different approaches to assessment, create ways to teach online, manage flexible learning environments, seek to be responsive to the needs of students with unique learning needs, and continually strive to support the learning of diverse students who may have experienced years of failure in our school systems. Navigating the different agendas, cultural contexts, and values that drive education in ways that enable improved valued student outcomes in literacy requires that educators expect unpredictable and diverse outcomes for different individuals and contexts (Cochran-Smith et al., 2014).

Creating PL opportunities to improve literacy demands that those responsible for leading PL, and the teachers they support, work within and across multiple and embedded systems where unpredictable and unforeseen consequences are inevitable and where many problems have no predictable or known solution (Heifetz, 2010). For example, teachers may be working in contexts where there has been a long history of student underachievement for specific groups of students with limited traction on improvement being made; where providing access to culturally sustaining and linguistically diverse pedagogy is an ongoing challenge; or where opportunities for teachers to engage in effective PL are limited due to geographic remoteness, or resource limitations. Heifetz and his colleagues refer to these sorts of problems as *adaptive challenges* (Heifetz,

2010; Heifetz et al., 2009; Heifetz & Linsky, 2017). Unfortunately, it is not possible to simply "fix" these problems, and attempts to do so in the past have often resulted in failure to improve. Instead, it is important that those responsible for PL recognize this complexity and learn to navigate through it (Heifetz, 2010; Le Fevre et al., 2020). PL is therefore complex—not just because of the range of people involved (policymakers, leaders, PL facilitators, teachers, students), but also because of the myriad interactions between and across these people and the unpredictable outcomes of these relations.

It can be tempting to think of PL as merely complicated. When something is complicated, you can take one piece at a time, work on it, and create improvement. Much like a jigsaw, you can work on one section at a time gradually contributing to completing the whole, yet complicated, picture successfully. When something is complex, it is much more challenging to achieve success because the parts of the puzzle are continually changing as you work on them. For example, student demographics, values, and needs change, as does curriculum content, the big agendas of a community may be in flux, assessment processes evolve, and leadership shifts. Teachers work in an environment influenced by a web of multiple layers and systems. For example, teachers have their own identity as a teacher, which is influenced by values and experiences developed over time from their past both within and beyond education. They have the context of the school they are working in, the skills, interests, values, languages, and cultures of the students they teach, and the diverse interests, concerns, and needs of the families and communities of these students. The leadership and PL context in which they work are also driven by multiple and diverse social, political, and cultural systems. What works with one group of students may not work with another group in a different context. This means it is not possible to rely on assumptions of linear cause and effect. Small events can have large and unpredictable effects and vice versa (Cochran-Smith et al., 2014), and consequences are often unintended.

Adaptive Challenges

Adaptive challenges are a powerful way of describing the sorts of problems educators face in working to improve education. Heifetz et al. (2009) outline some of the characteristics of adaptive challenges. For example, adaptive challenges are problems that have no predictable known solutions. They often feel uncomfortable and can be easy to deny or ignore. Responding to adaptive challenges usually requires changing the way we think and act, and this affects how we feel. In contrast to adaptive challenges, technical challenges can be solved with relative ease. They tend to have known solutions that can be taught to others (Heifetz et al., 2009).

An issue for PL is that the challenges faced in schools are often treated as though they are *technical* challenges when in fact they are *adaptive* challenges (Le Fevre et al., 2020). For example, a school might be implementing a new literacy program aimed at increasing the reading comprehension of high school students in content areas. On the surface this might appear to be a straightforward technical challenge; however, in fact, it is most likely to be an adaptive challenge because it requires teachers to reimagine their roles and professional responsibilities to include promoting literacy learning. Traditionally, this is not how a science or math specialist teacher views themselves, and the challenges of changing people's theories and beliefs about their work and identity are not straightforward (Richardson & Placier, 2001). In addition, there is a need to achieve a deep conceptual learning and understanding about literacy learning and to try new pedagogies and inquire into effectiveness for different students. These are all complex processes, and consideration of their interaction across a diverse staff with different skills, motivations, and values begins to reveal the depth of work needed to create and sustain changes like these.

PL facilitators work in contexts where uncertainty, ambiguity, and differing views are common. They work within nested complex systems seeking to address ongoing and important challenges related to critical issues such as equity that do not have predictable or consistently effective solutions. Possible solutions to adaptive challenges differ from common ways of operating and require continual learning (Heifetz, 2010). For PL facilitators to make progress in addressing adaptive challenges, PL must be approached in ways that develop adaptive expertise, and learning and innovation must move beyond existing approaches and expertise (Heifetz, 2010).

Using Adaptive Expertise to Address Adaptive Challenges

Leading PL that is effective in addressing urgent adaptive challenges such as creating equity demands having adaptive expertise (Hatano & Inagaki, 1986). Adaptive expertise is a way of working in complex environments that draws on developing deep conceptual knowledge and skills, acknowledging the role of emotion, and developing an evaluative inquiry stance (Le Fevre et al., 2016). Deliberate and continual evaluative inquiry helps educators to understand the diverse contexts they work in and to respond effectively. "Adaptive expertise is a way to characterize educational professionalism that emphasizes responsiveness, relationship, and a deep knowledge base from which to make decisions" (Le Fevre et al., 2020, p. ix).

Adaptive expertise informs a way of working to create improvement in education that is "rooted in curiosity, respect, self-knowledge, and a deep understanding of the role of language and culture in education" (Le Fevre et al., 2020, p. ix). The focus on developing expertise within schools makes PL more equitable and sustainable as it is not so dependent on external resourcing or external facilitators. Rather, it is a focus on a way of being and a way of working that can be interwoven through other, existing, PL initiatives.

Providing effective PL involves navigating complex structural challenges. For example, typically, only a finite level of resourcing is available, and those in remote geographic locations or economically underprivileged areas often have fewer resources and opportunities to engage. By focusing on developing adaptive expertise, capacity can be developed within and across schools. While external facilitation is a valuable resource, the intention is to develop capacity so that the leadership for PL can also come from within schools. Developing capacity for evaluative inquiry and acknowledging the role of emotion moves the responsibility for PL from an external compliance driver to an internal and collective responsibility that contributes to sustainability.

How Adaptive Expertise Can Be Developed

The stance that PL facilitators and leaders take can influence what and how people learn, and thus their capacity to change and bring about improvement in literacy education. Our research (Le Fevre et al., 2020) identified seven underlying stances that are key to adaptive expertise:

- Adopting an evaluative inquiry stance;
- Valuing and using deep conceptual knowledge;
- Being agentic;
- Developing awareness of cultural positioning;
- Recognizing the role of emotion;
- Bringing a systemic focus; and
- Being metacognitive.

These stances, or "ways of being" (Cochran-Smith & Lytle, 2009), can potentially underlie a range of approaches to PL. In other words, they are not PL approaches or programs, but a way of being as you engage in a range of approaches or programs. For innovative PL to be effective and sustainable, it is important to focus on the development of these ways of being for everyone involved—at multiple levels, for example, policymakers, leaders, PL facilitators, and teachers. The first step in developing these ways of being is to be aware of them. Understanding their importance is a necessary driver for supporting people to work this way. However, recognizing importance is not sufficient. Our work in schools revealed that intentionally teaching and engaging with these ways of being is also essential for creating improvement in teaching learning, classroom pedagogy, and ultimately, student outcomes.

PL has tended to focus on skills or strategies for teachers to adopt in order to support improvement in the learning and teaching of literacy. It is also critical to focus on the teacher's underlying beliefs and theories that influence both whether and how they will employ these new skills and strategies. These underlying theories and beliefs comprise a stance or way of being; the different ways of being are discussed next.

Adopting an Evaluative Inquiry Stance

An evaluative inquiry stance involves continually focusing on the outcomes of PL, that is, remaining focused on the impact on students. Collecting, interpreting, and using evidence and data are critical parts of an evaluative inquiry stance. PL facilitators who adopt such a stance continually ask themselves and others, "What evidence is there for this claim? How good is this evidence? And what other evidence or explanations might be important to consider?" (Le Fevre et al., 2020). An evaluative inquiry stance demands seeking evidence and views from a range of perspectives. For example, how are students experiencing the new literacy initiative? What do they see as opportunities for their learning? What gets in the way of their learning from their perspective? How do teachers view the new initiative? What are the views of family and communities? As a PL facilitator, it is important to be curious and open-minded. But being open-minded does not mean you cannot hold and advocate views and theories; what it does mean is that it is important to be willing to readily reexamine these views in the face of alternative or conflicting evidence and information (Hare, 2006).

Engaging in genuine inquiry is an important part of evaluative inquiry. Much inquiry that happens in schools is actually *pseudo-inquiry* (Le Fevre et al., 2014). Pseudo-inquiry is when people ask questions to which they already know the answer, or at least think they know the answer, either to test someone (e.g., "What does decoding mean?") or to be manipulative (e.g., "Do you think it's a good idea to miss the professional development meeting?"). Genuine inquiry is when you inquire from a stance of open-mindedness and a desire to know and to learn.

Keeping track of how often you and others engage in genuine inquiry can be a powerful way of beginning to notice what sort of inquiry is happening in the context of PL and for directing it toward genuine inquiry.

Another aspect of adopting an evaluative inquiry stance is what Heifetz et al. (2009) call "thinking experimentally." This kind of thinking opens you to learning and to the possibility that you might not be right (Hare, 2006; Heifetz et al., 2009). It involves being open-minded, managing ambiguity, being willing to commit to an intervention (while, at the same time, not being wedded to it), and being open to exploring unintended consequences.

The PL facilitators in our research intentionally practiced adopting an evaluative inquiry stance when planning their work with schools. For example, they had prompts to continually ask themselves and others, "Is this working? How do we know? What needs to change?" This meant having an environment where it was okay to change direction and not to get it right the first time, or even the second time. Instead, the facilitators were encouraged to notice when something was not working and to change direction without negative consequences. As one of the facilitators said, "It is okay for something to fail; what matters is that failure becomes part of an ongoing learning process, where we learn from that failure."

Valuing and Using Deep Conceptual Knowledge

Deep conceptual knowledge that enables people to interpret and understand new information distinguishes experts from novices (Bransford et al., 2000). "Deep knowledge allows people to work flexibly and responsively in complex and challenging settings" (Le Fevre et al., 2020). The types of conceptual knowledge that are relevant to literacy PL are varied, and include, for example, knowledge of how children learn, literacy concepts, the social psychology of the classroom, content knowledge, and adult learning theory.

The development of new knowledge that challenges existing theories and beliefs is a key aspect of developing adaptive expertise (Le Fevre et al., 2020). But what sort of conceptual knowledge matters? New knowledge that is developed in response to actual problems of practice in one's own context is more likely to promote sustainable change in practice than decontextualized knowledge. This means that engaging with actual problems of practice from one's own experiences is a powerful platform for learning. Knowledge building that is co-constructed between PL facilitators and teachers around actual practice was revealed to be a powerful way of learning that had an impact on practice in our research. When knowledge building is a one-way process from facilitator to teacher, effectiveness is compromised.

During the New Zealand research, the PL facilitators spoke about how they wanted the teachers they worked with in the schools to do things differently, but they were not succeeding. Specifically, they wanted the students to be able to read texts in the classroom that were written in the language spoken in their homes, rather than in English. The conversation among the facilitators focused on what they wanted teachers to be doing, that is, providing these texts. At this stage, the lead facilitator interrupted the conversation and said she was concerned that the facilitators were not framing the PL in such a way that teachers would understand that including books in the child's home language would be a powerful pedagogy. By focusing only on the surface features (the provision of a particular type of text), they were failing to engage with deep, conceptual understanding. Once facilitators engaged the teachers with the conceptual ideas, then they could begin to understand more fully what was going on for learners and why it was important to change their practice.

Being Agentic

Effective PL happens when professional developers, leaders, and teachers have a sense of their own agency and the agency of others. Having a sense of agency empowers people to feel that they can intentionally influence situations and that they are not simply in reactive mode responding to what is happening to them and others.

For example, a teacher might believe that they cannot make a difference to the learning of a particular group of students. As a result, the teacher might subconsciously hold low expectations for the particular groups of students and not feel agentic in their capacity to change these students' literacy achievement and educational outcomes. They may feel reluctant to employ new strategies, feeling that they may not be effective and will be unable to produce the desired outcome. This example demonstrates the importance and power of focusing on ways of being. Those teachers who hold an agentic stance and believe that they can intentionally influence the experiences of students will be more likely to engage fully with innovative strategies and hold high expectations of the students' capacity to learn. Being agentic is not sufficient, and teachers also require specialized knowledge and skills in how to support learning. However, specialized knowledge and skills in the absence of these ways of being are unlikely to be effective in creating long-term and sustainable improvement.

In addition to individuals needing to have a sense of their own agency, the idea of collective agency is also key (Donohoo, 2017). Collective agency involves the "perceptions and judgments of a group of educators regarding their ability to positively influence student outcomes"

(p. 102). Over the period of our 5-year study, it became apparent that the overarching narrative or "story" that the teachers used to explain what was happening in their schools influenced their own and others' sense of agency. For example, those teachers who had a sense that they could make a difference, that their students had the capacity to be engaged and to learn, felt more empowered to problem-solve, to share possible solutions, and to change pedagogy.

Being Aware of Cultural Positioning

Improving literacy outcomes for students often requires more than learning to do something differently; it requires questioning, challenging, and changing one's fundamental beliefs (Richardson & Placier, 2001; Timperley et al., 2017). People are culturally located. Each and every PL facilitator, leader, teacher, and student is culturally located in their own unique linguistic and cultural context. Some people share similar linguistic or cultural contexts to those represented in the dominant cultures of the school, while others do not, and this can influence opportunities for equity. Being aware of your own cultural positioning, the cultural positioning of those you work with, and the potential impact of this positioning on others is central to developing adaptive expertise.

In the New Zealand PL initiative, we encouraged people to be aware of their own beliefs and assumptions, their own linguistic and cultural positioning, and to consider how these beliefs might impact others. This can be a challenging situation because things that are common and familiar to us can be difficult to see. Sometimes we need to make the familiar strange (Erickson, 1986) to see our own culture and to be immersed in other cultures to understand them. Being aware of your own cultural positioning and questioning your own assumptions are both important because they help you to begin to see things from the perspective of others.

The following vignette describes one way in which the PL initiative helped facilitators to be aware of their own cultural positioning and to develop an understanding of what it means and why it matters.

> Tara, Mike, and Lui are literacy PL facilitators supporting teachers in schools with linguistically and culturally diverse students from Pasifika communities (Western Samoa, Tonga, and Niue) who are beginning learners of English. Tara, Mike, and Lui are European New Zealanders whose only language is English, and the teachers they support in schools are also English-speaking New Zealanders. As part of the PL initiative, these facilitators were immersed in a microteaching simulation where they were the student learning to read a text in the Samoan language. The language spoken throughout was Samoan. Following the

> approximately 15-minute lesson, the three facilitators debriefed how it felt to be the student, how they learned, what got in the way of their learning, and most importantly, what this meant for how they promoted the learning of teachers who work with students from linguistically and culturally diverse backgrounds. Extensive debriefing meant these facilitators had the opportunity to examine their own cultural positioning, to consider how it impacted the way they worked and to begin to understand the impact that the cultural positioning of others might have on their opportunities to learn. By increasing their understanding of some of the challenges faced by students and the pedagogical moves that supported them to learn, they were able to consider how to support teachers more effectively in working with students from diverse linguistic and cultural backgrounds.

This example illustrates how powerful it can be to actually experience in a small way what students might be facing and feeling in our classrooms. This is particularly important when teachers represent the dominant language and culture.

Recognizing the Role of Emotion

Research on PL often focuses on what people need to be able to know and do to be more effective. Less attention is given to the role of emotion in PL and change. Developing adaptive expertise involves specifically focusing on the role of emotion because emotion and feelings of vulnerability can be expected responses by teachers who are involved in new learning and change. Our research found that perceptions of risk are an inherent part of change when people are addressing adaptive challenges because, by definition, the outcome of the change is uncertain (Le Fevre et al., 2020). People have perceptions of risk when they fear they may lose something they value (Aven & Renn, 2009), and addressing adaptive challenges often generates a sense of loss for people (Heifetz et al., 2009). This perceived possible loss can take many forms. For example, they might fear that student achievement will decline; they might be uncertain that they have the necessary skills to change the way they teach and that they might lose a sense of their own competency in teaching and professional credibility; or they might be concerned that they will lose valuable time as it will take a lot of time to introduce the new pedagogy.

In our work with schools, we observed educators who were reluctant to try a new pedagogical approach even when evidence revealed that their existing approach was not working. For example, Kim had for several years taught elementary students who were recent immigrants to New Zealand and who were beginning learners of English. Kim recognized that the students became very engaged and interactive when they had opportunities to speak their own language and to interact in culturally sustaining ways when they participated in a cultural song and dance group with others from their country. She was also aware that in class during literacy teaching they struggled to engage with the basic reading materials in English. This was an ongoing challenge, and yet Kim continued to persist with the English resources and her approach, even when she was given new resources in the language of the students and was encouraged to integrate these materials into her program.

Kim was by all accounts a dedicated and caring teacher who wanted the best for her students, so why was this disconnect happening? She said she was worried that she would not know what the students were talking about; she had a perception of risk that she might lose control of the class, and she didn't want to lose face by showing her inadequacy with their language. Interestingly, once she had the opportunity to share these feelings and concerns with the professional learning facilitator, she took the next step in actually changing her pedagogy and using the new resources. Inquiring into the efficacy of existing pedagogies can create perceptions of risk. Teachers can perceive risk when they are to move beyond the known and familiar, even when the known and familiar are ineffective. Heifetz et al. (2009) explain:

> You know the adage "People resist change." It is not really true. People are not stupid. People love change when they know it is a good thing. No one gives back a winning lottery ticket. What people resist is not change per se, but loss. When change involves real or potential loss, people hold on to what they have and resist the change. We suggest that the common factor generating adaptive failure is resistance to loss. (p. 22)

Understanding what might be perceived as a potential loss is important for those leading PL and is a critical part of developing adaptive expertise. The effective leadership of PL focused on literacy requires that educators be able to recognize and connect with the values, beliefs, and anxieties of those impacted by a challenge. Discussing the fact that change involves possible perceptions of risk and that this risk is to be expected can go a long way in supporting teachers to navigate their own perceptions of risk and try new strategies. Adaptive change "involves tough tradeoffs, and the uncertainty of ongoing, experimental trial and error" (Heifetz et al., 2009, p. 23), and it is essential that those involved in PL both have support for themselves and support others to navigate through periods of possible disturbance and upset (Heifetz et al., 2009). Uncertainty is inherent in complex contexts (Le Fevre et al., 2020), and effective PL is responsive to the fact that people might perceive possible risks and that it can help them to navigate through these risks.

Bringing a Systemic Focus

Schools are embedded in a web of complex influences, notably, families, school districts, and the community. The impacts of inequity, poverty, and other negative social influences mean that "effectively addressing the existing disparity of outcomes for learners demands a focus on the big picture of system-wide improvement" (Le Fevre et al., 2020, p. 26). History has shown that making change that creates sustainable improvement in the student's academic and social outcomes requires paying attention to larger and interconnected systems—both within and beyond schools (Opfer & Pedder, 2011).

PL is often ineffective because it does not take into sufficient account how problems are embedded within larger interconnected systems. For example, one of the high schools we studied was prioritizing the improvement of student literacy. However, underachievement was part of a larger problem related to student attendance, which was connected to issues of family responsibility and the fact that many of the older students in the school were caring for younger children at home due to limited social and financial resources. This situation meant that they were either getting to school late or were not even attending school some days. Considering the larger systems that surround the identified problem is important if substantive and long-term change for improvement is to be achieved. A systemic focus creates the potential to involve people beyond schools who have the capacity to positively impact surrounding systems, for example, social workers, community groups, and families. Ongoing inequity, marginalization, and underachievement are systemic problems perpetuated over time and having a systemic focus is necessary for solving complex problems (Le Fevre et al., 2020).

When considering the systems that teachers work in, the most immediate systems include those that teachers have direct contact with (e.g., students and their families, other teachers, school boards). The interactions between these immediate systems influences teachers, their learning, and their capacity to change. So, too, do systems that exist beyond the most immediate such as school district boards and government policy. The fact that teachers operate within a complex web of systems cannot be ignored if PL is to be effective. Developing adaptive expertise includes paying attention to the most immediate systems that surround a teacher as well as the larger sociopolitical environment. In the high school where students were arriving late or not attending at all, the PL facilitator asked teachers to inquire into the individual situations of their students. They were then able to respond to the student needs by taking a multithronged approach, including changing timetabling, providing online virtual course support for students who could not attend, and contacting social service providers to provide further support for families.

Being Metacognitive

The final stance is being metacognitive or being aware of and having control of your own thinking and responses (Bransford et al., 2000). In many ways, this stance underlies the other stances already discussed. Being metacognitive is central to developing adaptive expertise as a PL facilitator, and it is important to have continual awareness of the decisions you make and the possible effects of these decisions on others. For example, in a middle school we worked in, we observed a facilitator working to encourage a small team of teachers to participate as a PL group. They observed each other in class and then later discussed the students' literacy learning opportunities students and the impact that the teachers' decisions had on these opportunities. Although the group of teachers met together, they didn't fully engage in the work of analyzing their own and others' practices. Aware of this, the facilitator had developed sufficient trust with the group that he was able to say what he had observed and ask why this might be happening. When we interviewed the facilitator, it was clear that he was continually metacognitive, thinking about his own thinking, feelings, and decisions and considering the impact (both emotional and cognitive) of his actions on the group. He realized that he was asking them to do too much too soon without sufficient scaffolding. The teachers were reluctant to observe each other's practice, and the facilitator was able to ask himself, "Why might this be the case?" "What might the teachers be experiencing?" "Why might this be a challenging thing to do if they are not practiced in it?" "How can I develop a safer place to support teachers so that they can explore their own and others' practices without judgment?"

Sustaining Improvement

How can we create opportunities for sustainable PL that can have a positive impact on valued student outcomes? Sustainability includes several dimensions, both in access for teachers and in outcomes for students. If PL is driven by a constant evaluative inquiry stance as one of the core ways of being, then there will be constant inquiry into the question "How are we doing?" The way in which this question is answered is an important aspect of adaptive expertise. In the past, the tendency was to evaluate outcomes by estimating an average effect. Rather than documenting simply "what works," by estimating an "on-average" effect, Bryk et al. (2015) suggest that it is important to learn how we are doing, what is working, for whom, and under what set of contexts and conditions. There is no "one size fits all" in understanding how to sustain the positive outcomes of PL.

This chapter has introduced several key components of creating adaptive expertise. An important goal in creating effective PL is to get beyond small, isolated pockets of improvement and to create larger-scale and wider system improvement (Bryk et al., 2015). It is important that educational improvement efforts not only reach large numbers of students, teachers, and leaders but that they reach them in deeply meaningful, effective, and sustained ways (Coburn, 2003). However, the temptation to scale up something that is working in one context to multiple contexts is a problem because "the push to implement 'good ideas' into rapid large-scale use rarely delivers on the outcomes promised" (Bryk et al., 2015, p. 468).

Gawande (2012) asks, "What if you built a car from the very best car parts? Well, it would lead you to put in Porsche brakes, a Ferrari engine, a Volvo body, a BMW chassis. And you put it all together and what do you get? A very expensive pile of junk that does not go anywhere." Gawande's point is this: adding more parts (e.g., new people, better tools, innovative literacy resources, more PL, modern classroom environments)—no matter how wonderful the parts–will not assure a quality outcome.

Scaling up effective literacy PL is about more than the sum of the parts. It can be tempting to take what is often referred to as *best practice* and try to implement it in a new context and then wonder why it does not work. Simply combining best practices will not necessarily lead to improvement. Instead, focusing on the underlying ways of being and creating adaptive expertise at multiple levels (e.g., policy, PL facilitators and leaders, teachers) provides a way for educators to be empowered to inquire into the effectiveness of practices that have been effective in other contexts, to keep student learning at the center of practice, and to continually seek more effective ways of working in complex environments. Traditional attempts to implement similar programs in different contexts are now being viewed as both unattainable and flawed. Rather, recent successes in attaining systemic and sustainable change point to the importance of prioritizing learning at all levels of our systems, developing adaptive expertise, and working collaboratively to meet the unique needs of diverse students in a range of contexts within a complex and changing world.

PL can have a powerful effect on teacher learning, educational change and valued student outcomes. There are many different and innovative initiatives for creating improvement in literacy-focused PL. Approaching these initiatives with a stance of adaptive expertise is an important consideration if the goal of creating sustainable improvement is to be attained.

REFERENCES

Aven, T., & Renn, O. (2009). On risk defined as an event where the outcome is uncertain, *Journal of Risk Research, 12*(1), 1–11.

Bransford, J., Brown, A., & Cocking, R. (2000). *How people learn: Brain, mind, experience and school.* National Academies Press.

Bryk, A. S., Gomez, L. M., Grunow, A., & LeMahieu, P. G. (2015). *Learning to improve: How America's schools can get better at getting better.* Harvard Education Press.

Coburn, C. E. (2003). Rethinking scale: Moving beyond numbers to deep and lasting change. *Educational Researcher, 32*(6), 3–12.

Cochran-Smith, M., Ell, F., Ludlow, L., Grudnoff, L., & Aiken, G. (2014). The challenge and promise of complexity theory for teacher education research. *Teachers College Record, 116*(5), 1–38.

Cochran-Smith, M., & Lytle, S. (2009). *Inquiry as stance: Practitioner research for the next generation.* Teachers College Press.

Donohoo, J. (2017). *Collective teacher efficacy research: How educators' beliefs impact student learning.* Corwin.

Elmore, R. F. (2016). "Getting to scale . . ." it seemed like a good idea at the time. *Journal of Educational Change, 17*(4), 529–537.

Erickson, F. (1986). Qualitative methods in research on teaching. In M. C. Whitrock (Ed.), *Handbook of research on teaching* (3rd ed., pp. 119–161). Macmillan.

Gawande, A. (2012). How do we heal medicine? TED Talk. Retrieved from *www.ted.com/talks/atul_gawande_how_do_we_heal_medicine/transcript?language=en.*

Hare, W. (2006). Why open-mindedness matters. *Think, 5*(13), 7–16.

Hatano, G., & Inagaki, K. (1986). Two courses of expertise. In H. Stevenson, H. Azama, & K. Hakuta (Eds.), *Child development and education in Japan* (pp. 262–272). Freeman.

Heifetz, R. A. (2010, Spring). Adaptive work. *The Journal of the Kansas Leadership Center,* pp. 72–77.

Heifetz, R., Grashow, A., & Linsky, M. (2009). *The practice of adaptive leadership: Tools and tactics for changing your organization and the world.* Harvard Business Press.

Heifetz, R. A., & Linsky, M. (2017). *Leadership on the line, with a new preface: Staying alive through the dangers of change.* Harvard Business Press.

Le Fevre, D., Robinson, V., & Sinnema, C. (2014). Genuine inquiry: Widely espoused but rarely enacted. *Educational Management Administration and Leadership, 43,* 883–899.

Le Fevre, D. M., Timperley, H., & Ell, F. (2016). Curriculum and pedagogy: The future of teacher professional learning and the development of adaptive expertise. In D. Wyse, L. Hayward, & J. Z. Pandya (Eds.), *The SAGE handbook of curriculum, pedagogy and assessment* (pp. 309–324). SAGE.

Le Fevre, D. M., Timperley, H., Twyford, K., & Ell, F. (2020). *Leading powerful professional learning: Responding to complexity with adaptive expertise.* Corwin.

Mason, M. (2008). What is complexity theory and what are its implications for educational change? *Educational Philosophy and Theory, 40*(1), 35–49.

Opfer, V. D., & Pedder, D. (2011). Conceptualizing teacher professional learning. *Review of Educational Research, 81*(3), 376–407.

Richardson, V., & Placier, P. (2001). Chapter 41: Teacher change. In V. Richardson (Ed.), *Handbook of research on teaching* (4th ed., pp. 905–950). American Educational Research Association.

Timperley, H., Ell, F., & Le Fevre, D. (2017). Developing adaptive expertise through professional learning communities. In A. Harris, M. Jones, & J. B. Huffman (Eds.), *Teachers leading educational reform: The power of professional learning communities* (pp. 175–189). Routledge.

Timperley, H., Ell, F., Le Fevre, D. M., & Twyford, K. (2020). *Leadership of professional learning: Practical strategies for impact in schools.* Australian Council for Educational Research.

CHAPTER 2

Innovative Hybrid Professional Learning at Redmond Mountain High School

Cynthia H. Brock, Leigh A. Hall, Erin E. Silcox, and Jeff Makelky

Watch a related video from the authors at this link.

Picture this. Fifteen teachers, the school principal, and two university teacher educators are all sitting in the library of Redmond Mountain High School (RMHS) in Wyoming, participating in a professional learning (PL) session. The five leaders of the PL session are RMHS teachers. Mary,[1] one of two math teachers at the school, has been teaching at RMHS for 21 years; Sylvia, one of two science teachers at the school, has been teaching at RMHS for 2 years; Amanda and Frances, both English teachers, have been teaching at RMHS for 10 years and 1 year, respectively; and Mike, one of two special education teachers, has been teaching at RMHS for 6 years. In this PL session, Mary, Sylvia, Amanda, Frances, and Mike each spent approximately 15 minutes sharing with their fellow teachers how they had been using literacy as a tool in their respective disciplines over the past 4 to 5 months.

Mary, Sylvia, Amanda, Frances, Mike, and their colleagues at RMHS had been participating in a collaborative PL initiative at their school for approximately a year and a half at the time the aforementioned PL session occurred. How did the RMHS collaborative PL initiative get started? What *was* the collaborative initiative? What made the collaborative initiative innovative? We briefly address these questions in the introduction

[1]The school's name and all teacher names are pseudonyms.

to this chapter, and we devote most of this chapter to unpacking the different components of the PL initiative. We end the chapter discussing how the PL initiative promoted equitable and sustainable PL among the teachers at RMHS. As well, we share RMHS's current PL plans and work.

How Did the Collaborative PL Initiative Get Started?

The superintendent of the school district where RMHS is situated had worked with Dr. Smith, a colleague from Western University (WU) specializing in adolescent literacy, in his previous position as a principal in a different district. When Dr. Smith was appointed to his position, the superintendent invited him to do a literacy presentation to the teachers at RMHS. Jeff (the fourth author of this chapter and the principal of RMHS) was impressed with Dr. Smith and her presentation; he was also concerned about his students' reading scores on state-level standardized tests. Jeff noticed that whereas RMHS students consistently scored above the state average on standardized assessments in math and science, they consistently scored below the state average in reading. He saw students' reading test scores as a problem to be addressed, and he knew that addressing this problem would require a schoolwide effort. He also believed it would be useful for his school to work with Dr. Smith and her colleagues. So, Jeff called the Literacy Research Center and Clinic (LRCC) at Western University, and the collaboration between RMHS and WU began.

What *Was* the Collaborative PL Initiative?

When Jeff called the LRCC at Western University, we had a collaborative conversation focused on (1) striving to understand what Jeff wanted to accomplish at his school, and (2) considering ways that we might work jointly with Jeff and the teachers and students at his school to achieve their goals. Drawing on the work of Taylor (2011), our first PL activity with RMHS—as in all schools with whom we do PL work—involved engaging in a schoolwide needs assessment. A schoolwide needs assessment helps us to understand what key stakeholders at the school (e.g., teachers, students, administrators, and specialists) see as important areas for instructional improvement, the extent to which different stakeholders are willing to engage in the work, and the nature of the school leadership structure that might support such work.

After engaging in this assessment, we worked with Jeff and the leadership team at RMHS to create an initial PL plan that would be flexible and adaptive to the needs of the teachers and students at RMHS. Key components of the co-developed plan, which are explained in more detail below, included (1) two to three face-to-face PL sessions each year designed around the school leadership team's suggestions for the content and focus of each session, (2) online micro-courses on topics that the teachers deemed important and that could be completed by teachers at their own pace, and (3) monthly check-ins with the RMHS leadership team via Zoom to determine what was working for teachers at the school and to problem-solve about anything that was not working.

What Made the Collaborative PL Initiative Innovative?

Traditional PL approaches are often short-term, hierarchical, one-size-fits-all models of teacher training (Lieberman & Miller, 2014). They are short-term because outside "experts" typically present at a school once or twice; they are hierarchical because the outside "expert" tells the educators at the school what they "need to know" about a topic or issue; and they are one-size-fits-all because the outside "expert" typically shares the same message with different schools in different contexts.

Perhaps not surprisingly, these traditional approaches have been criticized for a host of reasons. First, teachers are viewed as passive recipients of information rather than active constructors of knowledge. Second, often little or no follow-up takes place relative to teachers' actual instruction in their classrooms after the outside "expert" session(s). Third, these traditional approaches to PL rarely result in meaningful teacher or student learning (Lieberman & Miller, 2014).

As a field, we know that successful PL approaches are (1) context-embedded, (2) tailored to teachers' and students' unique instructional needs in specific contexts, and (3) democratic and co-constructed (Brugar & Roberts, 2017; Koellner & Jacobs, 2015). In these more successful PL approaches, collaborative inquiry among educators provides a sense of ownership and sustained, active engagement in PL focused on teachers' instructional needs to support student learning (Risko & Vogt, 2016; Timperly et al., 2020).

We included the following features of our collaborative work with RMHS to strive to make the work innovative. First, our work with RMHS was co-designed with the teachers and administrators and tailored to their specific needs. Second, Leigh (the second author of this chapter) developed online micro-courses for the teachers and administrators at RMHS to address the content areas on which they wanted to focus. Third, the professors at WU provided face-to-face PL sessions several times across the year designed specifically around the content areas on which the teachers wanted to focus. Fourth, Cindy (the first author of this chapter) met with the RMHS leadership team each month to discuss teachers' successes and challenges regarding the implementation of instructional ideas about which they were learning and striving to implement in their classrooms. Finally, across time, the RMHS teachers themselves became the PL presenters, sharing with their colleagues their successes and challenges as they implemented instructional ideas.

Now, having briefly introduced our collaborative PL initiative, we delve more deeply into each component of the work. In doing so, we paint a more detailed picture of the nature of our collaborative work.

The Major Components of Our Collaborative Work at RMHS

The Literacy Needs Assessment

Because we knew from the onset that we wanted to tailor our collaborative PL work to RMHS's specific needs (Brugar & Roberts, 2017), we worked with RMHS teachers, students, and administrators to ascertain what they were currently doing with respect to informational text reading and writing. In short, we conducted a needs assessment, which included the following mutually agreed-upon components: visits to teachers' classrooms, selected interviews, teacher surveys, and student surveys.

Classroom Observations

The teachers at RMHS welcomed us into their classrooms, and Leigh and Cindy spent an entire day visiting the different classes across the school. Because we knew that RMHS educators and administrators wanted to improve their students' informational text reading and writing, we focused our observations on (1) whether teachers engaged with informational texts in their respective classes, and (2) if they did, the ways they did so.

Whereas we observed some examples of engagement with informational texts (e.g., one English teacher was asking her students to read about Malcolm X and consider different cultural lenses with which different readers might interpret the text), we did not see many instances of teachers engaging with informational text reading or writing across our day of observations. We did, however, learn about a unique reading instructional practice at RMHS: The school had a schoolwide reading program, which we learned more about in our interview with Jeff and describe below.

Selected Interviews

After visiting most classrooms across the school, we then spoke with Jeff, as well as the district language arts specialist[2] who worked at RMHS. In our discussion with Jeff, we (1) asked him to share his central goal(s) for our collaborative work and (2) posed questions and offered suggestions regarding our initial interpretations of our visits to RMHS teachers' classrooms.

With respect to the central goal for our collaborative work, Jeff stated, "Well, it's pretty basic; we just want to improve our overall reading." Jeff explained that his students scored lowest on the state standardized test on informational reading.[3] He reasoned that if his students were learning what they needed to know about informational reading, their test scores should be higher.

Regarding our questions and observations from our classroom visits, we mentioned that we did see some engagement with informational text reading and writing across the day, but not much. We suggested to Jeff that a schoolwide focus on disciplinary literacy could strengthen students' learning about, and engagement with, informational texts.

In our discussion, we asked Jeff to tell us more about the schoolwide reading initiative we had observed. Jeff mentioned that the schoolwide reading initiative had been part of the school culture for quite some time. In fact, it was started before Jeff's tenure at RMHS. He explained that the school's goal with the schoolwide reading initiative was to foster "the excitement, enthusiasm, and enjoyment of reading." Because students were divided across all teachers at the school for this reading initiative, groups were small (typically 12 to 14 students per group), and students usually stayed with the same teacher for their 4 years in high school. As we concluded our discussion of the schoolwide reading initiative, Jeff stated: "I'm open for suggestions or whatever you think we should do to maximize that period, to better use it."

Teacher and Student Surveys

Jeff was clearly interested in maximizing the use of the schoolwide reading initiative to promote student learning about informational text reading

---

[2]The district language arts specialist shared wonderful ideas for how we might work with content-area teachers to foster more meaningful engagement with informational texts. Due to space constraints, we do not focus on our conversation with her in this chapter.

[3]We note here that RMHS scores for information text reading were just slightly below the state average, but Jeff, and the teachers at his school felt that they could do better.

and writing. Thus, we created surveys about this reading initiative that we asked teachers and students to complete. We asked teachers to tell us how they engaged in this schoolwide reading initiative, what they saw as the goals of this reading time, what they were doing with their students during this time, what was working with this reading time, what possible suggestions they had for revisiting the use of this reading time, and so on.

Overwhelmingly, the teachers wanted to keep the schoolwide reading time focused on reading for enjoyment and striving to get students interested in, and engaged with, reading. We did learn, however, that teachers used a wide variety of different practices during this time including, but not limited to (1) students reading a chapter of a book at a time and then discussing the chapter with the group, (2) popcorn/round-robin reading, (3) teacher read-alouds, (4) reading and journal writing, and the like.

Most of the students at the high school (i.e., 143) filled out the student surveys about the schoolwide reading program. When asked to describe what occurred in classes during the schoolwide reading sessions, student responses resembled faculty responses. However, because the students' experiences varied based on the group they were assigned to, we got a sense of the frequency of different literacy-related practices in classrooms. For example, overwhelmingly students said that most of their time was spent engaging in silent reading and discussing what they read. The next most prevalent type of reading was round-robin or popcorn reading. Students also reported teacher read-alouds, some writing in response to reading, and some vocabulary work. However, these three practices were not as common across the classrooms.

When asked about the goals for schoolwide reading, overwhelmingly students responded that central goals included reading more, getting better at reading, reading for pleasure, and finishing entire books. A limited number of students also mentioned raising standardized test scores, engaging in skills-building (e.g., vocabulary and comprehension), and having parties after finishing entire books or 600+ minutes of reading. Thus, we noted that students' goals and teachers' goals for schoolwide reading overlapped considerably; most people in both groups saw reading books for enjoyment and pleasure to be central goals for schoolwide reading time.

Needs Assessment Summary Comments

Taken together, our analysis across the components of the needs assessment revealed two general areas where we could begin to work to improve students' informational text reading and writing: the way teachers engaged with students during schoolwide reading time, and the way teachers used literacy tools (i.e., reading, writing, and discussion) during instruction in their content areas. We knew that teachers would need to learn more about possible ways to adjust their literacy-related instruction in these two contexts. It is to this issue that we now turn.

Online Micro-Courses

Having conducted our needs assessment, we collaborated with Jeff to create a plan that could support the staff's PL goals. We agreed that teachers would benefit from a sustained approach over the course of a school year and beyond. Teachers needed regular opportunities to learn, apply, and receive feedback on a variety of instructional approaches that could support their students' literacy development.

We immediately ran into a practical issue. The distance between our university and RMHS limited how often we could be physically present at RMHS. However, we recognized that PL did not have to happen entirely face-to-face. Leigh proposed that we use this situation as an opportunity to try a different approach to PL. Rather than only come to RMHS for two or three times, we could design an online experience for teachers that would give them access to content when they needed it and allow for ongoing support from university collaborators. Our in-person work together could then concentrate on where teachers needed additional learning and support.

Leigh got straight to work on creating an approach for PL at a distance. While she oversaw the creation of the content and the approaches for online mentoring, Cindy worked with the leadership team on understanding their needs, creating goals, and planning our in-person visits.

In designing the courses, the team agreed that all teachers should take a course that would help them understand the concept of disciplinary literacy. This course was foundational to them in achieving their overarching PL goals as a school, and we agreed it was important for everyone to have this shared knowledge. From there, teachers would be free to pick and choose from a menu of options that included topics on vocabulary, comprehension, and writing instruction.

Since an important component of our process was giving teachers access to information about high-quality, research-supported literacy instruction, Leigh designed the courses to be asynchronous and on-demand. This allowed teachers to access them when it served them best and they were ready to learn the information. There were no official start or end dates for the courses, allowing teachers to (1) begin when it was convenient for them, (2) work at their own pace, and (3) return to any of the content as needed.

It is important to note that Jeff, the school principal, took micro-courses along with the teachers at his school. As an instructional leader at his school, Jeff modeled the importance of continuing to engage in his own PL around literacy (Robinson et al., 2008). Because everyone at RMHS was taking micro-courses and striving to apply what they were learning in their instruction, the school was developing a common language and common practices built around literacy instruction. The common language and practices being co-developed at RMHS provided a platform for meaningful discussions about teaching and student learning when Jeff visited classrooms to observe instruction.

Leigh worked to identify current and former teachers who specialized in literacy education and could create a range of content. Over the course of the year, these creators were able to develop 43 courses. All courses were housed on Thinkific, a platform that allows for the creation and sharing of online courses. Fifty-four percent of the courses (n = 23) took 5 hours for teachers to complete, and 46% (n = 20) took 15 hours for teachers to complete.

Each course followed the same format. Teachers were first given an overview of the course and the objectives it covered. They then completed a pretest to assess their understanding of the course objectives. Once the pretest was completed, teachers gained access to the course content and were able to progress through the remainder of the course.

The course content was largely video-based and divided up into chapters. Each chapter focused on teaching one objective. At the end of each chapter, there was a challenge where teachers demonstrated their knowledge of what they had learned in that section by either (1) explaining their understanding of the concepts presented in the course, or (2) applying concepts to their instruction and discussing what happened. Completing challenges was optional, and teachers could decide if they wanted to complete all, some, or none within a course. Teachers completed a posttest at the end of each course so that we could measure their learning. After they completed the posttest, they received a certificate.

In addition to having unlimited access to content, teachers also had access to a private site where they could share and discuss their work. They were able to ask for help from us or their colleagues at any time. This approach allowed us to better understand teachers' successes and struggles and shaped our thoughts on planning their in-person experiences.

Monthly Planning Meetings

To have a viable collaboration that would make a difference with respect to teacher and student learning, we knew that we would need ongoing collaboration. Jeff already had a leadership team established at his school. Consequently, we did not need to create a leadership team specifically for this collaborative PL endeavor. RMHS leadership team members included Jeff and teacher representatives from across different subject areas.

As a group, we decided that we would (1) co-create specific goals, which are described below, (2) seek input from the faculty on the goals before finalizing them, (3) ask leadership team members to check in with colleagues prior to our monthly meetings to see how teachers were progressing on completing micro-courses and practicing the skills and strategies learned from the micro-courses with the students in their own classes, (4) problem-solve together whenever teachers raised concerns, questions, or issues with the PL work in which we were all engaging, and (5) collaboratively make decisions about the focus for face-to-face PL sessions that were led by university colleagues toward the beginning of the PL process.[4] Members of our monthly planning group also decided to revisit the nature of the work we were doing together to make sure that the tasks in which we were engaging were working to foster teacher and student learning at RMHS.

We co-created a two-pronged approach to our collaborative work about reading and writing informational text at RMHS. The first prong focused on the existing schoolwide reading program and included the following two goals:

- All students engage in meaningful reading and discuss what they read.
- All students read a variety of fiction and nonfiction genres throughout the school year.

The second prong (i.e., a disciplinary literacy content goal) focused on ways that each teacher could use literacy tools such as reading, writing, talking, and viewing in their content-area instruction. Our goal for the second prong was stated as follows: Teachers will implement disciplinary literacy practices within their core subjects.

Sample Face-to-Face PL Session

We conducted two to three face-to-face PL sessions with RMHS each of the years we worked together. We share one sample face-to-face PL session in detail here to illustrate (1) how we made decisions about the conceptual focus for PL sessions and (2) the way PL sessions led by university collaborators were typically conducted with RMHS colleagues.

As noted, one of the many topics addressed at monthly leadership team meetings included discussions of plans for face-to-face PL sessions at RMHS. Recall, too, that one micro-course that folks at RMHS could

[4]As our introductory vignette illustrated, however, the RMHS teachers themselves led face-to-face PL sessions as our collaborative work progressed.

choose focused on vocabulary. Several teachers at RMHS had taken the vocabulary micro-course, and they wanted additional work on vocabulary. Also, some teachers at RMHS were concerned about their students' SAT scores. When this information was brought to one of the monthly leadership team meetings, the leadership team decided that an upcoming face-to-face PL session should focus on vocabulary. While discussing the potential vocabulary focus for the PL session, one of the teachers mentioned Beck's work on tiered vocabulary instruction (Beck et al., 2013). Thus, the leadership team chose Beck et al.'s (2013) vocabulary work—especially choosing and teaching Tier Two vocabulary words—as a PL focus. See Beck et al. (2013) for a discussion of Tier Two vocabulary words.

Whereas Cindy, Leigh, and Erin (the first, second, and third authors of this chapter, respectively) were originally scheduled to co-lead this PL session, road closures due to inclement weather prohibited Leigh and Cindy from making the 5-hour drive to RMHS. Erin lived only an hour from RMHS, and because the roads were not closed between her home and RMHS, she drove to RMHS to lead the PL session on her own. Erin had developed the PL session after talking with Leigh and Cindy about the focus the RMHS teachers wanted for their PL work. We briefly outline key aspects of Erin's PL session to illustrate how we strove to co-create meaningful face-to-face sessions geared to the specific needs of RMHS teachers.

Introducing the PL Vocabulary Session

First, prior to the day of the PL session, Erin had asked the teachers to bring texts relative to their unique disciplines to the session. Erin wanted the teachers to draw on materials that they normally use to choose Tier Two words on which to focus for their instruction. Second, Erin's interactive presentation included an infographic with a URL. The URL was chock-full of practical resources for identifying and teaching Tier Two words that the teachers could take back to their classrooms to use immediately after the PL session. Erin's objectives for the PL session were written as follows: By the end of this session, you will be able to (1) define Tier Two vocabulary, (2) choose Tier Two words to teach, and (3) incorporate Tier Two words into your instruction.

Engaging in the PL Vocabulary Session

Rather than just telling the teachers about Tier One, Two, and Three words, after defining the different tiers of words, Erin asked the teachers to engage with her and with one another as they explored and debated the differences between Tier One, Two, and Three words. See Beck et al. (2013) for a discussion of Tier One, Tier Two, and Tier Three vocabulary words. As the teachers identified which tiers different words belonged to, Erin asked them to draw on the definitions and examples she had provided in the infographic to justify their assertions. Once teachers had experienced identifying Tier Two words, Erin provided instruction on how to choose Tier Two words for weekly instruction. Then, she showed video clips of teachers engaged in effective teaching of Tier Two words, and she shared key practices for effective vocabulary instruction.

Finishing the PL Vocabulary Session

In the final portion of the PL session, Erin asked the teachers to use the infographic to guide them in the process of choosing Tier Two words for their respective subject areas. She also asked the teachers to begin planning how they would teach these words to their students. In addition to discussing ways to implement Tier Two vocabulary instruction in their own classrooms, teachers began to discuss how they could choose Tier Two words to feature schoolwide so that teachers across school subjects were all reinforcing key Tier Two words across each week. According to Jeff, choosing and teaching Tier Two words schoolwide is a practice that continues today at RMHS.

The PL Vocabulary Session: Concluding Comments

When we debriefed about this PL session after Erin implemented it, we identified several features that made it successful overall. First, most of the teachers were internally motivated because they had chosen the focus for the session; in short, the session was specifically designed to address the needs of the teachers at RMHS. Second, the session was highly interactive. Erin did not talk *at* the teachers; rather, she designed a series of experiences in which teachers engaged to explore the underlying concepts pertaining to choosing and teaching Tier Two vocabulary. Finally, much like the teachers at this school had adopted a whole-school reading approach, the RMHS teachers decided to implement a whole-school approach to Tier Two vocabulary word instruction.

We think it is important to point out that not everything went perfectly with this PL session, just as not everything went smoothly in our overall collaborative PL work across time. For example, with respect to this PL session, some teachers expressed concern about having sufficient time to teach Tier Two words in their disciplines given the difficulty of finding time to teach all their academic content. Some teachers also expressed concern about knowing enough to effectively teach Tier Two words in their classrooms since the vocabulary instructional strategies introduced in this session were new to some teachers.

Conclusion: Promoting Equitable and Sustainable Change at RMHS

The collaborative, innovative hybrid PL approach that we co-developed at RMHS included the following components: a needs assessment designed to ascertain current informational text instructional practices; online micro-courses tailored to the instructional needs of the teachers at RMHS; monthly planning meetings between the leadership team at RMHS and the WU; two to three face-to-face PL sessions each year; and a culminating PL session whereby the teachers at RMHS shared their learning and experiences with one another. With respect to this last item, we come full circle to the beginning of this chapter whereby we presented a brief vignette of five teachers who led one of the culminating PL sessions at RMHS. Toward the end of our collaboration, teachers shared with colleagues many literacy-related instructional approaches they had learned about and were implementing in their respective classes.

Overall, we judge our collaborative PL work to have been effective for several reasons. Two practices at RMHS were already in place that contributed to our successful school–university partnership. First, the teachers and administrators at RMHS had been engaging in PL communities (PLCs) since 2014. Thus, teachers and administrators had already spent time thinking and working together to foster positive change to promote student learning in their school.

Second, as an experienced and successful high school principal, Jeff[5] knew that he wanted to continue to foster *collective efficacy* at RHMS (i.e., the shared belief that a school's staff can have a positive impact on student learning; Goddard et al., 2004). One of Jeff's goals as an instructional leader was to ascertain common interests and common ground on which teachers could focus to promote student learning (Robinson et al., 2008). Hence, Jeff played a crucial role in (1) narrowing down our PL focus to working on schoolwide reading instruction and disciplinary literacy instruction within content area classrooms, and (2) leading the focused ongoing work and reflection across the years of our school–university collaboration.

With respect to the role WU colleagues played in the school–university collaboration, as university colleagues, we had already worked extensively with different schools and districts in our state. In all of our PL work, we seek to (1) understand current literacy-related practices at schools by implementing literacy needs assessments, (2) draw on

[5] Jeff was named the Wyoming State Principal of the Year in 2020.

research-based literacy practices as a foundation for collaborating with the teachers, teacher leaders, and administrators at each school to tailor PL work to the specific needs and interests of each school with whom we work, and (3) collaboratively work with schools to put into place iterative structures and systems whereby school personnel engage in an ongoing process of inquiry and knowledge building (Timperley et al., 2020).

In short, both the school and university partners had established certain practices and systems prior to our collaborative work that contributed to the success of our collaboration. However, we also worked together across an extended period of time to assess the specific needs of RMHS and co-develop and co-implement a PL plan tailored to those needs. Our collaborative plan included an ongoing system of checks-and-balances. Each month when we met, we problem-solved what was working and what was not. Then, we adjusted our work together to address concerns along the way.

We draw on two of many possible examples of evidence to support our assertion that we co-constructed an effective school–university PL partnership. After Erin's face-to-face PL session at RMHS, Jeff provided schoolwide PL time for the entire staff to complete the micro-courses on vocabulary instruction. (Recall that only a few micro-courses were completed by the entire staff. Then, staff members had options for additional micro-courses they wished to complete.) Next, the RMHS leadership brainstormed ways to continue to work on vocabulary on a schoolwide basis. The school decided to continue to work together to support one another in effectively choosing and teaching Tier Two vocabulary words. Moreover, the school chooses three new Tier Two words each week as a whole-school focus. (This activity is in addition to Tier Two vocabulary work that individual teachers perform in their classrooms.) These schoolwide focus words are shared during morning announcements; anyone walking into Jeff's school will see these words displayed on a reader-board in the front entrance to the school. In addition, Tier Two words from across the year are displayed near the front entrance of the school (see Figure 2.1). Finally, the leadership team encouraged teachers to continue choosing and teaching Tier Two words as well as identify crucial Tier Three words for their respective disciplines to teach.

Across time, Jeff and the teachers at RMHS have seen a rise in ACT scores with respect to informational text reading. We suggest that test scores are improving because of high-quality instruction at RMHS. Thus, test scores are the result of high-quality instruction rather than the central goal for Jeff's school (Raphael et al., 2014). As we have long known, there are no quick fixes for raising standardized test scores (Allington & Walmsley, 1995); rather, higher standardized test scores are a result of sustained high-quality instruction.

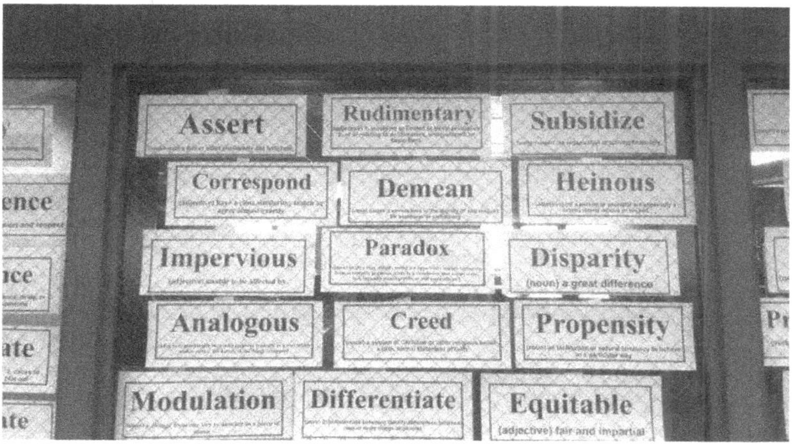

FIGURE 2.1. Tier Two words near the front entrance at RMHS.

Final Thoughts

The PL collaboration between RMHS and the LRCC created accessible opportunities for sustainable PL for the following reasons. The RMHS principal and his school leadership team drove the PL initiative. Members of the university and the RMHS leadership team co-developed a cohesive schoolwide plan to improve students' informational text reading. The online micro-courses developed for RMHS were geared toward the needs of the teachers at RMHS, and teachers exercised choice in micro-course selection. Finally, across time, the teachers and administrators at RMHS developed a self-sustaining culture of learning from, and with, one another that extended beyond the life of the school–university PL collaboration.

REFERENCES

Allington, R., & Walmsley, S. (1995). *No quick fix: Rethinking literacy programs in America's elementary schools.* Teachers College Press.

Beck, I., McKeown, M., & Kucan, L. (2013). *Bringing words to life: Robust vocabulary instruction* (2nd ed.). Guilford Press.

Brugar, K., & Roberts, K. (2017). Seeing is believing: Promoting visual literacy in elementary social studies. *Journal of Teacher Education, 68*(3), 262–279.

Goddard, R., Hoy, W., & Hoy, A. (2004). Collective efficacy beliefs: Theoretical developments, empirical evidence, and future directions. *Educational Researcher, 33*(3), 3–13.

Koellner, K., & Jacobs, J. (2015). Distinguishing models of professional development: The case of an adaptive model's impact on teachers' knowledge, instruction, and student achievement. *Journal of Teacher Education, 66*(1), 51–67.

Lieberman, A., & Miller, L. (2014). Teachers as professionals: Evolving definitions of staff development. In L. Martin, S. Kragler, D. Quatroche, & K. Bauserman (Eds.), *Handbook of professional development in education: Successful models and practices PreK–12* (pp. 3–21). Guilford Press.

Raphael, T., Vasquez, J., Fortune, A. J., Gavelek, J. R., & Au, K. (2014). Sociocultural approaches to professional development. In L. Martin, S. Kragler, D. Quatroche, & K. Bauserman (Eds.), *Handbook of professional development in education: Successful models and practices, PreK–12* (pp. 145–173). Guilford Press

Risko, V., & Vogt, M. (2016). *Professional learning in action: An inquiry approach for teachers of literacy.* Teachers College Press.

Robinson, V., Lloyd, C., & Rowe, K. (2008). The impact of leadership on student outcomes: An analysis of the differential effects of leadership type. *Educational Administration Quarterly, 44*(5), 635–674.

Taylor, B. M. (2011). *Catching schools: An action guide to schoolwide reading improvement.* Heinemann.

Timperley, H., Ell, F., Le Fevre, D., & Twyford, K. (2020). *Leading professional learning: Practical strategies for impact in schools.* Victoria, Australia: ACER Press.

CHAPTER 3

Professional Learning Designed to Cultivate Continuous Learning and Innovation

Cynthia Greenleaf, Mira-Lisa Katz, Mary Stump, and Gayle Cribb

Watch a related video from the authors at this link.

This chapter examines how a professional learning model (PL) grounded in an instructional framework and its organizational principles and practices create fertile conditions for sustained literacy learning and practice. Over the past 25+ years, thousands of middle and high school teachers have engaged in Reading Apprenticeship PL, developed by the Strategic Literacy Initiative (SLI) at WestEd. This chapter describes the Reading Apprenticeship approach and "makes it real" by following the PL journey of Gayle Cribb, who taught high school history in a small district in northern California for 32 years.

Gayle enacted Reading Apprenticeship in her classroom, participated in the project's inquiry networks, and led schoolwide literacy reform. Her story illustrates Reading Apprenticeship's generative model of distributed leadership and learning, as Gayle becomes a Reading Apprenticeship practitioner, facilitator, coach, co-designer of PL in new environments (hybrid, online), and researcher. We describe how the practices of our R&D organization help Gayle and thousands of teachers across the country thrive through grant-funded opportunities to collaborate, to innovate to meet new challenges, and to validate this work by contributing new tools and knowledge and assisting in the dissemination of these innovations through professional development, presentations, and publications.

We argue that the outcomes of PL we describe here are best gauged by attending to these long-term impacts and the collegial engagements and diffusion networks intentionally fostered by the project (Penuel et al., 2012; Sun et al., 2013). After relating characteristics of the Reading Apprenticeship instructional framework and elements of the PL model, we then articulate the key principles underlying this PL approach and the structures that support sustained growth for teachers and for the field.

Introducing the Reading Apprenticeship Instructional Framework

As its name suggests, Reading Apprenticeship is at heart a partnership of expertise, drawing both on what subject-area teachers know and do as discipline-based readers and on adolescents' unique and often underestimated strengths as learners. Reading Apprenticeship aims to help students become better readers of a variety of texts by making teachers' discipline-based reading processes and knowledge visible to students and by making the students' reading processes and the social contexts, strategies, knowledge, and understandings they bring to the task of making sense of subject-matter texts visible to the teacher and to one another. Through ongoing *metacognitive conversations* that make these usually tacit processes visible and explicit, students gain insight into their own reading processes and acquire a repertoire of problem-solving strategies with the varied texts of the academic discipline. As depicted in Figure 3.1, Reading Apprenticeship involves teachers in orchestrating and integrating four interacting dimensions of classroom life in order to draw on adolescents' particular strengths to help them develop the knowledge, strategies, and dispositions they need to become more powerful readers, in an environment rich with opportunities for students to learn with complex subject-matter texts.

These four interacting areas of classroom life—social, personal, cognitive, and knowledge-building dimensions—are woven into subject-area teaching through metacognitive conversations. Rather than focus on implementing a specific teaching strategy or strategies (e.g., cooperative group learning, integrated strategy instruction), Reading Apprenticeship engages teachers and students alike in metacognitive, text-based inquiry, thus *learning by doing*. Teachers and students work collaboratively to make sense of texts, while simultaneously engaging in a conversation about what constitutes reading in specific academic disciplines as well as how they are going about it. New knowledge, strategies, and dispositions develop in an ongoing conversation in which teacher and students think about and discuss their personal relationships to reading, larger issues of

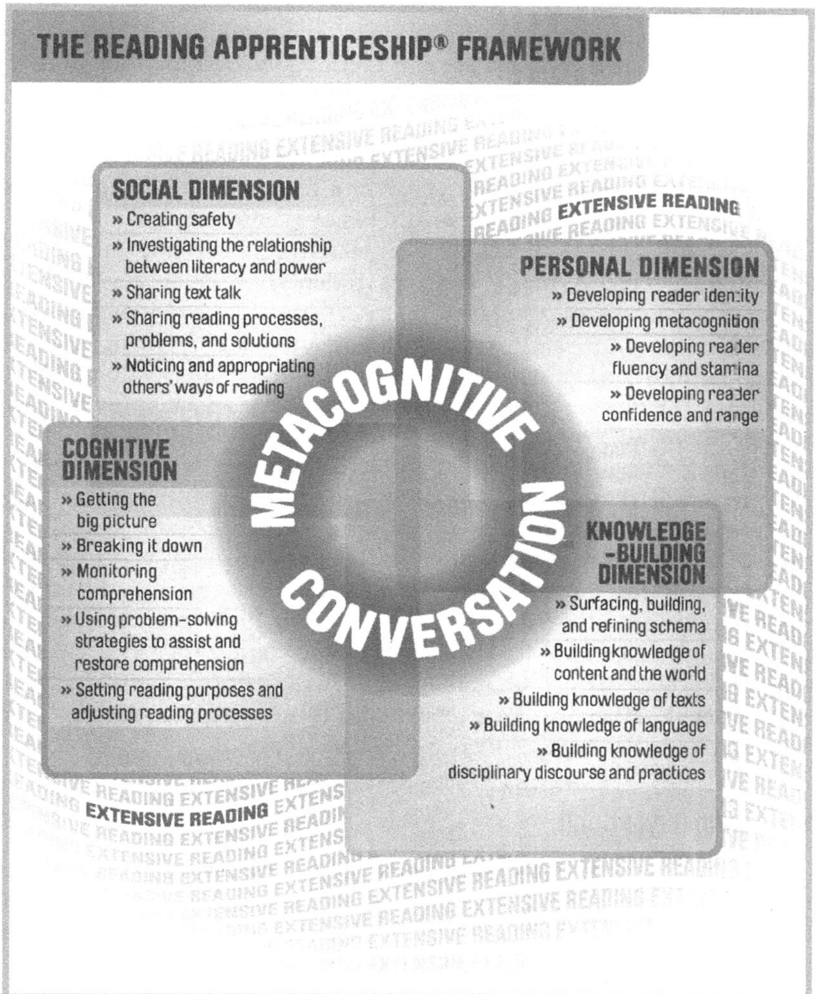

FIGURE 3.1. Reading Apprenticeship framework. Reprinted by permission of WestEd.

literacy and power, the social environment and resources of the classroom, their mental processes, the language structures and varied ways of conveying meaning used in particular types and modalities of texts, and the kinds of knowledge needed to make sense of reading.

Metacognitive conversations occur through many means—class discussions between teachers and students, small-group conversations, written reflections and logs, think-alouds, and "talking to the text" in annotations. As such conversations and reflections become routine, they offer students ongoing opportunities to consider what they are doing as they read and to assess how well their strategies and approaches are working for them, changing their approach to suit their purposes as they read. Repeated opportunities to make sense of a text individually, in pairs or small groups, and in facilitated class discussions center on students' voices, interpretations, and perspectives, demonstrating their importance and allowing teachers access to the resources students bring to bear in learning.

With students' voices at the center of learning activities, Reading Apprenticeship routines support risk taking and foster shifts in students' understandings of themselves as learners. Ongoing metacognitive conversation about text is simultaneously formative assessment, as teachers dynamically adjust instructional activities to support students' sensemaking. Nesting this work within routines that support students' sense of safety and value deepens the apprenticeship and the learning that it supports. Several rigorous studies of Reading Apprenticeship have shown positive impacts on teacher practice and student learning, and thus have paved the way for further expansion of the model through dissemination grants that enable Reading Apprenticeship PL to reach teachers in diverse geographical, policy, and demographic contexts across the nation (Fancsali et al., 2015; Goldman et al., 2019; Greenleaf et al., 2011; Sommers et al., 2010). Also see research on Reading Apprenticeship summarized in CASEL.org and EvidenceforESSA.org.[1]

Introducing Gayle Cribb

Gayle Cribb first encountered Reading Apprenticeship as a veteran teacher in 2001 when SLI offered PL at no cost through a state grant that supported outreach to low-income areas. She enacted Reading Apprenticeship in her classroom, saw positive changes in her students, and went on to participate in inquiry networks, lead schoolwide literacy reform, and facilitate Reading Apprenticeship PL in very diverse settings as part of Reading Apprenticeship's expert teacher consultant pool. She also participated in research first as a "subject" and later as a researcher and author. Gayle's learning and growth accumulated over time, enabling her to lead from the wisdom of her own practice and increasingly cultivate strong instructional practice more broadly by supporting other teachers to have similar learning and teacher leadership opportunities. Readers can see Gayle teaching and read some of her publications at *www.ReadingApprenticeship.org*.

[1] *https://pg.casel.org/reading-apprenticeship; www.evidenceforessa.org/programs/reading/reading-apprenticeship.*

Effective PL and the Reading Apprenticeship Approach

Recent research syntheses have attempted to derive characteristics of PL that can meaningfully change teachers' instructional practices, students' opportunity to learn, and, importantly, students' achievement. For example, Desimone's influential work suggests that professional development is most effective when (1) it centers on content; (2) is aligned with the goals of school and districts in which teachers work; (3) engages teachers actively; (4) is collaborative; and (5) is of sufficient duration (Desimone & Stuckey, 2014). Research has demonstrated that engaging with academic content, pedagogy, and evidence of student learning can foster knowledge and pedagogical content knowledge development in ways that inform daily instruction (Darling-Hammond et al., 2009; Dillon et al., 2011; Gersten et al., 2010; Yoon et al., 2007). To this knowledge based on effective professional development, Kennedy adds the importance of inquiry as a mode of teacher learning (Kennedy, 2016).

Engaging Teachers Actively through Inquiry in Reading Apprenticeship PL

The characteristics of effective PL outlined in this research literature result from meta-analyses of a broad range of studies in varied circumstances and from addressing distinct PL topics and needs. The characteristics of effective PL derived from meta-analyses are, therefore, by definition, abstracted from practice. In laying out the ways Reading Apprenticeship embodies these effective characteristics, however, specifics matter. Reading Apprenticeship is focused on building the capacity of teachers across the subject areas and secondary and postsecondary grade levels to advance students' literacies, which will enable their engagement and success in subject-area learning. It is important, then, to detail what "engaging teachers actively" means with regard to this ambitious aim.

Just as the Reading Apprenticeship instructional framework guides teachers in designing and reflecting on the classroom learning environment, attending to personal, social, cognitive, and knowledge-building dimensions, PL is itself guided by the framework. Inquiry is the central mode of learning in the Reading Apprenticeship classroom; in parallel, active inquiry is central to Reading Apprenticeship PL for teachers. Facilitated enactments of text-based inquiry routines mediate the social and personal elements of teacher learning as teachers encounter, consider, and reject or embrace new ways of thinking about texts in the context of teaching their subject areas. Facilitated and supported discussion is as vital to the PL community as it is to the classroom community. In Reading Apprenticeship PL, this commitment to inquiry as a mode of learning for teachers and their students is embodied in the conversational routines and structures of the PL experience.

Reading Apprenticeship facilitators work from highly designed agendas and their own knowledge and classroom practice to engage teachers in inquiry routines designed to surface their literacy histories and identities as subject matter teachers. Carefully sequenced learning experiences have teachers begin Reading Apprenticeship PL by inquiring into their own content knowledge, reflecting on their reading and literacy habits and experiences in a variety of contexts, and recalling the impulses and interests that initially inspired them to become teachers of their particular disciplines. Reading process inquiries engage teachers in tackling complex texts as naïve readers and sharing what they did to make sense of these challenging pieces. Still other inquiries help teachers identify features of texts that offer learning opportunities and challenges, or zero in on their unarticulated knowledge about discipline-specific texts, purposes for reading, and reasoning processes that constitute expert practice.

To articulate these hidden processes of reading and reasoning, teachers may utilize specific strategy routines (e.g., clarifying, word learning, questioning) and then reflect not only on what they learned about expert reading processes, but also on the utility of particular pedagogical routines for supporting comprehension. Teachers then use these insights to design and facilitate similar inquiries in their classrooms. Gayle describes how this PL entered into her classroom instruction.

> Initially, I model (for students), articulating my own processes as a reader as I read aloud. My students and I begin looking at specific places in the text where we have problems understanding, where we have to slow down, where we are uncertain. We talk about what we might do to figure things out, we test various strategies, we talk about whether or not a particular strategy worked, and if so what we understand as a result. A lighter tone develops as reading becomes less of a mystery and more of a project that we work on together in class. (Cribb quoted in Schoenbach, Greenleaf, & Murphy, 2012, p. 89)

Reflecting the central importance of student voice in the Reading Apprenticeship model, multiple learning inquiries focus on making sense of student thinking. For example, after tackling inquiries into their own sensemaking with a text, teachers may view videos of Reading Apprenticeship classrooms in which students are engaged in text-based discussion about the same piece, or pour over student annotations on the text they read. They are supported to notice what students are doing to make sense of texts—are they drawing on personal knowledge and experience, looking up vocabulary, consulting other texts, talking with peers, tapping genre knowledge, parsing sentences, drawing graphics? To what extent are their moves echoing what teachers themselves did in making sense of the same text? The inquiry focused on noticing what students are doing to make sense of texts helps teachers identify strengths and learning needs evident in what students say or write, to interrogate their own assumptions about students, and to practice interpreting student voices with deeper insight over time.

Through all of these inquiries, teachers experience metacognitive conversation, reading, and grouping routines that they are then encouraged to implement in their classrooms with students. This active and experiential dimension of PL—the apprenticeship based on Vygotsky's zone of proximal development (Vygotsky, 1978)—makes potential changes in instructional practice visible and nameable, and therefore more attainable and easier to sustain and build upon over time in the classroom. The Reading Apprenticeship model reflects the understanding that for practice to become truly responsive to student needs and to the varied contexts of teachers' work, teachers must be encouraged to be adaptive and generative in their use of specific practices (Ball & Cohen, 1999; Gillis, 2014; Kennedy, 2016).

The Content of Reading Apprenticeship PL: Fostering a Collaborative Literacy Learning Environment

Similarly, it is important to detail what "centering on content" means in the context of the ambitious goals of the Reading Apprenticeship instructional framework. Many programs of professional development will address specific instructional strategies. Others will focus on enriching teachers' understanding of their subject areas, such as science concepts, or disciplinary pedagogical approaches, such as using primary source documents in history teaching. While instructional strategies and subject area knowledge are important, our understanding of the "content area" for PL in literacy is rooted in long-term collaborative inquiry into the problem of secondary students' inexperience, discomfort, and difficulties making sense of complex, academic materials.

In our many investigations into students' literacy histories, experiences of shame and powerlessness are common and can be life-shaping incidents that influence students' future literacy engagement and the investments they are willing to make in learning. Elsewhere, we have described the pain students experience in school regarding reading and the many ways they compensate for perceived weaknesses (see Greenleaf et al., 2001; Greenleaf & Hinchman, 2009; Greenleaf & Valencia, 2017; Litman & Greenleaf, 2014).

But such stories are equally true for teachers, regardless of how successful they may be as adult readers in particular circumstances. For example, in PL inquiries, teachers may relate how painful experiences with literary interpretation turned them off to reading literature. Yet they joyfully engage with nonfiction texts in their subject areas without realizing the deep reservoir of literacy knowledge they have developed with these texts, how that knowledge makes the sensemaking work feel easier, and what their deep engagement offers to less experienced readers. They may tell us how struggling to comprehend college texts in particular subjects shaped their choice of major and led to their teaching biology, say, instead of the career they had planned in medicine. They may describe standing outside the book mobile to request books by name, since as children in segregated communities, they weren't allowed to enter the community library. They may offer the ways that reading provided momentary escapes from bewildering and unsettling family or community circumstances and trauma. In Reading Apprenticeship PL, preparing teachers to support students in meaning making with text draws on these inquiries into teachers' own literacy lives, acknowledging how sensemaking implicates the whole self, all of one's experiences reading in community and school, across time.

Making sense of text similarly taps into the whole world of familiar and unfamiliar text types and textual practices common to academic and disciplinary work, for both students and teachers (Goldman et al., 2016). Teachers can be more effective when they are aware of the language experiences that shape the ways readers draw inferences and interpret text signals (Fang & Schleppegrell, 2010; Phillips Galloway et al., 2020; Skerrett, 2020), as well as the processes that readers engage in with texts while making meaning (Kintsch, 1998; Perfetti, 1999), including how readers recruit everyday interpretive practices from their social and cultural contexts to comprehend texts (Lee, 2020; Lee & Spratley, 2010). Making sense of text draws on everything that readers know and have experienced, as well as what they don't know and have difficulty imagining (Cervetti & Wright, 2019).

In Reading Apprenticeship, the content of PL thus includes more than a focus on reading strategies or text structures and features. Through collaborative inquiry, teachers are supported in learning how to create classroom environments in which the work of understanding complex text is a shared venture; in which already knowing is not as celebrated as coming to know (learning); in which disclosing difficulties understanding text supports problem solving for all rather than being labeled a weakness or liability; in which students' varied social and cultural experiences and knowledge count and are recognized as assets as they are put to use in collaborative sensemaking (Schoenbach et al., 2012; Schoenbach & Greenleaf, 2009).

The Reading Apprenticeship PL approach is therefore shaped by theoretical frameworks and current research understandings from psychology and the learning sciences as well as from literacy research. To create collaborative learning environments, whether in PL or in the classroom, understanding learners' socioemotional learning needs is key. Educators' recent focus on the role of socioemotional dispositions and strategies in learning has drawn renewed attention to the long-studied roles that motivation and emotional responses have been shown to play in learning (Farrington et al., 2012; Yeager & Walton, 2011; CASEL.org). Recent research has underscored the importance of learning cognitive, metacognitive, and attentional self-regulation strategies (Afflerbach & Cho, 2009; Guthrie & Klauda, 2016); the centrality of social and cultural practices that influence and shape knowledge (National Academies of Sciences, Engineering, and Medicine, 2018); conceptions of self, agency, and learning that enable growth rather than rendering it seemingly futile; and the necessity of building stamina and perseverance in the face of challenge—when students may otherwise give up and give in (Duckworth et al., 2011; Dweck, 2006; Dweck & Molden, 2005; Duckworth, 2016; Duckworth & Quinn, 2009).

Creating an effective learning environment for teacher collaboration requires this same set of understandings, with added sensitivity to the specific needs of adult learners (Darling-Hammond et al., 2009, 2017; Desimone, 2009; Hill et al., 2013; Merriam & Bierema, 2014; Trotter, 2006). Just like their students, teachers must feel safe to ask questions, voice confusion and disagreements, and bring their own experiences to the collaborative learning environment. In describing therapeutic environments in which people are able to build resilience after experiencing trauma, Walsh (Walsh, 2002, 2007) enumerates characteristics that could apply equally well to the supportive classroom culture for literacy learning that is the focus of Reading Apprenticeship PL:

- "Normalizing struggle"—recasting challenges as shared, comprehensible, manageable, and meaningful to tackle
- Making implicit theories about learning explicit and open to revision
- Drawing out and affirming strengths; recognizing resourcefulness, persistence, and problem solving
- Prioritizing communication processes that clarify ambiguities and encourage expression and empathetic response
- Encouraging collaborative problem solving and mutual support to meet challenges

The Duration of Reading Apprenticeship PL

There have been many iterations of Reading Apprenticeship PL over the years to accommodate the varied needs of teachers working in diverse school and district contexts. In each iteration, these core elements—inquiry enactment as a way of learning, tackling complex texts, literacy engagement and sensemaking processes, and developing a socioemotionally informed learning environment—remain constant. Advocating that PL be "of sufficient duration" in response to the one-shot workshop approach typical of teacher learning offerings, Reading Apprenticeship takes place in multiple in-person and online experiences over time (Darling-Hammond et al., 2017). Recognizing that teacher learning is a complex and interactive process, learning institutes and PL communities (PLCs) punctuate the school year so that teachers (as learners) have access to the necessary resources (tools, time, and people) to experience new ways of thinking about their own practice. Regularly spaced learning across the school year offers teachers opportunities to reflect individually and collaboratively on practice, to enact new practices in their own classrooms, to discuss and reflect on associated successes and challenges, and to plan next steps for continuing the cycle of learning and deepening practice.

When educators are given the opportunity to work in a group or team over extended periods of time, transformation in teacher practices occurs. As it did for Gayle when she was in the classroom, so it did when she apprenticed history teacher Crystal Maglio, who eventually became a design research partner. Crystal gives voice to the hard work and identity shifts that take place—for both teachers and students—when engaged in deep learning with complex texts. In a 2016 reflection, which became part of an open resource history unit she and Gayle designed, Crystal articulated how insights she gained in PL inquiries led to shifts in her practices that were new but initially uncomfortable to enact in the classroom.

> When I look back at video clips [of my own teaching] . . . I can see how hard I am working to hold back from validating students' interpretations and, instead, am trying to push the meaning-making back to the students. This was a huge struggle for me internally, and I got a lot of push back from the students, which made it even harder. At one point—in a moment I like to think of as "the mutiny"—one student raised his hand to protest the "new way" of doing things. He accused me of leaving them hanging by not explaining the texts. I tried to communicate that I wanted to give them the power to decide what the texts meant for themselves. And, part of me still felt like I was guilty as charged; I wasn't "helping"—at least not in the old way. And I didn't yet understand the new way enough to have confidence in

> it. However, with Gayle's support and encouragement, I persisted. (Maglio, 2016, "Crystal's Reflection," p. 4)

Key Principles of the Reading Apprenticeship Approach

On the one hand, PL can be described as a curriculum or set of lesson plans, complete with material resources to support teacher learning. Reading Apprenticeship institutes, courses, books, videos, and other materials (tools) can be seen in that light. On the other hand, PL can be understood as a profession-long enterprise of ever deepening expertise. This understanding of, and commitment to support, ongoing teacher and student literacy growth is at the heart of the work done to build Reading Apprenticeship over nearly three decades.

Beyond the characteristics and theoretical influences described above, then, Reading Apprenticeship is founded on a set of principles that have shaped its growth and impact: a commitment to equity; collaborative design; asset orientation; teachers' passion for their subject area; and a positive socioemotional learning climate. These principles are fundamental to the work and success of the project, yet commitments such as these are not often discussed in the evidence base, nor are they listed as characteristics of high-quality PL. We share them here because they create the fertile ground for the project's continuous growth and innovation. We illustrate these principles and their impact through Gayle's growing contributions to her students, fellow teachers, and the field.

Equity

Access to high-quality learning for both teachers and their students has driven the development of Reading Apprenticeship PL, tools, and materials since 1995. Through grants from philanthropic and government agencies focused on enhancing opportunities for students who are most often underrepresented in higher education, our aim has been to guide teachers and staff to support "engaged, advanced literacy for all." In conjunction with this commitment is a focus on high-quality PL for all teachers. Equity and access are not separate concepts or activities we "do" but instead are baked into each principle articulated below and at each level of our work—from the framework itself, to how we design teacher PL and research, to how we allocate resources and function as an organization.

In the classroom, Reading Apprenticeship promotes a view of students as *inexperienced with*, rather than *incapable of*, tackling the challenges of discipline-specific literacy. We view all students as capable of reading and learning from complex texts. Regardless of their past school experience and performance and student identity, in Reading Apprenticeship classrooms, everyone can "play," and there are multiple entry points and levels to meet each student's needs. Students are consistently invited into collaboration and are supported to participate in the enterprise of making sense of text and creating new knowledge.

Reading Apprenticeship routines help teachers support students to understand the "how" of learning—that asking questions, being aware of when you are confused, and seeking support from teachers and peers who have different backgrounds, interpretations, and experiences are all part of school and life. Teachers also inquire into students' interests, experiences, and cultures, designing lessons that draw on those interests, build on those strengths, and track their change over time. Students' voices and perspectives are thus the center of classroom instruction, which takes the form of extended meaning making about texts and content. As students build their capacity for learning, self-awareness, and sensemaking, teachers introduce increasingly complex texts and disciplinary ways of reading.

Gayle recalls coming into teaching with a clear sense of mission that resonated with Reading Apprenticeship.

> "I came into teaching with a clear commitment to equity. As a college student, I learned Spanish as part of that, trained as a bilingual teacher, and chose a district with socioeconomic and ethnic diversity. I was also committed to history. I wanted all my students to have access to the discipline I had come to value. I wanted them to understand the epistemology of history, to seek out and know how to grapple with multiple perspectives, to think historically, and to be able to reason and think critically. I wanted them to have these powerful tools for understanding their present through an inquiry into the past. Before encountering Reading Apprenticeship, I had worked hard at engaging my students in this endeavor and was successful to some degree, but few students could handle many of the texts, so I became better at delivering the content without so much text in an effort to give all of my students access. With Reading Apprenticeship, my students learned to engage with complex texts, and the rigor I had always believed was possible began to emerge."

In PL, Reading Apprenticeship facilitators likewise reach for the engagement of each and every teacher in a course, regardless of their past experience and performance and teacher identity. Mirroring what we do with students in a classroom, we attempt to take every teacher where they are, and work with them to expand their insights and repertoire. Because of our organizational commitment to equity, we intentionally offer PL to teachers in diverse and under-resourced settings, especially seeking out teachers who may have had few opportunities due to their location or their school system's resources. We seek large grant work for evidence-based projects, especially those that include scale and reach—often choosing to work with thousands of educators across multiple regions and contexts when we could limit work to a single district.

For example, one recent initiative involved work with seven states and included teachers of low-wealth students in both urban San Francisco Unified and rural Fresno County. In another initiative, we engaged teachers and leaders from Chicago Public Schools and a small, off-road remote school in Alaska. In yet another, we worked with teachers in New York City and in Arizona's native reservations. Solving the challenge of maintaining high quality and impact and living the principles articulated below, while working at scale, is indeed part of making evidence-based PL more accessible to ever more educators. In each setting, we find teachers eager for intellectually challenging work and ready to collaborate with colleagues to improve student learning experiences and outcomes.

Collaborative Design

Recognizing the challenges that teachers face in helping a wide range of students engage in rigorous academic reading to learn subject matter, Reading Apprenticeship classroom routines have always been designed in collaboration with teachers with the goal of identifying and sharing effective ways to advance students' literacy engagement and achievement. The model is one of *distributed expertise,* relying on teachers and their students to tap the resources they bring to the learning environment. Reading Apprenticeship research and PL staff engage experienced Reading Apprenticeship teachers in *Inquiry Networks* explicitly devoted to building new tools and approaches through joint inquiry into specific literacy phenomena. We work with teacher colleagues to develop tools and practices for teacher and student learning, designing and redesigning for specific, intended outcomes (such as drawing students' affective responses into the work of learning, and engaging students to notice and share their confusions, to learn to generate specifically scientific or historical questions of texts, to do intertextual referencing, and to develop disciplinary argumentation from multiple sources).

Collaborative design may involve teachers as partners in design-based research projects or in the design of instructional routines, PL, curriculum, or their own research. Teachers collect evidence from students to gauge the promise and potential of new instructional routines. Successful routines for teacher and student learning emerge from this iterative design process, enabling teachers new to Reading Apprenticeship to benefit from the work of predecessors. Over time, Gayle participated in all of these endeavors. Although not every teacher participates at the level experienced by Gayle, many do.

> "When we were working on Project READI, we had a Teacher Inquiry Network with a focus on disciplinary argumentation. I facilitated the history group. We wanted to become aware of how we read as we develop historical arguments. The professional development team designed an inquiry to capture our processes as we read historical texts under two different circumstances. For one set of primary sources, we provided a claim and asked teachers to read the texts in order to support the given claim. For the second set of primary sources, we asked teachers to read the texts and create claims. Then we had a metacognitive conversation in which we described the specific moves we had made as readers in each circumstance. We were surprised to discover how very different our processes were! That "ah ha" then affected how Crystal and I designed the unit for our research (Cribb, Greenleaf, & Maglio, 2018) and, because it had big implications for what students learn how to do with historical texts, we incorporated a similar inquiry into one of our history argumentation modules for PL."

Asset Orientation

Teachers and students bring unique assets into the classroom learning community in the form of language, knowledge, life experiences, and interests. Reading Apprenticeship recognizes these as key resources to draw upon as learners focus on sensemaking with complex texts in various subject areas. The Reading Apprenticeship PL model immerses teachers in experiential learning through literacy inquiry with complex texts, practices that they are supported to integrate into their subject-area teaching. As teachers become reacquainted with their academic and discipline-specific literacy expertise through collaborative inquiries into their own and their colleagues' reading, they are increasingly able to reimagine what they and their own students can accomplish. Importantly, explorations of classroom videos and student work support teachers in building insight into student meaning making. The approach is therefore dynamic and responsive; it is rooted in the act of teaching and learning with text. This requires reframing learning equally in the classroom and in the PLC as a *partnership of expertise*.

As a novice Reading Apprenticeship teacher in 2004, Gayle reflected on how experiencing one metacognitive learning routine, "Thinking Aloud," and then later facilitating it with colleagues and her own students, brought about shifts in her understanding of both reading and her students.

> I now think that reading is thinking—that it is in the interaction between the author and the reader that the meaning is constructed. It matters what the reader brings to the reading in terms of experience and prior knowledge, as well as what the reader expects to get from the reading and his or her own processes for doing so . . .
>
> I find that I am more curious than I used to be about what exactly my students are thinking when they are reading. I listen more closely for how they are trying to make sense of the piece and ask them more questions about their process. I am less urgent about identifying and providing that missing piece of information or logic. I am more expectant about learning something about my students or the text or life from their particular reading of the text. . . . I can't help but think that my students feel this shift toward peerness, however subtle, and respond in kind. (Cribb quoted in Strickland & Kamil, 2004, pp. 240–241)

Socioemotional Learning Climate

Embarking on new teaching approaches unavoidably requires risk-taking. Teachers and the work they do are embedded in systems that make demands on their time and constrain their decision making to varying degrees. Reform mandates shift, often without consideration of valuable ongoing work. Well-meaning administrators pepper the faculty with multiple, often simultaneous and sometimes contradictory, reform initiatives, often without regard to how they can be addressed and integrated into the central work of teaching. There is little time in the teaching day to think, consolidate learning, and imagine new ways to engage learners.

Students and communities are impacted by trauma—from natural disasters, to bullying and gun violence, to pandemics and their accompanying disruptions and distress. Reading Apprenticeship facilitators work from an understanding of the important social and emotional dimensions of learning, as they work with teachers who are often overwhelmed and frazzled, want to do well by their students, yet experience little autonomy or recognition. Just as in the Reading Apprenticeship classroom, PL depends on building a climate of trust and care in order to build teachers' hope, resilience, and agency to embrace new ideas and build the courage to enact new approaches to teaching. As Gayle notes,

"One of the things I needed to learn as I transitioned from teaching students in the classroom to facilitating professional learning was how much I was asking of teachers. Though I had been in the trenches myself, my own learning curve had happened over the course of a decade. I had forgotten how tightly we hold to what we have figured out in the classroom, to our teacher identities, our beliefs, and our practices. I needed to attend to the emotional work entailed in teachers considering significant pedagogical shifts.

Passion for Learning

Underlying the notion of distributed expertise in Reading Apprenticeship PL is a deeply held set of assumptions: Teachers, especially those at the secondary level, have expertise in a subject matter and, at some point, they loved history, art, math, physics, or literature; however, when teachers are discouraged, working in dysfunctional settings, overworked, and pressed by everyday crises, their passion and idealism can get buried. One of the outgrowths of text-based inquiry routines in Reading Apprenticeship is the engagement in deep subject matter learning that occurs while reading something complex. These inquiries often reawaken the passion that brought teachers to their disciplines in the first place. In the classroom, these same routines support students' deep engagement in thinking and talking—especially when coupled with interesting texts—sparking students' innate curiosities and often leading them to new discoveries. Not much is more compelling than the light in students' eyes when they step into the joy of curiosity. Reading Apprenticeship PL draws these key moments of student engagement in learning into view through video inquiries, formative assessment, and ongoing teacher reflection.

Gayle captures this kind of reengagement in her passion for history in a recent reflection on her choice to engage in an inquiry group focused on her subject area.

"When SLI formed a History Teacher Inquiry Group to develop disciplinary literacy knowledge and tools specific to history, I volunteered. I opted into these opportunities because I enjoyed the intellectual stimulation, the learning, the collaboration, and how what I learned fed my classroom practices. We were gaining nuance in understanding how we read as people interested in history, with historical questions. Those insights were useful in resisting the pressures of convention and making room for something different from the way history and social studies were typically taught at the secondary level. We were homing in on what I had loved as an undergraduate student of history."

Structuring for Equitable Access and Sustained Support

PL as Ongoing Research and Development

Developing and supporting learners' growth in text-based inquiry is demanding, both for teachers in the classroom and for facilitators in the PL setting. Mediating such learning requires one to assess the learning situation, to read the resources in the group, to make decisions about how to challenge and support particular learners—in particular disciplines, and at particular moments in the learning journey. Reading Apprenticeship PL routines are meant to guide and support teachers in practicing and refining this very complex decision making. Through metacognitive conversational routines, ongoing formative assessment is built into PL and classroom engagements. Because Reading Apprenticeship facilitators are drawn from diverse settings and subject areas and are themselves expert Reading Apprenticeship teachers, they are able to *lead from practice* in PL.

To ensure the PL routines are supporting particular groups of learners, research and professional development design staff engage in what is essentially an ongoing project of iterative, formative design research at multiple levels—analyzing and reflecting on interactions with facilitators, teachers, and students in order to create and refine enabling conditions for learning. Similarly, as mediators of teacher learning, Reading Apprenticeship facilitators continually reflect on what they need to do next to support deeper learning with particular groups of teachers—be their shared focus a content area, grade level, or course-type—and respond to the continually changing context, as society and the field of education change over time. Ongoing research and development processes can themselves present opportunities for teacher PL and validation, as Gayle describes.

> "To my good fortune, my classroom was selected for observation and data collection as part of a Reading Apprenticeship R&D project. I was partnered with a brilliant researcher, Cindy Litman, who asked amazing questions, shared observations, listened to me work out my thinking, and collaborated on lesson design. Later, some of those lessons were filmed for use in professional learning and some of the data has made its way into various publications. As classroom teachers, much of the time we work in isolation. Much of what we do is invisible, even to our students. So, having another educator in my classroom, thinking with me about my work, was rich and enormously validating. For many of us, the creativity, care and intelligence we pour into our lessons never moves beyond our classroom walls. There

are few mechanisms that allow that good work to be shared, so to be able to make a contribution to the field was a gift."

From the outset, SLI's leadership identified the need for this work and carried out studies to provide evidence of its effectiveness, enabling the project to continue securing funding for the kind of work Gayle and so many others experienced. The project intentionally invested funding resources in researcher/practitioner partnerships to iteratively design, test, and refine teacher-informed tools to be broadly disseminated. This research agenda was grounded in an ongoing commitment to gauge success by examining impact on teacher practice, on students' opportunities to learn, on students' literacy learning outcomes, and on informing the discourse of the field. This ongoing focus led to greater opportunities to disseminate Reading Apprenticeship, replicate prior research, as well as conduct new studies to deepen the knowledge base of the field. Gayle's continued professional growth was supported by these new opportunities.

> "In 2010, SLI won federal grants for two big projects which included teacher leadership and teacher-researcher partnerships. I was invited to take on new roles, as I left the classroom and became both part of a PL design team and a research team. Both roles were challenging—designing for teachers, rather than students, and participating in what was a new field for me, the academic world of literacy research. Key to being able to step into those roles successfully were SLI's valuing of my expertise as a classroom teacher, insistence that my voice be heard, and support for the learning I needed to do."

Communities of Learners

Fostering a learning environment that provides access to and builds on the resources already present in learners, including teachers, through metacognitive conversation requires the development of robust learning communities. One way the principle of *leading from practice* informs Reading Apprenticeship PL design is that we seek to start working with teachers who opt in from a school site, rather than working with entire faculties who are mandated to attend. This is particularly important when focused on discipline-specific literacy instruction, since many subject area teachers regard literacy as being outside of their purview.

Starting with a subset of teachers who choose to participate in PL also enables the more intrepid explorers on a school staff to try out core Reading Apprenticeship routines in their subject areas and to begin leading from their own practice, thereby developing evidence of successful implementation and student engagement for their less eager colleagues and beginning their own journeys as *teacher leaders*. To seed the growth of site-based communities of practice, teachers are invited to participate in multi-site Reading Apprenticeship PL institutes and courses with colleagues, as *subject-based and/or cross-subject area teams*. Site-based teams are connected across schools in PL *networks*, enabling fertile ideas and solutions to implementation dilemmas to travel from site to site.

Over time, additional *cohorts* of teachers from school sites participate in Reading Apprenticeship. Teacher leaders at the school site are often key in encouraging their colleagues to participate. Through resources and materials as well as focused PL opportunities, Reading Apprenticeship supports site-based PLCs to grow in order to sustain and deepen their work to advance student literacy learning.

Additionally, Reading Apprenticeship facilitators engage in a community of practice led by the organization, providing collegial support for ongoing learning, as well as an improvement and innovation resource for high-quality dissemination. SLI's capacity to consistently implement PL at a national scale, while also remaining responsive to local conditions, is dependent upon this community. Gayle believes that Reading Apprenticeship facilitators remain engaged because they value one another and have a shared commitment to teaching, PL, and continuous improvement.

> "As a facilitator community, we appreciate opportunities to collaborate with one another. Facilitating this complex professional learning is challenging. The local contexts are each unique, and the field of education is constantly changing as new knowledge, initiatives, reforms, and politics develop. We strive for flexible fidelity—understanding Reading Apprenticeship and the design of the professional learning deeply enough that we can respond to the needs of particular groups of educators. Because the knowledge base of Reading Apprenticeship continues to build, our professional learning offerings continue to evolve. We love getting a chance to try out a new inquiry; recalibrate by tackling a new text together; work through a new facilitation agenda; or share perceptions, insights, and questions about a particular context or a new development in our contexts (e.g., online learning; digital texts; wearing masks due to pandemics). We treasure the expertise in the room and value learning from one another."

Multiple Entry Points and Sustained Support

As described above, from the outset of this work SLI has engaged teachers as way-makers, explorers who can chart a new course and lay out stepping stones for others. Creating access to high-quality, continuous PL is central to improvement and equity for both teachers and students. Rather than minimize the demand PL can place on burdened school sites and teachers, we opt to create access via multiple entry points and levels of investment, from instantly accessible digital resources on the web to comprehensive multi-year, district and statewide literacy initiatives.

To meet the needs of diverse districts and individuals, Reading Apprenticeship includes PL engagements of varied lengths (in-person, online, and hybrid options), and we publish affordable, practical books with tools so that any educator can take up this work with their students and have models for expanding the work to a department, school, or districtwide initiative. Reading Apprenticeship online PL gives educators more scheduling options, expands accessibility for rural educators, and increases all educators' interactions with experts and colleagues over the school year without the expense of travel. We have intentionally designed online learning to include the extended synchronous inquiries, discussion, and interaction that embody our commitment to supporting teachers socially and personally as they engage in new forms of practice (Archer et al., 2018; Katz et al., 2019).

To create PL experiences that are responsive to local contexts while building capacity to sustain inquiry and continuous learning, we work with the many layers of leadership that sustain PL over time—support agencies, teacher leaders, and administrators. These local partners often hold long-term expertise and knowledge about education policies and PL in their area and can inform the project of ways to integrate local reform initiatives with Reading Apprenticeship. We design and convene networks, as well as instructional leadership teams, building the pipeline of access through additional training for Teacher Leaders and administrators. These layers of support enable schools to provide principled, ongoing assistance for teachers at their sites and extend the impact and ongoing refinement of Reading Apprentice immeasurably, as Gayle's own PL journey attests.

> "When I look back at my history in Reading Apprenticeship, I appreciate the opportunities I was afforded, over time. This was not a "one and done" training. In fact, our administrators signed an agreement that we would not be expected to present something to our colleagues when we finished the first three days, but would be given that year to implement and to continue learning. The implication was that this was not a small project, or a simple practice. We were encouraged to try things and to bring back our successes and challenges to the Reading Apprenticeship network. Opportunities for continuing to learn emerged in subsequent years, as SLI won new grants, and my district was able to allocate resources to allow us to continue deepening our understanding. Our student teachers learned the approach

from us because that was just "how things rolled" in our classrooms. In periods when we did not have access to further PL, we had the book and we had protocols for inquiries and assessments that we could use in house to keep moving forward.

"As a facilitator, I was initially skeptical that Reading Apprenticeship could be learned in an asynchronous online format. After having taught many of those courses, I can attest that, if people do the work, they can make tremendous progress in understanding Reading Apprenticeship and transform their practices. I have met teachers who read the book and say it changed how they taught, and teachers who got some exposure from a teacher-led inquiry at school and now sought in-person PL. From an equity lens, I am so pleased that there are multiple ways to begin, and multiple ways to continue to learn."

The books Gayle refers to—*Reading for Understanding: How Reading Apprenticeship Improves Disciplinary Learning in Secondary and College Classrooms* and *Leading for Literacy: A Reading Apprenticeship Approach*—enable individual teachers and teams at school sites to walk well-marked and principled pathways on their own, through book study groups (Schoenbach et al., 2012, 2017). Likewise, the website *www.ReadingApprenticeship.org* offers classroom videos to share what Reading Apprenticeship looks like across secondary and college levels and in different subject areas. Lesson resources, curriculum units that model and support text-based inquiry, teacher team tools, research reports and tools are also available on the website at no cost. These portable tools offer additional points of access, seeding the field and distributing expertise across time by designing and mediating teachers' experiences as they continue to deepen their practice with Reading Apprenticeship teaching and learning. Over time, teachers expand their pedagogical content knowledge and expertise as well as their confidence as strategic designers of learning opportunities for their students.

Conclusions

In this chapter, we have described long-term investments we have intentionally made as a collaborative R&D project to foster ongoing literacy growth among teachers and students across subject areas and grade levels. Our work has proceeded by acknowledging and tapping into distributed expertise and teacher ownership to build the capacity and generativity of teachers and education leaders. When defining PL as a single experience or series of institutes or workshops, measuring the value added from such inputs in terms of teacher change or student outcomes is necessarily limited in scope and, often, in magnitude. Yet a far different view of *impact* emerges when viewing a larger program of capacity building and investment in teacher leadership over time. When there are central organizing projects like the Strategic Literacy Initiative that can invest in and support work over time, professional expertise can be continuous. As Gayle's professional growth and the reach of her impact on the field illustrates, the value added of such work defies easy quantification.

By holding true to a vision of deep literacy learning as the means through which teachers and their students can continuously improve, we have created tools and learning opportunities and resources that have reached over 10,000 teachers and more than 1,500,000 students. And while multiple rigorous randomized controlled trials have measured and certified the efficacy of the Reading Apprenticeship PL model in its impact on teacher practice, as well as student literacy and subject matter learning (Greenleaf et al., 2011; Goldman et al., 2019), such measures, as Gayle's professional journey attests, reveal only a small part of the long-term, sustained impact of this work. And while Gayle Cribb is a remarkable professional, she is one of the hundreds of Reading Apprenticeship leaders and facilitators working to transform the literacy learning opportunities of middle and high school students across the nation. We intend her story to be illustrative, emblematic of the reach each teacher can have when equipped with the knowledge, tools, agency, support, and generativity that a program of deep inquiry-based learning such as Reading Apprenticeship can offer. Each Reading Apprenticeship facilitator and experienced teacher leader could offer a similarly unique story of sustained professional growth and impact.

Likewise, the work we have described in this chapter is replicable. We have attempted to lay out the key principles and core values, the investments and ongoing iterative development that can build and magnify outcomes over time. This work can be taken up by others with different goals and focus areas for teacher and student growth. Universities, regional education support centers, and school districts can support ongoing and collaborative R&D to tackle long-term problems of practice (Coburn & Penuel, 2016). In such work, sustained PL with ongoing support for teacher growth is a necessary component. All too often, schools and systems invest in publisher-based and short-term workshops that show little impact on teacher practice or student learning.

The longer-term investment is difficult to ensure, given constraints of budget and time; yet this is where a central R&D role can be key to building and sustaining teacher leadership and capacity. Scholars, groups of scholars within universities or organizations like WestEd, education agencies, and school districts can support work over time through intentional fund raising for educator/researcher partners with a long-term and sustained focus. Enlightened school and district leaders can shift a focus on short-term solutions to an investment in longer-term growth and teacher leadership. External funding organizations can assist in holding the vision and focus on capacity building through the tumult and change that often surround schools and teachers. Such support can take the field of PL beyond narrow understandings of effectiveness and impact to embrace a long view of teacher learning.

At the end of the day, transformation is not brought about by teaching specific routines or telling people what to do; transformation occurs when we go deep into what it means to teach and learn. In the work of Reading Apprenticeship, we have designed for scale and have intentionally made iterations on the model over time, always in partnership with teachers. Ours is a story about what ongoing collaborative R&D, through funding and consistent focus, has enabled us and so many educators to do by engaging teachers as essential leaders and owners of this work so that it can spread, grow, develop, and ultimately transform the field.

REFERENCES

Afflerbach, P., & Cho, B. Y. (2009). Identifying and describing constructively responsive comprehension strategies in new and traditional forms of reading. In S. E. Israel & G. G. Duffy (Eds.), *Handbook of research on reading comprehension* (pp. 69–90). Routledge.

Archer, J., Katz, M. L., Charney-Sirott, I., Howlett, H., & Max, J. (2018, April). Implementing online professional learning communities: Insights from WestEd's Blended Professional Development Model. Mathematica Policy Research. Retrieved from *https://readingapprenticeship.org/articles/implementing-online-professional-learning-communities.*

Ball, D., & Cohen, D. (1999). Developing practice, developing practitioners: Toward a practice-based theory of professional education. In L. Darling-Hammond & G. Sykes (Eds.), *Teaching as the learning profession: Handbook of policy and practice* (pp. 3–32). Jossey-Bass.

Cervetti, G. N., & Wright, T. S. (2020). The role of knowledge in understanding and learning from text. In E. B. Moje, P. Afflerbach, P. Enciso, & N. K. Lesaux (Eds.), *Handbook of reading research* (Vol. V, pp. 237–260). Routledge.

Coburn, C. E., & Penuel, W. R. (2016). Research–practice partnerships in education: Outcomes, dynamics, and open questions. *Educational Researcher, 45*(1), 48–54.

Collaborative for Academic, Social and Emotional Learning. (2015). *2015 CASEL guide: Effective social and emotional learning programs—Middle and high school edition.* Author.

Cribb, G. (2004). Teaching reading strategies at the secondary level. In D.

Strickland & M. L. Kamil (Eds.), *Improving reading achievement through professional development* (pp. 140–142). Christopher-Gordon.

Cribb, G., Maglio, C., & Greenleaf, C. (2018). Collaborative argumentation: Tenth graders read modern Iranian history. *The History Teacher* (Long Beach, CA), *51*(3), 477–526. Retrieved from *www.societyforhistoryeducation.org/pdfs/M18_Cribb_Maglio_and_Greenleaf.pdf.*

Darling-Hammond, L., Hyler, M., & Gardner, M. (2017). *Effective teacher professional development.* Learning Policy Institute.

Darling-Hammond, L., Wei, R. C., Andree, A., Richardson, N., & Orphanos, S. (2009). *Professional learning in the learning profession: A status report on teacher development in the United States and abroad.* National Staff Development Council.

Desimone, L. (2009). Improving impact studies of teachers' professional development: Toward better conceptualizations and measures. *Educational Researcher, 38*(3), 181–199.

Desimone, L., & Stuckey, D. (2014). Sustaining professional development. In L. Martin, S. Kragler, D. Quatroche, & K. Bauserman (Eds.), *Handbook of professional development in education: Successful models and practices, Prek-12* (pp. 467–482). Guilford Press.

Dillon, D. R., O'Brien, D. G., Sato, M., & Kelly, C. M. (2011). Professional development and teacher education for reading instruction. In M. L. Kamil, P. D. Pearson, E. B. Moje, & P. B. Afflerbach (Eds.), *Handbook of reading research* (Vol. IV, pp. 655–686). Routledge.

Duckworth, A. (2016). *Grit: the power of passion and perseverance.* Scribner.

Duckworth, A. L., Grant, H., Loew, B., Oettingen, G., & Gollwitzer, P. M. (2011). Self-regulation strategies improve self-discipline in adolescents: Benefits of mental contrasting and implementation intentions. *Educational Psychology, 31*(1), 17–26.

Duckworth, A. L., & Quinn, P. D. (2009). Development and validation of the Short Grit Scale (Grit-S). *Journal of Personality Assessment, 91*(2), 166–174.

Dweck, C. S. (2006). *Mindset: The new psychology of success.* Random House.

Dweck, C., & Molden, D. (2005). Self-theories: Their impact on competence motivation and acquisition. In A. Elliot & C. Dweck (Eds.), *Handbook of competence and motivation* (pp. 122–140). Guilford Press.

Fancsali, C., Abe, Y., Pyatigorsky, M., Ortiz, L. Hunt, A., Chan, V., . . . Jaciw, A. (2015, December) The impact of the Reading Apprenticeship Improving Secondary Education (RAISE) Project on Academic Literacy in High School: A report of a randomized experiment in Pennsylvania and California schools. *Research Report: An Empirical Education Report.* Retrieved from *www.empiricaleducation.com/pdfs/RAISEfr.pdf.*

Fang, Z., & Schleppegrell, M. J. (2010). Disciplinary literacies across content areas: Supporting secondary reading through functional language analysis. *Journal of Adolescent and Adult Literacy, 53*(7), 587–597.

Farrington, C. A., Roderick, M., Allensworth, E., Nagaoka, J., Keyes, T. S., Johnson, D. W., & Beechum, N. O. (2012). *Teaching adolescents to become learners: The role of noncognitive factors in shaping school performance.* Consortium on Chicago School Research.

Gersten, R., Dimino, J., Jayanthi, M., Kim, J. S., & Santoro, L. E. (2010). Teacher study group: Impact of the professional development model on reading instruction and student outcomes in first grade classrooms. *American Educational Research Journal, 47*(3), 694–739.

Gillis, V. (2014). Disciplinary literacy. *Journal of Adolescent and Adult Literacy, 57*(8), 614–623.

Goldman, S. R., Britt, M. A., Brown, W., Cribb, G., George, M., Greenleaf, C., . . . Project READI. (2016). Disciplinary literacies and learning to read for understanding: A conceptual framework for disciplinary literacy. *Educational Psychologist, 51*(2), 219–246.

Goldman, S. R., Greenleaf, C., Yukhymenko-Lescroart, M., Brown, W., Ko, M., Emig, J. M., . . . Britt, M. A. (2019). Explanatory modeling in science through text-based investigation: Testing the efficacy of the Project READI intervention approach. *American Educational Research Journal, 56*(4), 1148–1216.

Greenleaf, C., & Hinchman, K. (2009). Reimagining our inexperienced adolescent readers: From struggling, striving, marginalized, and reluctant to thriving. *Journal of Adolescent and Adult Literacy, 53*(1), 4–13.

Greenleaf, C. L., Litman, C., Hanson, T. L., Rosen, R., Boscardin, C. K., Herman, J., . . . Jones, B. (2011). Integrating literacy and science in biology: Teaching and learning impacts of reading apprenticeship professional development. *American Educational Research Journal, 48*(3), 647–717.

Greenleaf, C., Schoenbach, R., Cziko, C., & Mueller, F. (2001). Apprenticing adolescent readers to academic literacy. *Harvard Educational Review, 71*(1), 79–129.

Greenleaf, C., & Valencia, S. (2017). Missing in action: Learning from texts in subject-matter classrooms. In K. A. Hinchman & D. A. Appelman (Eds.), *Adolescent literacy: A handbook of practice-based research* (pp. 135–155). Guilford Press.

Guthrie, J. T., & Klauda, S. L. (2016). Engagement and motivational processes in reading. In P. Afflerbach (Ed.), *Handbook of individual differences in reading: Reader, text, and context* (pp. 41–53). Routledge.

Hill, H. C., Beisiegel, M., & Jacob, R. (2013). Professional development research: Consensus, crossroads, and challenges. *Educational Researcher, 42*(9), 476–487.

Katz, M. L., Stump, M., Charney-Sirott, I., & Howlett, H. (2019, September/October). Traveling with Integrity: Translating face-to-face teacher professional learning to blended spaces. *Journal of Adolescent and Adult Literacy, 63*(2), 217–223.

Kennedy, M. M. (2016). How does professional development improve teaching? *Review of Educational Research, 86*(4), 945–980.

Kintsch, W. (1998). *Comprehension: A paradigm for cognition.* Cambridge University Press.

Lee, C. D. (2020). Social and cultural diversity as lens for understanding student learning and the development of reading. In E. B. Moje, P. Afflerbach, N. K. Lesaux, & P. Enciso (Eds.), *Handbook of reading research* (Vol. V, pp. 37–56). New York: Routledge.

Lee, C. D., & Spratley, A. (2010). *Reading in the disciplines and the challenges of adolescent literacy.* Carnegie Foundation of New York.

Litman, C., & Greenleaf, C. (2022). Traveling together over difficult ground: Negotiating success with a profoundly inexperienced reader in an Introduction to Chemistry class. In K. Hinchman & H. Thomas (Eds.), *Best practices in adolescent literacy* (3rd ed., pp. 205–229). Guilford Press.

Maglio, C. (2016, June 16). World History unit. Reading Apprenticeship. Retrieved from *https://readingapprenticeship.org/resource/world-history-high-school.*

Merriam, S. B., & Bierema, L. L. (2014). *Adult learning: Linking theory and practice.* Jossey-Bass.

National Academies of Sciences, Engineering, and Medicine. (2018). *How People Learn II: Learners, contexts, and cultures.* National Academies Press.

Penuel, W. R., Sun, M., Frank, K. A., & Gallagher, H. A. (2012). Using social network analysis to study how collegial interactions can augment teacher learning from external professional development. *American Journal of Education, 119*(1), 103–136.

Perfetti, C. A. (1999). Comprehending written language: A blueprint of the reader. *Neurocognition of Language, 167,* 208.

Phillips Galloway, E., Brown, J., & Uccelli, P. (2020). Broadening the lens on the science of reading: A multifaceted perspective on the role of academic language in text understanding. *Reading Research Quarterly* (Special Issue: The Science of Reading: Supports, Critiques, and Questions), *55*(1), 331–345.

Schoenbach, R., & Greenleaf, C. (2009). Fostering adolescents' engaged academic literacy. In L. Christenbury, R. Bomer, & P. Smagorinsky (Eds.), *Handbook of adolescent literacy research* (pp. 98–112). Guilford Press.

Schoenbach, R., Greenleaf, C., & Murphy, L. (2012). *Reading for understanding: How reading apprenticeship improves disciplinary learning in secondary and college classrooms.* Jossey-Bass.

Schoenbach, R., Greenleaf, C., & Murphy, L. (2016). *Leading for literacy: A reading apprenticeship approach.* Jossey-Bass.

Skerrett, A. (2020). Social and cultural differences in reading development: Instructional approaches, learning gains, and challenges. In E. B. Moje, P. Afflerbach, P. Enciso, & N. Lesaux (Eds.), *Handbook of reading research* (Vol. V, pp. 328–344). Routledge.

Somers, M. A., Corrin, W., Sepanik, S., Salinger, T., Levin, J., & Zmach, C. (2010). *The Enhanced Reading Opportunities Study Final Report: The Impact of Supplemental Literacy Courses for Struggling Ninth-Grade Readers. NCEE 2010-4021.* National Center for Education Evaluation and Regional Assistance.

Sun, M., Penuel, W. R., Frank, K. A., Gallagher, H. A., & Youngs, P. (2013). Shaping professional development to promote the diffusion of instructional expertise among teachers. *Educational Evaluation and Policy Analysis, 35*(3), 344–369.

Trotter, Y. D. (2006). Adult learning theories: Impacting professional development programs. *Delta Kappa Gamma Bulletin, 72*(2), 8.

Vygotsky, L. S. (1978). *Mind in society: The development of higher psychological processes.* (M. Cole, V. John-Steiner, S. Scribner, & E. Souberman, Eds., & Trans.). Harvard University Press.

Walsh, F. (2002). A family resilience framework: Innovative practice applications. *Family Relations, 51,* 130–137.

Walsh, F. (2007). Traumatic loss and major disasters: Strengthening family and community resilience. *Family Process, 46*(2), 207–227.

Wells, G. (2007). Semiotic mediation, dialogue and the construction of knowledge. *Human Development, 50*(5), 244–274.

Yeager, D. S., & Walton, G. M. (2011). Social-psychological interventions in education: They're not magic. *Review of Educational Research, 81*(2), 267–301.

Yoon, K. S., Duncan, T., Lee, S. W.-Y., Scarloss, B., & Shapley, K. (2007). *Reviewing the evidence on how teacher professional development affects student achievement* (Issues & Answers Report, REL 2007-No. 033). U.S. Department of Education, Institute of Education Sciences, National Center for Education Evaluation and Regional Assistance, Regional Educational Laboratory Southwest.

CHAPTER 4

Enhancing Secondary Teachers' Opportunities to Learn about Comprehension in Culturally Sustaining Ways

Sarah M. Lupo, Dianna R. Townsend, and Rachel Knecht

Watch a related video from the authors at this link.

Hannah (all names in this chapter are pseudonyms) is a ninth-grade English teacher in an urban high school in a city that houses a refugee center. Her school hosts a multilingual population of students who speak 47 different languages. All ninth-grade English teachers in this district are required to teach certain books each year, including *To Kill a Mockingbird* by Harper Lee. Hannah cares deeply for her students, and she is dismayed that she has struggled for the past several years to engage her students with this book. She has tried assigning chapters for students to read for homework and providing time for her students to read independently in class, but when she asks her students questions about the book, they seem unable to tell her what happened in the text.

In her teacher training courses, Hannah learned a variety of comprehension strategies to support students, such as teaching students how to make connections or predictions to support their understanding of the book. Although she employs these strategies, her students often focus on irrelevant details and only seem to have a literal understanding of the text. She has discussed this problem at length with her principal, who has told her that according to a recent standardized reading comprehension test, many of her students read below grade level. Hannah takes this to mean that her students cannot understand the book because it is too challenging for them to read independently. She finally settles on reading the entire novel out loud to her students, constantly stopping to explain the book to her students and model comprehension strategies. This takes 8 weeks, and Hannah is deeply unsatisfied with the results.

Much of what Hannah learned in her preservice methods courses focused on literary analysis. She has now had ample classroom experience to understand that she needs more and better approaches for supporting students with histories of reading difficulty. Hannah's story is likely familiar to secondary teachers across all disciplines, who are often contending with a large number of adolescents who have not met proficiency benchmarks for literacy (National Center for Education Statistics, 2019). As such, it is imperative to explore effective professional learning (PL) around literacy for secondary teachers.

This chapter shares an innovative PL initiative for secondary teachers' professional knowledge and practice related to engaging *all* secondary readers with complex texts. First, we present the principles of professional learning that have guided our work with preservice and in-service teachers. Next, we outline what teachers of secondary content areas need to know about reading comprehension and how they can use texts as scaffolds to build knowledge and support comprehension through use of the Quad Text Set (QTS) framework (Lewis et al., 2014; Lupo et al., 2018). Then, we discuss how designing and using QTSs across secondary content areas afford opportunities to build that essential professional knowledge around reading comprehension and prompt important reflections and pedagogical planning related to culturally sustaining pedagogy (CSP; Alim & Paris, 2017). Finally, we share an example of our innovation, the Quad Text Set Professional Learning (QTS-PL) initiative that explores how to support secondary teachers in scaffolding reading comprehension in the content areas in culturally sustaining ways.

Guiding Principles of PL for Literacy in Secondary Classrooms

As Hannah's experiences illustrate, professional learning in secondary literacy needs to be designed to simultaneously support reading comprehension and learning disciplinary content for *all* learners. Although students with the most significant histories of reading difficulties will need substantial scaffolding to engage in reading in content-area classrooms (Fagella-Luby et al., 2012), teaching reading comprehension and disciplinary content is not an either/or proposition. Effective secondary literacy instruction involves scaffolds to support all readers with challenging texts (Lupo et al., 2019), and effective PL follows suit (Townsend, 2014).

For professional learning broadly, there are established principles that should inform the design and implementation of a PL experience. Specifically, teacher knowledge is most likely to be impacted in PL experiences that include a content focus; opportunities to engage in active learning; coherence with teachers' existing knowledge and beliefs, as well as with broader policies and reforms; a duration of at least several months; and collective participation with colleagues from the same school, grade level, or department (Desimone, 2009). Ultimately, effective professional development should deepen teachers' content knowledge, change their beliefs, and improve their practice in order to improve student learning (Desimone, 2009).

However, these ingredients are not a guarantor of impact. Opfer and Pedder (2011) argue that "teacher learning must be conceptualized as a complex system rather than as an event" (p. 378). Such a perspective allows for a more nuanced examination of why PL based on the established principles does not always yield the desired impact on teachers or students. Importantly, teacher learning is more likely to be effective if schoolwide goals and values are reflected in professional development activities (Penuel et al., 2007). Our PL approach is based on the literacy needs of adolescents, the professional learning needs of teachers, and the established principles for PL. Our innovation also includes consideration of how PL interacts with the larger, complex systems in which teacher learning typically takes place.

What Do Secondary Teachers Need to Know about Comprehension?

Let's think about Hannah again as a touchstone for the professional knowledge related to comprehension that teachers need. Through our work with teachers and our review of related scholarship, we have identified three specific learning opportunities for Hannah that will likely make a big difference for her and her students. Specifically, secondary teachers often need opportunities to learn about (1) how comprehension works, (2) what instructional routines and scaffolds support comprehension, and (3) how comprehension processes interact with students' cultural and linguistic backgrounds and identities.

First, Hannah needs opportunities to deepen her knowledge of the comprehension process and what happens in adolescents' minds as they process texts. She may have the misconception that comprehension is a set of skills that can be taught in isolation (such as finding the main idea or identifying plot structures), rather than a multifaceted, complex process that has many influences. Several influences that Hannah would want to integrate into her instructional decision making are how readers' interests and motivations affect their understanding of a text (Guthrie & Wigfield,

1997), as well as how background knowledge plays a critical role in shaping a reader's comprehension (Anderson, 2013; Kintsch, 2013).

Second, in addition to learning more about how comprehension works in adolescents' minds, Hannah would need opportunities to build instructional practices that will both *support* and *improve* her readers' comprehension of various texts. Additionally, Hannah would benefit from learning that adolescents can benefit from reading a range of texts at varying levels of challenge, with appropriate scaffolding (Elish-Piper et al., 2014; Shanahan, 2015). As part of these learning practices, Hannah would likely appreciate support in both building her toolbox of instructional scaffolds to increase readers' comprehension and selecting the kinds of texts that can serve as scaffolds themselves.

Third, given the wide-ranging multicultural and multilingual backgrounds of Hannah's students, it is critical for teachers to also consider how to center students' linguistic and cultural resources as they support their understanding. Comprehension does not occur in a cultural or linguistic vacuum; rather, it is housed in culturally and linguistically specific ways of knowing and of using language (Lee, 2020). Culturally Sustaining Pedagogy (CSP; Alim & Paris, 2017; Paris, 2012) offers a powerful lens for exploring comprehension in linguistically and culturally relevant ways. It is an approach to teaching and learning that centers students and seeks to honor and sustain their cultural identities and linguistic repertoires. *Sustain* is the key word here, and it defines how CSP builds on earlier frameworks of cultural relevance and responsiveness. Sustaining culture involves creating instructional space for recognizing and honoring the many different cultural ways of knowing and being and using language that learners bring to a classroom.

Overall, without a strong understanding of the comprehension process and of the kinds of texts and instructional routines that can support it in culturally sustaining ways, *To Kill a Mockingbird* and many other texts will remain a frustrating and unengaging endeavor for many students and teachers. Effective professional learning can support teachers in building this knowledge and practice, but traditional professional learning has fallen short of this pursuit. Instead, traditional comprehension professional learning tends to create "strategy junkies" (Fisher & Frey, 2008), that is, teachers who are eager for generic literacy strategies they can immediately apply, often without a full understanding of when, why, and how to use those strategies (Wilson et al., 2009). As a result, teachers often complete PL with a set of new tools (i.e., instructional strategies) that they are unable to use in targeted ways to support adolescent readers.

Instead, literacy-focused professional learning should help educators engage in practice and reflection about comprehension instruction, including text selection and content-specific literacy skills that both develop learners' comprehension skills and support learning from texts

(Brevik, 2014; Hall, 2005). Doing so will ultimately demystify the comprehension process for both teachers and students. An important outcome of this greater attention to the comprehension processes is ***sustainable knowledge gains*** for teachers. When teachers know how comprehension works and can anticipate where it might break down, they can use instructional scaffolds in targeted ways. In the following section, we unpack just how powerful Quad Text Sets can be for supporting teacher learning around comprehension, text selection, and instructional scaffolding.

QTSs: A Vehicle for Teacher Learning

What Are QTSs?

A QTS has four types of texts (see Figure 4.1), starting with a *target* text. A target text both addresses a core content learning objective and is challenging for readers in the absence of scaffolding. For example, students in a high school earth science class may be working on science standard HS-ESS3–2: "Evaluate competing design solutions for developing, managing, and utilizing energy and mineral resources based on cost-benefit ratios" (Next Generation Science Standards [NGSS], 2013).

As students explore this standard, the teacher selects the target text *How a Wind Turbine Works* (Department of Energy, 2014a) to illustrate one way to design an alternative energy resource. In this text, the teacher has identified challenges around the complexity of both language and the concepts. The text contains a great deal of academic and discipline-specific vocabulary, such as *horizontal*, *upwind*, and *nacelle*. Additionally, the concept of turning wind into energy is abstract, difficult to visualize, and as such, not easy for adolescents to understand. Consequently, the

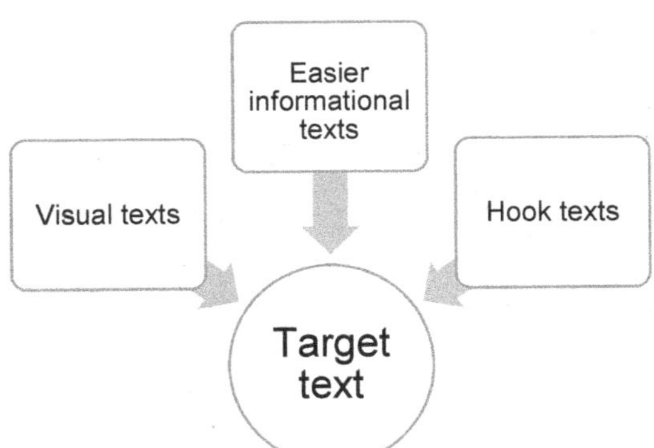

FIGURE 4.1. The Quad Text Set framework.

teacher has deemed this an appropriate "target" as it both meets content learning objectives and serves as an appropriately challenging text for students to tackle in order to improve comprehension.

Then, the teacher selects easier informational and visual texts (the second and third types of text) to build relevant knowledge to support learners in understanding the target text. For example, before engaging in the target text about how wind turbines work, students can read about the importance of clean energy in the text *Cool Jobs: Harnessing the Power of the Wind* by Kathiann Kowalski (2016). In this text, the author explains the challenge of developing wind turbine farms that are both cost effective and efficient, explaining that shifting winds and the speed at which wind hits the turbine blades both impact the turbine's ability to harness energy. This text contains more informal language and vocabulary and simpler syntax, making this an easier text for students to comprehend than the target text, which explains related concepts with more complex language and syntax. Additionally, the teacher then selects visual text(s), such as the infographic "Understanding the Grid" from Energy.gov (2014), which explains how electricity is collected at a source (i.e., wind farms) and is transported to various places that it is used (see Figure 4.2). This visual helps adolescents conceptualize the abstract idea of collecting and distributing energy.

Lastly, for the fourth type of text in a QTSs, teachers include text(s) that will serve to "hook" the readers' interest in order to motivate them to *want* to read about the topic. A hook text can help students relate to the topic, but also understand *why* it is important to learn about this topic. This is also an opportunity to connect ideas they are learning about with equity and diversity issues. For example, the teacher selects the article "Energy Access Is Not Equal; This Ann Arbor Organization Is Trying to Change That" by Jaishree Drepaul-Bruder (2018). This article helps readers get excited about the topic because they can see the real-life implications of energy, and it also highlights equity issues around energy to inspire students to work toward energy solutions for a more equitable future (see Table 4.1 for the entire text set).

QTSs differ from other kinds of text sets. Often, text sets are thematically arranged without much attention to text difficulty, student engagement, or motivation, or to how texts can scaffold one another. For example, a set of texts from 19th-century American poets might allow for opportunities to compare and contrast the themes and metaphors referenced by different poets in that era. While this may be a valuable set of texts for students to explore, none of them explicitly scaffold each other with comprehension support or knowledge-building. However, QTSs are intentionally designed to support students' comprehension of one target text using three related texts that serve as scaffolds for knowledge,

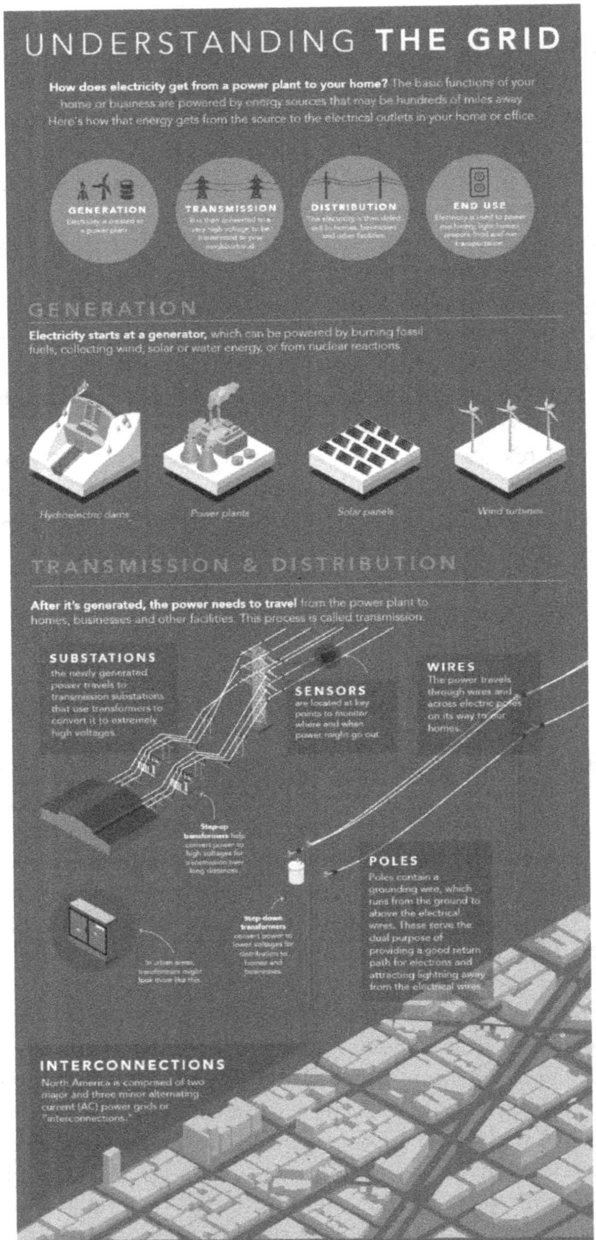

FIGURE 4.2. Clean energy infographic. Available at *www.energy.gov/articles/infographic-understanding-grid.*

TABLE 4.1. Clean Energy Quad Text Set Example

Learning objective. Students will be able to evaluate and design different cost-effective solutions for producing clean energy.
Target text. "How Wind Turbines Work" (retrieved from *www.energy.gov/articles/how-wind-turbine-works*).
Informational text. "Cool Jobs: Harnessing the Power of the Wind" by Kathiann Kowalski (retrieved from *www.sciencenewsforstudents.org/article/cool-jobs-power-wind*).
Visual text. Energy.gov Infographic: "Understanding the Grid" (retrieved from *www.energy.gov/articles/infographic-understanding-grid*).
Hook text. "Energy Access Is Not Equal; This Ann Arbor Organization Is Trying to Change That" by Jaishree Drepaul-Bruder (retrieved from *www.secondwavemedia.com/concentrate/features/uejl0478.aspx*).

language, and motivation. Further, QTSs can be designed with a CSP lens that helps adolescents learn from increasingly challenging texts while *also* creating spaces to explore and sustain cultural and linguistic knowledge. As such, QTSs can be a vehicle for learning both about comprehension and how to teach it with a lens of culturally sustaining pedagogy (see Figure 4.3).

QTSs as a Vehicle for Learning How Comprehension Works

By utilizing QTSs, teachers begin to view comprehension as a meaning-making process that happens across texts, rather than a singular or isolated act. In addition, teachers have opportunities to explore what kinds of background knowledge are most relevant for a target text, which helps them better understand the relationship between knowledge and comprehension. Overall, QTSs can help teachers understand that successful comprehension involves integrating new knowledge *across texts* with readers' prior knowledge (Kintsch, 2013). Designing a strong QTS affords teachers the opportunity to learn how comprehension operates in three layers: literal, inferential, and critical (see Figure 4.4). These three layers of comprehension build on one another to support the goal of reading: critical understanding of a text.

The literal level involves understanding the factual details of a text (Kintsch, 2013). For example, in the following excerpt of the target text about types of wind turbines, understanding that wind turbines usually have a horizontal axis and can either be faced upwind or downwind represents a literal layer of understanding of the text (see Figure 4.4).

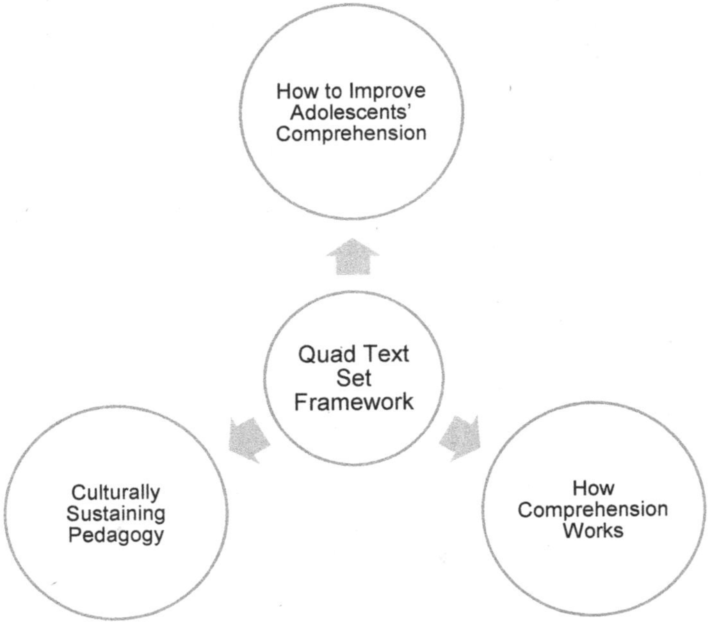

FIGURE 4.3. The Quad Text Set Professional Learning (QTS-PL) initiative for secondary teachers.

> TYPES OF WIND TURBINES
>
> There are two basic types of wind turbines: those with a horizontal axis, and those with a vertical axis. The majority of wind turbines have a horizontal axis: a propeller-style design with blades that rotate around a horizontal axis. Horizontal axis turbines are either upwind (the wind hits the blades before the tower) or downwind (the wind hits the tower before the blades). Upwind turbines also include a yaw drive and motor—components that turns the nacelle to keep the rotor facing the wind when its direction changes. (Department of Energy, 2014b)

The literal layer of understanding forms the basis for the next layer, the inferential level, which is often referred to as "reading between the lines." At the inferential layer, readers make inferences about the text using their own background knowledge to make sense of texts. With QTSs, readers have opportunities to build relevant background knowledge through the three scaffolding texts before they get to the target text, which builds their literal understanding and thus provides a stronger base for developing the inferential layer of comprehension. For example, when reading the wind turbine text above, a reader might remember from one of the supporting texts that wind energy farms earn money based on how much energy is produced, which in turn is based on the amount of wind a turbine receives. Then, while reading this passage, the reader may infer that wind turbines come in different shapes and sizes in order to maximize the harnessable power of wind (see Figure 4.4).

Finally, the inferential layer of understanding supports students in reaching the level of critical comprehension. The goal of comprehension is not simply to find the main idea of a text, or even to learn basic information about a topic like wind turbines. Rather, the goal of comprehension happens in this third layer, in which the reader is able to critically evaluate what they read, including whether or not what they are reading is true. Readers often do this by synthesizing ideas read in one text with ideas read in others. For example, after reading both the informational text about the importance and difficulty of finding clean energy sources that are also cost-efficient, students are better positioned to critically evaluate the target text. They can use what they learned from both texts to make inferences and evaluate information, which in this case, can result in an understanding of how turbine technology can be altered to be a cost-efficient source of clean energy (see Figure 4.4).

Further, at the critical level of comprehension, the reader would understand the knowledge from the text well enough to make it part of their own knowledge base and *apply* their knowledge to a new situation. For example, a teacher could have students design different aspects of wind turbines to operate under specific conditions. Finally, by approaching comprehension this way, readers can evaluate issues of access to energy

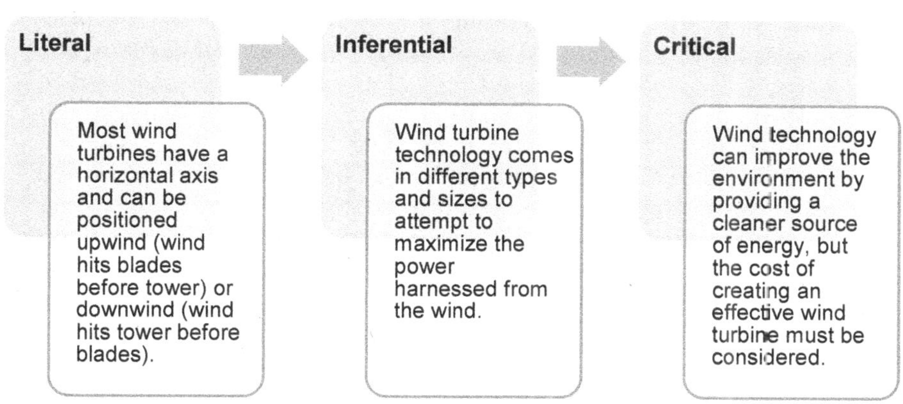

FIGURE 4.4. Layers of understanding types of wind turbine text.

and how climate change affects different groups of people in the United States in unequitable ways.

QTSs as a Vehicle for Learning How to Scaffold Comprehension

In addition to supporting teacher knowledge about how comprehension works, designing QTSs also affords opportunities to learn how to integrate instructional scaffolds into reading. Just by virtue of creating a cohesive and engaging QTS, teachers have "built-in scaffolding" for the target text because readers have opportunities to build important background knowledge in accessible and engaging ways. Further, designing and using QTS also encourages teachers to think about *activity* factors related to reading. For example, as teachers design QTS, they will consider purposes for reading, guiding questions that will help readers attend to specific concepts and text structures, and think-aloud models that can demonstrate to readers how to make connections and how inferences across texts can help facilitate readers' comprehension. Further, it is important for teachers to consider the sociocultural context (RAND, 2002) when creating scaffolds, including the literacy practices and beliefs of the teacher, the school, and the local community. This is why culturally sustaining pedagogy is critical to supporting readers and reading comprehension.

QTSs as a Vehicle for Engaging in CSP

CSP is a recently conceptualized framework that expands on the complementary frameworks of culturally responsive teaching (Gay, 2018) and culturally responsive pedagogy (Ladson-Billings, 2014). As Alim and Paris (2017) explain, "CSP seeks to perpetuate and foster—to sustain—linguistics, literate, and cultural pluralism as part of schooling for positive social transformation. CSP positions dynamic cultural dexterity as a necessary good, and sees the outcome of learning as additive rather than subtractive, as remaining whole rather than framed as broken, as critically enriching strengths rather than replacing deficits" (p. 1). This definition states important distinctions, such as additive versus subtractive and whole versus broken. By attending to these distinctions, we honor multiple cultures and ways of using language, while at the same time countering narratives that position some groups of learners as "different," "less than," or "in need of." The word "sustain" is a unique contribution to the body of work on cultural responsiveness. It suggests that classrooms should both honor and sustain students' cultures, languages, and ways of knowing. To work toward these goals, Alim and Paris (2017) advocate for celebrating all the cultural and language resources students bring to the classroom; providing opportunities for students to draw on and expand their cultural and language knowledge; avoiding deficit models and the privileging of one way of knowing above others; and emphasizing representation and role models in curricular materials.

QTSs can allow for two important CSP principles to be realized: (1) sustaining and building on cultural and language knowledge, and (2) integrating representation and role models into curricular materials. First, our cultural and linguistic resources are part of us and therefore part of our comprehension processes. In other words, the meaning-making processes of reading comprehension are influenced by cultural and language resources, as well as epistemologies, that learners bring to a text (Lee, 2020). The deep involvement with texts that is part of work with QTSs pushes all students to draw on what they know and how they know it. As a result, there is instructional space for students to share how they interpret language, make meaning from text, and draw on their own cultural and linguistic lived experiences. At the same time, within QTSs, readers have opportunities to build background knowledge that supports their understanding of complex texts. So, when students' cultural and linguistic knowledge is not aligned with a given target text, all students have opportunities, via the other three texts, to add to their own funds of knowledge to support their meaning-making with the target text.

The second way that QTSs can be realized with a CSP lens relates to the important idea that *representation matters*. The texts that make up QTSs are ideal for sharing expertise and perspectives from people from many backgrounds. For example, a QTS in biology with some of Darwin's writings as the target text might include an informational text on Ynez Mexia (Massive Science, 2021), a Mexican American botanist who completed college in her 50s and went on to discover 500 new plant species around the world. Or a QTS with a document from the Lewis and Clark expedition as the target text might include the picture book *American Slave, American Hero: York of the Lewis and Clark Expedition* (Pringle, 2006). In this way, QTSs integrate representation with knowledge-building and meaning-making rather than positioning diverse texts as supplementary, or worse, as an after-thought or add-on. These texts are usually not privileged or readily available in many classrooms, but the QTS design provides teachers with opportunities and reflective space to find and teach voices that might otherwise be (QTS) marginalized or silenced—voices that mirror and represent many of our students. Related to representation and equity, QTSs can also be used to help adolescents develop more critical perspectives and work toward remedying some of the injustices in our current society (Lewis & Flynn, 2017). In particular, young adult literature or current events can be used to support students in exploring equity issues, including gender identity, racial discrimination, and climate change (Lewis & Strong, 2020).

The QTS-PL Initiative

Drawing on established principles of PL and the potential of QTSs as a vehicle for learning about comprehension and CSP, we offer the QTS-PL initiative. As we explain later in this section with specific examples, the QTS-PL initiative includes the established principles of PL: a content focus, active learning, coherence, sufficient duration, and collective participation (Desimone, 2009). Table 4.2 provides a brief overview of what each principle looks like with the QTS-PL initiative.

What Does This Look Like?: Implementation of the Initiative with Riverside District Team Learning

Sarah (first author) implemented this year-long initiative in the Riverside School District (RSD), which is an urban district in a large city. The majority of the students in the district are African American (59%), with approximately 15% of students identified as English learners, 15% are identified as having a disability and 74% as economically disadvantaged. Each school was instructed to send teams of teachers and leaders to the professional learning, which included a principal or assistant principal, instructional coaches, reading specialists, English teachers, special educators, and Teaching English as a Second Language (TESOL) teachers. In total, there were 22 participants across 10 middle and high schools, and 17 participants at the 10 schools agreed to take part in the study.

The school teams participated in eight sessions of professional learning. The first session focused on mindsets, showing both how all children are capable of rigorous reading and the consequences of low expectations. In the second session, we shared research around text complexity and the comprehension processes to help teachers rethink approaches to comprehension instruction that favor matching adolescents with texts at their so-called level. The third session centered on how to develop and use quad text sets. The remaining sessions focused on continuing to develop teachers' understanding of comprehension, with an emphasis on how to scaffold readers' understanding of the QTS texts.

Within each of the sessions we built in opportunities for teachers to plan and practice. For example, at the beginning of each session, teachers had an opportunity to reflect on what they had implemented since the last session, often sharing about how their knowledge was extended and

TABLE 4.2. The QTS-PL Initiative with Components of Effective PL

Effective PL component	The QTS-PL initiative
Content focused	The language and literacy demands of each discipline are unique, rich, and challenging (Fang et al., 2006; Goldman et al., 2016), and the more time teachers have to grapple with these demands, the better. Secondary teachers, in particular, are invested in their own disciplines, but they rarely have sufficient time to develop deep professional knowledge as to what it means to support students with reading comprehension. The QTS-PL initiative allows for a simultaneous focus on comprehension alongside disciplinary content.
Active learning	With the QTS-PL initiative, teachers have opportunities to explore their own standards, learning objectives, and texts. Their choice of materials is never prescribed, nor are the purposes for reading delineated. Rather, teachers actively select important challenging readings, define the purposes for reading, and identify texts that serve as scaffolds for the challenging texts. And, within a year-long, sustained, professional learning initiative, teachers have ample opportunity to work through the plan–practice–reflect cycle (Darling-Hammond et al., 2017).
Coherence	Coherence in regard to both individual teachers and systems in a school is important in the context of teacher learning. Most prominently, supporting teachers with the development and instruction of QTSs has powerful implications for teachers' individual systems of knowledge, beliefs, and practices. Teachers' practices with comprehension support are often informed by too few opportunities to learn how comprehension works. The QTS-PL initiative is also well aligned with important factors in school-level systems, which are beholden to standards across disciplines that call for meaningful work with complex texts (National Council for the Social Studies [NCSS], 2013; National Governors Association Center for Best Practices & Council of Chief State School Officers, 2010; NGSS, 2013).
Sufficient duration	The QTS-PL initiative involves a year of PL opportunities. Teachers participate in eight to nine PL modules, which can be facilitated either in person or online, increasing access to the PL. Over the course of the year, teachers also work through several planning–practice–reflection cycles and analyze their students' comprehension successes and challenges with the target texts in each text set.
Collective participation	The QTS-PL initiative is designed for secondary teachers in content-area teams. While there are certainly advantages to working across content areas and grade levels, the opportunity to explore content-area texts and related background knowledge with colleagues is powerful.

challenged, as well as questions they still had. In each session, teachers had several opportunities to design text sets and scaffolds for those texts that they would use in upcoming units of study. As they created these text sets and scaffolds, they engaged in "Collegial Conversations." In these conversations, three to four teachers shared their disciplinary purposes for reading, their texts, their scaffolding, and their consideration of whose voices and lives were represented, and their students' responses to the QTS. The PL facilitators provided coaching or feedback throughout the process to support teachers in their design and use of the QTS framework.

Additionally, teachers were asked to share their beliefs and practices regarding support of readers' comprehension before and after the intervention as well as to provide feedback on the information provided after each session in the form of a survey. Analysis of the surveys revealed that prior to the start of the intervention, there was little agreement about how to support readers across various roles within schools and across the district. Further, many participants struggled to articulate the strengths of readers who scored poorly on standardized assessments or to define what kinds of supports helped these readers improve.

After the intervention, however, most of the participants were able to articulate a strengths-based approach to supporting their learners, one that valued readers' funds of knowledge and recognized their areas of growth. For example, participants shared that students' strengths included "their funds of knowledge and bringing their experiences to the table when it comes to reading." Additionally, participants were able to clearly name and articulate when and how to use a variety of scaffolds to support learners. For example, participants reported that one way to support students in reading a particularly challenging social studies text was to "build vocabulary and knowledge and provide an application of what is learned in the text," as well as "provide a text on a similar topic to build students' knowledge."

The QTS-PL initiative in practice made it clear that many secondary teachers can benefit from opportunities to build professional knowledge around comprehension, complex texts, scaffolding, and CSP (see Figure 4.5). One specific finding was that QTSs were one of the most popular tools that participants learned across the year; QTSs provided the "glue" that helped teachers understand the process of comprehension and scaffolding more deeply. Another substantive finding was that participants shifted their thinking to view texts themselves as scaffolds. For example, when asked how to support readers, one participant mentioned that they would "find shorter articles for students to read prior to reading a novel." Others viewed motivational supports as key to supporting adolescents' reading of rigorous texts; while explaining the importance of hook texts, one person reported:"my goal is to build interest in reading."

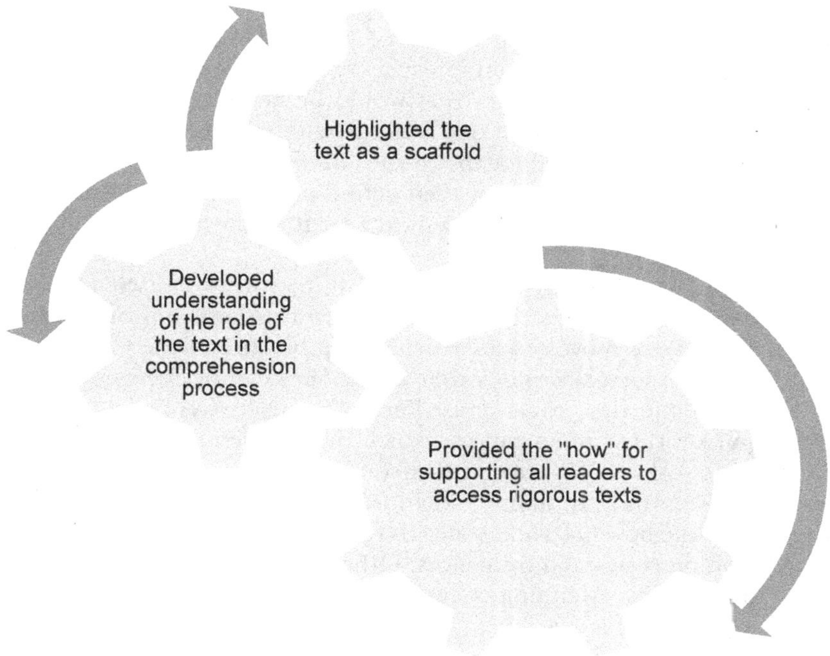

FIGURE 4.5. Benefits of the QTS-PL initiative.

An additional finding was that participants' understanding of comprehension shifted as they saw the role of the text in the comprehension process differently, and participants noted their ability to modify texts to support students' reading in a variety of ways. For example, several teachers cited the importance of providing easier informational texts to support students' knowledge base and therefore comprehension of the target text. Others noted that they could modify the text itself, for example, "reformatting the text to include visuals or definitions of key vocabulary." Additionally, QTS provided a missing piece to the puzzle as it helped teachers understand *how* to provide rigorous reading for students they had identified as having reading challenges. For example, one teacher mentioned that having various levels of texts, both easier and more rigorous ones, was "essential to students' success."

The last important finding was that the QTS-PL experience is the development of teacher leaders who can institute real change within their schools. The RSD-PL experience was designed to develop teacher leaders who would bring ideas back to the school and implement change across their professional learning communities and teacher teams. By design, administrators attended with their teachers so that they could further support others in the school in implementing these ideas, as well as help provide any structural changes that would be necessary to improve literacy outcomes. For example, one administrator realized the importance of common planning time for their teams in order to create quality QTS across disciplines, and noted in their action plan at the last session that they would rearrange the schedule next year to allow for more common planning time.

Finally, we found that the QTS-PL initiative lends itself to a virtual, accessible, differentiated model. The last three sessions of the RSD PL initiative were moved to a virtual setting because of the COVID-19 pandemic. The virtual sessions were accessible to all teachers, regardless of schedules and time constraints. Further, teachers were able to spend more time on the components for which they needed more practice and less time on others. We noticed that some teachers were learning about comprehension in a substantive way for the first time and needed extra time to explore how QTS and scaffolds that accompany it align with comprehension processes and influences. Other teachers were more ready to build in culturally sustaining components. This built-in and self-selected differentiation that is possible in a virtual setting honors teachers' agency and their professional assessment of their own learning needs.

Revisiting Hannah's Experiences with Complex Texts

After engaging in the QTS-PL initiative, Hannah took a different approach to teaching the required novel *To Kill a Mockingbird*. She first thought about the comprehension process itself, and she knew that it involved integrating prior knowledge with new knowledge gained in the book. For the first time, Hannah began to consider what she wanted her students to *learn* as a result of reading this novel. This insight prompted her to reflect on the novel itself, and she realized that although she appreciated the classical literature of *To Kill a Mockingbird*, she also was concerned about the racial messaging in the book, a concern of many teachers and scholars today (e.g., Venkatraman, 2020). She decided that she would like her students to read this text more critically to evaluate some of these messages and to compare experiences in the book to more current events.

As such, she developed a QTS to support students in reading this novel using a more critical lens (see Table 4.3). She began her unit with a newspaper article (Romero, 2020) about a black man who was freed from jail after being wrongfully convicted for raping a white woman. She chose this article both to "hook" her readers by highlighting the importance of exploring racial issues in the U.S. justice system and to set the stage for the need to approach texts from the 1960s written about the

1930s period of U.S. history with a critical race lens. To build relevant background knowledge, she decided to intersperse informational texts between the chapters of the novel. She chose to juxtapose excerpts from the nonfiction novel *Just Mercy: A Story of Justice and Redemption* by Bryan Stevenson (2014) as well as a historical account of the little-known but extremely devastating and deadly Tulsa Race Massacres (History.com, 2021) between chapters of the novel. Her point was to encourage her students to use a wider historical lens for exploring the themes of this book. She also included visual texts, including a TED talk by Baratunde Thurston (2019), on how to reconstruct responses to racism, along with providing time and space for her students to critically evaluate some of the themes of *To Kill a Mockingbird*.

As Hannah had learned in her professional development sessions, she also altered the *activity*, to support her students' understanding of the texts and help her students activate and use their knowledge to make meaning. As such, Hannah began each day with different types of writing around the relevant themes in the book or related texts, asking students to reflect on their own knowledge and experiences as a means of helping them use their knowledge to make sense of this text. For example, to help them connect to the characters' experiences in *To Kill a Mockingbird,* she asked her students to reflect on a time when they were not treated well as a means of helping them connect to the characters' experiences in *To Kill a Mockingbird*.

Rather than reading the text out loud to her students, Hannah provided various scaffolds to support their reading, including partner reading, fluency support, and reading guides to support understanding of challenging concepts and vocabulary. By valuing her students' knowledge, respecting their perspectives, and believing they were capable of reading grade-appropriate texts with scaffolding and supports, Hannah developed a context in which her students (the reader) could interact with texts (*To Kill a Mockingbird* and the supporting texts from her QTS) with appropriate activities (e.g., fluency and vocabulary supports, guiding questions, and think-aloud models) that scaffold their understanding (see Table 4.3).

Conclusion

This QTS-PL initiative supports secondary teachers in developing (1) a deep understanding of how comprehension works, (2) guidelines for selecting important disciplinary readings with accompanying scaffolding texts, (3) instructional strategies for comprehension that can be used in targeted ways to meet disciplinary objectives, and (4) adopting a culturally sustaining lens on reading comprehension and text selection. Further,

TABLE 4.3. Hannah's Revised QTS with Instructional Scaffolds and CSP Connections

Learning objective: Students will be able to evaluate the themes of the novel and form opinions about issues related to social justice.

	Texts	Scaffolds	Connections to CSP
Target text	*To Kill a Mockingbird* by Harper Lee	Reading guide to provide a visual of key abstract concepts and to prompt thinking and connections across texts Scaffolded partner reading to support fluency Journaling techniques, such as considering a time when they weren't treated well	Students read this novel with a critical lens to explore and grapple with some of the covert and overt racism themes of the novel
Hook text	NBC News "Black man freed after 44 years in prison for wrongful conviction of raping a white woman"	K-W-L chart to consider what students know and want to learn about racial issues with the U.S. justice system	Students can consider different ways that the racial system is unjust in the United States.
Informational texts	History.com "Tulsa Race Massacre" *Just Mercy: A Story of Justice and Redemption* by Bryan Stevenson	Double-entry journal to identify key quotes about what happened historically, and then reflect on those quotes Scaffolded partner reading to support fluency	Students can consider unmentioned histories and how Black histories have been silenced
Visual texts	"How to Deconstruct Racism, One Headline at a Time" by Baratunde Thurston Pictures of civil rights movement march on Washington, 1963 (Life.com), and Black Lives Matter marches, 2020 (*NY Times*)	ReQuest questioning strategy to support thinking and discussion around the TED talk and the photographs Journaling techniques to allow for self-reflection	In the TED talk, students can consider how racism is still present today and what actionable steps can be taken to reduce both small and large acts of racism In the pictures, students can consider how action has led to, and continues to lead to, a decrease in racist practices in the United States

by supporting teachers with a deep understanding of how comprehension works, they can better evaluate texts for the comprehension stumbling blocks their students will undoubtedly hit as well as select texts thoughtfully with an eye on representation and equity. This is critical professional knowledge (Snow et al., 2005), but secondary teachers rarely have the time to build it. When teachers have the knowledge and confidence to select texts, they can explore resources that bring a variety of perspectives, experiences, and role models into their classrooms. This innovative approach supports the development of their professional knowledge, beliefs, and practices related to literacy in the content areas.

REFERENCES

Alim, H. A., & Paris, D. (2017). What is culturally sustaining pedagogy and why does it matter? In D. Paris & H. S. Alim (Eds.), *Culturally sustaining pedagogies: Teaching and learning for justice in a changing world* (pp. 1–20). Teachers College Press.

Anderson, R. C. (2013). Role of the reader's schemata in comprehension, learning, and memory. In D. E. Alvermann, N. J. Unrau, & R. B. Ruddel (Eds.), *Theoretical models and processes of reading* (6th ed., pp. 476–488). International Reading Association.

Brevik, L. M. (2014). Making implicit practice explicit: How do upper secondary teachers describe their reading comprehension strategies instruction? *International Journal of Educational Research, 67,* 52–66.

Darling-Hammond, L., Hyler, M. E., & Gardner, M. (2017). *Effective teacher professional development.* Learning Policy Institute.

Department of Energy. (2014a, June 20). How a wind turbine works. Energy.gov. Retrieved from *www.energy.gov/articles/how-wind-turbine-works.*

Department of Energy. (2014b, November 17). Understanding the grid [Infographic]. Energy.gov. Retrieved from *www.energy.gov/articles/infographic-understanding-grid.*

Desimone, L. M. (2009). Improving impact studies of teachers' professional development: Toward better conceptualizations and measures. *Educational Researcher, 38*(3), 181–199.

Drepaul-Bruder, J. (2018, October 31). Energy access is not created equal. This Ann Arbor organization is trying to change that. Second Wave Media. Retrieved from *www.secondwavemedia.com/concentrate/features/uejl0478.aspx.*

Elish-Piper, L., Wold, L. S., & Schwingendorf, K. (2014). Scaffolding high school students' reading of complex texts using linked text sets. *Journal of Adolescent and Adult Literacy, 57*(7), 565–574.

Fagella-Luby, M. N., Graner, P. S., Deshler, D. D., & Drew, S. V. (2012). Building a house on sand: Why disciplinary literacy is not sufficient to replace general strategies for adolescent learners who struggle. *Topics in Language Disorders, 32*(1), 69–84.

Fang, Z., Schleppegrell, M. J., & Cox, B. E. (2006). Understanding the language demands of schooling: Nouns in academic registers. *Journal of Literacy Research, 38*(3), 247–273.

Fisher, D., & Frey, N. (2008). Comprehension instruction in action. In C. C. Block & S. R. Parris (Eds.), *Comprehension instruction. Research-based best practices* (2nd ed., pp. 258–270). Guilford Press.

Gay, G. (2018). *Culturally responsive teaching: Theory, research, and practice* (3rd ed.). Teachers College Press.

Goldman, S. R., Britt, M. A., Brown, W., Cribb, G., George, M., Greenleaf, C., . . . Project READI. (2016). Disciplinary literacies and learning to read for understanding: A conceptual framework for disciplinary literacy. *Educational Psychologist, 51*(2), 219–246.

Guthrie, J. T., & Wigfield, A. (Eds.). (1997). *Reading engagement: Motivating readers through integrated instruction.* International Reading Association.

Hall, L. A. (2005). Teachers and content area reading: Attitudes, beliefs and change. *Teaching and Teacher Education, 21*(4), 403–414.

History.com Editors. (2021, April 19). Tulsa race massacre. History.com. Retrieved from *www.history.com/topics/roaring-twenties/tulsa-race-massacre.*

Kintsch, W. (2013). Revisiting the construction–integration model of text comprehension and its implications for instruction. In D. E. Alvermann, N. J. Unrau, & R. B. Ruddel (Eds.), *Theoretical models and processes of reading* (6th ed., pp. 807– 839). International Reading Association.

Kowalski, K. (2016, March 10). Cool jobs: The power of the wind. ScienceNews for Students. Retrieved from *www.sciencenewsforstudents.org/article/cool-jobs-power-wind.*

Ladson-Billings, G. (2014). Culturally relevant pedagogy 2.0. *Harvard Educational Review, 84*(1), 74–135.

Lee, C. D. (2020). Social and cultural diversity as a lens for understanding student learning and the development of reading comprehension. In E. B. Moje, P. P. Afflerbach, P. Enciso, & N. K. Lesaux (Eds.), *Handbook of reading research* (Vol. V, pp. 37–56). Routledge.

Lee, H. (1960). *To kill a mockingbird.* Lippincott.

Lewis, W., & Flynn, J. E. (2017). Below the surface level of social justice: Using quad text sets to plan equity-oriented instruction. *The ALAN Review, 45*(1), 22–31.

Lewis, W. E., & Strong, J. Z. (2020). *Literacy instruction with disciplinary texts: Strategies for grades 6–12.* Guilford Press.

Lewis, W. E., Walpole, S., & McKenna, M. C. (2014). *Cracking the Common Core: Choosing and using texts in grades 6–12.* Guilford Press.

Lupo, S. M., Strong, J. Z., Lewis, W., Walpole, S., & McKenna, M. C. (2018). Building background knowledge through reading: Rethinking text sets. *Journal of Adolescent and Adult Literacy, 61*(4), 433–444.

Lupo, S. M., Tortorelli, L., Invernizzi, M., Ryoo, J. H., & Strong, J. Z. (2019). An exploration of text difficulty and knowledge support on adolescents' comprehension. *Reading Research Quarterly, 54*(4), 1–23.

Massive Science, adapted by Newsela Staff. (2021, March 7). Meet Ynes Mexia, late-blooming botanist whose adventures rivaled Darwin's.

Newsela. Retrieved from *https://newsela.com/read/botanist-ynes-mexia/id/2001019071/?search_id=fb099ff5-e61a-4807-bb33-9c1e7a55b329.*

National Center for Education Statistics. (2019). National assessment of educational progress report card: 2019 NAEP reading assessment [Data set]. The Nation's Report Card. Retrieved from *www.nationsreportcard.gov/highlights/reading/2019.*

National Council for the Social Studies. (2013). *The college, career, and civic life (C3) framework for social studies state standards: Guidance for enhancing the rigor of K–12 civics, economics, geography, and history.* National Council for the Social Studies.

National Governors Association Center for Best Practices & Council of Chief State School Officers. (2010). *Common Core State Standards: English language arts and literacy in history/social studies, science, and technical subjects, Appendix A.* Authors.

The New York Times. (2020, June 1). In photos: Protestors march in cities across America. *The New York Times.* Retrieved from *www.nytimes.com/article/pictures-george-floyd-protests-photos.html.*

NGSS Lead States. (2013). *Next generation science standards: For states, by states.* Authors.

Opfer, V. D., & Pedder, D. (2011). Conceptualizing teacher professional learning. *Review of Educational Research, 81*(3), 376–407.

Paris, D. (2012). Culturally sustaining pedagogy: A needed change in stance, terminology, and practice. *Educational Researcher, 41*(3), 93–97.

Penuel, W. R., Fishman, B. J., Yamaguchi, R., & Gallagher, L. P. (2007). What makes professional development effective?: Strategies that foster curriculum implementation. *American Educational Research Journal, 44*(4), 921–958.

Pringle, L. (2006). *American slave, American hero: York of the Lewis and Clark expedition* (C. Van Wright & Y.-H. Hu, Illus.). Calkins Creek.

RAND Reading Study Group, & Snow, C. (2002) *Reading for understanding: Toward an R&D program in reading comprehension.* RAND Corporation.

Romero, D. (2020, August 27). Black man freed after 44 years in prison for wrongful conviction of raping white woman. NBC News. Retrieved from *www.nbcnews.com/news/us-news/black-man-freed-after-44-years-prison-wrongful-conviction-raping-n1238557.*

Shanahan, T. (2015). What teachers should know about Common Core: A guide for the perplexed. *The Reading Teacher, 68*(8), 583–588.

Snow, C. E., Griffin, P., & Burns, M. S. (2005). *Knowledge to support the teaching of reading: Preparing teachers for a changing world.* Jossey-Bass.

Stevenson, B. (2014). *Just mercy: A story of justice and redemption.* Spiegel & Grau.

Thurston, B. (2019). How to deconstruct racism, one headline at a time [Video]. TED Conferences. Retrieved from *www.ted.com/talks/baratunde_thurston_how_to_deconstruct_racism_one_headline_at_a_time/details.*

Townsend, D. (2014). Who's using the language? Supporting middle school students with content area academic language. *Journal of Adolescent and Adult Literacy, 58*(5), 372–383.

Venkatraman, P. (2020, June 19). Weeding out racism's invisible roots: Rethinking children's classics. *School Library Journal*. Retrieved from *www.slj.com/?detailStory=weeding-out-racisms-invisible-roots-rethinking-childrens-classics-libraries-diverse-books*.

Wilson, N. S., Grisham, D. L., & Smetana, L. (2009). Investigating content area teachers' understanding of a content literacy framework: A yearlong professional development initiative. *Journal of Adolescent and Adult Literacy, 52*(8), 708–718.

CHAPTER 5

Situated Professional Learning through Targeted Reading Instruction

Building Teacher Capacity and Diagnostic Practice

Steven J. Amendum, Heather H. Aiken, Mary Bratsch-Hines, and Leslie M. Babinski

Watch a related video from the authors at this link.

Ms. Green, a second-grade teacher in rural North Carolina, described her approach to teaching reading. "I don't really know what to do," she said. "Sometimes I feel like a robot just going through the motions. I went to school to get a reading specialist degree, but I'd rather teach math." For too many early elementary teachers, knowing how to teach reading can feel like a mystery. Teachers often rely on packaged reading programs and assessments to guide their reading instruction. Recent media reports describe teachers' lack of knowledge to teach reading effectively (e.g., Shanahan, 2020), and teachers may be feeling added pressure as they work with their youngest readers.

Learning to read in early elementary school has lasting impacts into adolescence and adulthood. However, up to 20% of children find learning to read challenging, even when they receive high-quality instruction in their general education classroom. Children who do not read proficiently by the end of third grade are at heightened risk of not graduating from high school (Hernandez, 2011). The most recent National Assessment of Educational Progress (NAEP) results showed that 65% of fourth graders were not able to interpret texts and use their understanding of a text to make evaluations or draw conclusions (National Center for Education

Statistics, 2020). One important way to improve reading achievement is to engage elementary teachers in effective professional learning (PL) to provide and sustain effective evidence-based reading instruction, particularly for children who demonstrate difficulty learning to read (Allington, 2013).

In an attempt to address and improve classroom teachers' reading instruction, research studies have often focused on classroom teacher quality (Garet et al., 2008; Goldhaber et al., 2015; Hanushek, 2016; No Child Left Behind Act of 2001; Public Law 107-110, 2001; Risko et al., 2008). However, studies that examine distal features of teacher quality (such as teacher experience, highest level of education, and other qualifications) exhibit weak relationships with students' reading achievement (e.g., Hanushek, 2016; Kainz & Vernon-Feagans, 2007). Therefore, rather than focus on characteristics of *teachers*, researchers, administrators, and practitioners have given increased attention to the development and evaluation of PL programs intended to enhance and improve *teaching* (e.g., teachers' reading instruction).

PL programs often demonstrate positive effects on teaching or teacher outcomes, such as the degree to which teachers use explicit reading instruction or teachers' heightened content knowledge about reading (Garet et al., 2008; Institute of Education Sciences, 2008). Nonetheless, demonstrating positive effects on student achievement is much more difficult. Although the effect of PL programs on teacher learning and instruction is important, the link between teachers' PL and improved student outcomes is essential. To that end, researchers examined rigorous studies on teachers' PL and found characteristics of PL that were positively related to student achievement (Desimone & Garet, 2015; Yoon et al., 2007). These characteristics included (1) a longer duration of PL (14+ hours), (2) delivery of PL by experts or highly trained researchers, and (3) follow-up support for teachers to extend and solidify their learning (Yoon et al., 2007).

In the remainder of this chapter, we describe PL within a particular innovative model, Targeted Reading Instruction (TRI; formerly called Targeted Reading Intervention), which meets the characteristics outlined above (Desimone & Garet, 2015; Yoon et al., 2007). TRI teachers deliver diagnostic evidence-based reading instruction as the context for PL. Specifically, TRI's PL model prepares early elementary classroom teachers to use specific strategies within the TRI framework of one-on-one teacher–student lessons and is unique in employing virtual real-time instructional coaching (e.g., Amendum et al., 2011; Bratsch-Hines et al., 2020; Vernon-Feagans et al., 2013, 2015). TRI has been evaluated in Title I schools in primarily rural communities and has shown improvements in students' decoding and reading comprehension (Amendum et al., 2011; Vernon-Feagans et al., 2013, 2018) as well as with multilingual learners from urban, suburban, and rural schools with positive results for decoding (Amendum et al., 2018). Data from TRI studies have now been evaluated by independent organizations (e.g., What Works Clearinghouse, 2017; Evidence for ESSA), which have endorsed TRI as one of only a few promising reading programs. We now describe TRI's diagnostic evidence-based reading instruction as the context for TRI PL, and then delve into how the characteristics of TRI PL support sustainability and equity.

What Is TRI's Instructional Context for Professional Learning?

TRI instruction was designed for early elementary students who are not yet reading and/or who have challenges mastering specific reading skills (such as phonemic awareness, decoding, fluency, or vocabulary development). A primary goal of TRI is to enable classroom teachers to learn to differentiate literacy instruction to meet the specific needs of individual students (Fuchs et al., 2014; Grimm et al., 2018; Shanahan et al., 2010). TRI teachers work with an individual student for 15 minutes a day over a period of 8 to 10 weeks. Working with individual students allows TRI teachers to rapidly integrate TRI practices into their instruction. Over the course of the year, a TRI teacher works with three students, learning how to tailor each lesson to match each reader's specific needs. Every week, a TRI literacy coach provides virtual real-time coaching and feedback to the classroom teacher.

TRI Instructional Levels

Teachers learn to pace lessons through an evidence-based scope and sequence so that students move quickly through four color-coded TRI levels (Pink, Blue, Green, Purple). At all levels, teachers learn the importance of having the student "do the work" as they develop segmenting, blending, and vocabulary skills; practice fluent reading; and engage in reading connected text using books that build reading comprehension. *Pink* shows teachers how to assist students who have not yet developed letter sound or alphabetic knowledge and who may have little experience with texts. Teachers introduce the alphabetic principle and emphasize phonemic awareness as students work with short vowels in the context of two- or three-sound words. Teachers also introduce blends and consonant digraphs (*sh*, *th*, *ch*, *wh*, *ng*) at this level. *Blue* shows teachers how to assist students with the same skills in Pink, but within the context of four- to six-sound words. *Green* shows teachers how to effectively introduce long-vowel patterns as well as diphthongs (*oi*, *oy*, *au*, *aw*, *ow*, *ou*) and *r*-controlled vowels (the distinct sound of a vowel followed by an /r/, such as *ar* and *er*). *Purple* shows teachers how to provide students with practice in "chunking" words, breaking them into smaller parts to aid in decoding, moving from two-syllable words to three-, four-, and five-syllable words.

TRI Activities

Three primary activities comprise each 15-minute TRI lesson: *Rereading for Fluency*, *Word Work*, and *Connected Text Reading*. With coaching support, teachers adjust components within activities to meet the needs of an individual student.

Rereading for Fluency (~2 Minutes)

The student rereads part or all of a text read in the previous lesson's Connected Text Reading (Rasinski, 2003). Teachers engage with students using modeling, echo-reading, and choral reading to scaffold fluent expressive reading with some or all of the text, depending on the child's skill level. The teacher emphasizes reading connected text with appropriate prosody and timing (Rasinski, 2006).

Word Work (~6 Minutes)

The teacher uses interactive instructional activities to engage students as they manipulate, say, and write words (Bear et al., 2012; Solari et al., 2018), as well as brief strategies to help the student understand word meanings (Gärdenfors, 2017). Teachers help students learn sound–symbol relationships within words (Piasta & Wagner, 2010); make connections between the sounds of words and word meanings (Strom & Neuman, 2016); and build decoding fluency within words as well as across connected text (López et al., 2011). By focusing on skills within the meaningful context of whole words, students have the opportunity to define and use each word before trying to decode it, highlighting the role of vocabulary in word recognition and listening/reading comprehension (Austin & Vaughn, 2019; Language and Reading Research Consortium, 2015).

Connected Text Reading (~7 Minutes)

At the lower levels (Pink, Blue, and Green), teachers utilize texts matched to Word Work (e.g., short words with short vowel sounds) and the students' individual needs. The use of these texts provides students with the opportunity to apply the recently studied phonics patterns in connected text, increasing success and motivation (Cheatham & Allor, 2012; McIntyre et al., 2006). Once students attain a basic level of decoding knowledge, these initial texts are replaced with progressively more complex texts, including a large number of nonfiction texts. Teachers learn to pay particular attention to scaffolding students' ability to summarize, answer questions, predict, make connections, and make inferences, integrating classroom comprehension objectives into the lesson (Cohen et al., 2009; Foorman et al., 2016). Further, by immediately practicing new skills in the context of reading connected text, students see the "why" behind the activities, allowing them to transfer the skills to other learning opportunities and content.

Opportunities for Sustainable and Equitable PL through the TRI

TRI teachers build their knowledge of reading instruction through the act of teaching reading. This TRI PL process is based on the idea of *situated learning* (Brown et al., 1989), which maintains that learning and action are based in authentic situations (Langer, 2009). Within situated learning, instruction and learning occur in the social contexts in which new knowledge is to be applied. Some have described situated learning as "apprenticeship learning" (Korthagen, 2010, p. 99), and situated learning theory suggests that teachers' PL should be embedded in their everyday work context while they are engaged in daily instruction. Moreover, TRI PL is designed to initially address teachers' *practices*, based on the theory that change in practice will lead to change in student outcomes and later change in teacher knowledge and beliefs (Guskey, 2002). In other words, seeing their students achieve rapid reading growth will lead teachers to apply TRI practices throughout their classroom instruction.

The situated nature of TRI PL is operationalized through two methods to enhance teacher learning. First, teachers attend two initial days of TRI training (historically in-person on-site at schools, but now also available virtually), which includes watching training videos, observing coaches modeling TRI activities, practicing the activities through role playing, and implementing the activities and strategies with students. Additionally, teachers practice utilizing assessment data through a gradual release (Pearson & Gallagher, 1983) to plan TRI lessons for students. The initial TRI PL provides teachers with a basic understanding of the TRI structure and activities and gives them an opportunity to meet their coach face-to-face.

Second, teachers receive additional learning opportunities through weekly virtual coaching sessions during the teacher's one-on-one instruction with a student. TRI coaches are former teachers who hold a master's degree, extensive classroom teaching experience, and literacy expertise. TRI coaches are expected to (1) ensure that teachers are fully implementing TRI, emphasizing teacher skills in matching TRI activities and strategies to student needs; and (2) provide teacher support, including specific positive feedback individualized to each teacher. Coaches observe and interact during a TRI session while a teacher works with a student, offering real-time feedback and support on the implementation of TRI activities and strategies as teachers differentiate instruction to match the needs of individual students. After each coaching session, the TRI coach provides the teacher with written feedback to recap salient points from the coaching session and provide specific positive feedback. TRI coaches support and build teachers' capacity to use diagnostic thinking, so teachers internalize a refined understanding of reading development and differentiated diagnostic instruction (Porche et al., 2012).

TRI's situated model of PL creates accessible opportunities for both sustainable and equitable PL for teachers. For sustainability, teachers learn methods that are transferable to all students, learn how to make evidence-based instructional decisions, maintain a focus on student needs, and learn information that can be shared with others. To address equity, TRI PL is differentiated for teachers, and highly accessible content is focused on supporting all students' acquisition of reading skills; support is provided for teachers to help students they may have struggled to assist in the past. Each method is explored below, with voices from teachers[1] who participated in the TRI PL process providing introductions.

Sustainable PL through the TRI

Learning Transferable Teaching Methods

The sustainability of TRI PL is highlighted by teachers' learning of evidence-based diagnostic teaching strategies and methods that are transferable to all students (Amendum et al., 2011). The PL process, situated within the context of real-time instruction, supported teachers as they developed pedagogical skills in ways that allowed them to transfer their

[1]The research reported here was supported by the Institute of Education Sciences, U.S. Department of Education, through Grant No. R305A160255 to the University of Delaware, Steven J. Amendum, Principal Investigator. The opinions expressed are those of the authors and do not represent the views of the Institute or the U.S. Department of Education.

new learning beyond the one-on-one context and in sustainable ways. One teacher described her experience with TRI:

> "The activities, I think, are amazing . . . I started to incorporate some of those things [in] whole group. I saw a difference with my kids and how I spoke with them. . . . And I think TRI helped me in that sense and helped improve how I taught as a teacher."

Although teachers provide TRI instruction to individual students, teachers experience a range of student skills and instructional strategies within the TRI framework and become expert at matching particular evidence-based instructional strategies to individual students' needs. Over time, teachers apply these learned skills and strategies more broadly within the classroom to meet the needs of all students. One teacher noted, "I incorporated several of the strategies, even into whole group phonics learning." Through this process teachers who receive TRI PL, on average, become better reading teachers for all their students (Amendum et al., 2011). As their enhanced instructional practice positively impacts student outcomes, changes to teachers' knowledge and beliefs often follow (Guskey, 2002).

Making Evidence-Based Instructional Decisions

The diagnostic-focused TRI PL approach empowers teachers to make evidence-based instructional decisions for their students, particularly those who may be having difficulty with reading acquisition. Maintaining a focus on student needs along with providing supports for teachers, such as TRI materials and coaching, enables teachers to make evidence-based instructional decisions within the TRI framework, rather than relying on a lock-step highly scripted scope and sequence. However, some teachers specifically credited the systematic sequence of activities and instruction for students' progress. The TRI provides a structured scope and sequence that allows teachers to witness students' acquisition of skills and subsequent reading growth as they enhance their own instructional practice. As one teacher said,

> "[I saw] huge impacts with their just being able to break words apart or their decoding and knowing how to put words together, how to chunk [parts of] words. And just it made a huge difference with the two students. . . . So, just in their reading skills, their confidence . . . so I think it was very beneficial."

Through the structured diagnostic focus, the TRI PL process supports sustainability by both building teacher capacity to make evidence-based decisions and providing high-quality diagnostic instruction to meet the needs of all students. Another teacher captured this sentiment: "I love the way TRI did step-by-step of building the words together [to help students] how to read."

Maintaining a Focus on Student Needs

TRI focuses on sustainable PL by maintaining teachers' attention on diagnostic student-focused content to acquire knowledge (Guskey, 2002). Changes in practice and knowledge building are framed through the child's progress rather than through teacher behaviors and characteristics. One teacher said:

> "I like the fact that when I would finish the lesson [my coach] . . . would always say, 'So how do you think it went?,' you know, 'How do you think the child's proceeding?' or 'Would there be anything you would do differently?' And I had a chance to diagnose and just apply what I thought the child needed and adjust my course during the session."

As highlighted above, teachers valued the role of the TRI coach in providing support to teachers' learning related to matching instruction to their students' needs. To sustain knowledge acquired during the TRI PL process, teachers learn to focus on each child's performance to shape their day-to-day instruction. Teachers review each day's instruction and student performance to determine each subsequent day's instructional activities. The 15-minute TRI lessons are fast-paced and packed with activities and strategies that can be flexibly applied and transferred to a range of student needs. By maintaining this focus on addressing student needs in the classroom, teachers are able to engage in the PL in a nonthreatening way that enhances their own learning and practice.

Learning Information to Share with Others

The diagnostic TRI approach to PL centers teachers' learning around transferable diagnostic strategies and students' assets and needs, and empowers teachers to make evidence-based instructional decisions. TRI provides a highly effective scope and sequence that rapidly accelerates students' reading skills. Instead of relying on a highly scripted set of materials, teachers learn how to vary their instruction for each student by pacing lessons and adapting activities to match the needs of individual students. Building teacher capacity for reading instruction within the TRI context provides teachers with information they can share with other professionals (e.g., ESL teachers, special education teachers) and parents.

> "Overall, I just love it. I still have the materials. I plan to use it next year, you know, because this COVID thing happened. And then I guess more, we're going to really need TRI next year."

Moreover, the TRI process provides teachers with concrete and recorded evidence that children may be in need of additional services as well as language to describe students' particular challenges. This allows teachers to move away from blanket phrases (e.g., *poor reader*). Modeled after the conversations with TRI coaches, based on their new learning and enhanced practice, teachers' language often shifts to more specific language. For example, they might discuss a student's performance with specific skills: challenges with initial/medial/final sounds, knowledge of specific letter sounds, the ability to segment but not yet blend, the ability to remember certain long vowel patterns but not others, strategies used to read multisyllabic words or specific observations of a student's vocabulary knowledge, fluency skill, or reading comprehension.

Equitable PL through the TRI

Differentiating Highly Accessible PL

TRI coaches provide professional development that is timely, differentiated, and equitable. Teachers especially benefit from TRI's differentiated model of adult learning. Because teachers are provided with individualized weekly virtual coaching for the full school year, TRI coaches are able to provide them with equitable PL customized to each teacher's needs. In this way, PL is differentiated for teachers, providing each teacher with what they need to focus on the unique needs of their classrooms and students.

> "I think that immediate feedback is a benefit. I think having them also right there in the moment to quickly correct things . . . she could tell the student was having trouble understanding—which made it a lot more clear for my student to learn. And then it was kind of like an 'aha' moment for me. . . . So I think that just having that support right then and there when needed was very helpful. I think it is hard to come by that in classrooms."

In some instances, teachers like the one described above need specific guidance on how to implement TRI practices. In these cases, coaches may model or guide a teacher step-by-step through the activity. Other teachers may benefit from support on differentiating instruction, specifically tailoring TRI activities to meet a student's needs. Teachers often describe the importance of the specific positive feedback provided by their TRI coach and the value of the real-time feedback while providing direct instruction to a student. One teacher noted: "I definitely liked one-on-one coaching. I like in-the-moment coaching, especially with someone that is open, but is also allowing you to do the work."

Moreover, TRI's virtual delivery model supports equity for PL in that teachers from anywhere can engage with TRI coaches. Teachers have participated in TRI PL from rural, suburban, and urban schools and districts. Some teachers and schools have participated from geographically remote areas, where they often have limited access to evidence-based PL (Amendum et al., 2011).

Focusing on Supporting Students' Reading Skill Acquisition

TRI PL also promotes equity in the classroom through a focus on the needs of students, specifically those facing challenges with learning to read. For example, TRI PL focuses on teachers' concrete application of PL in the classroom to support students' acquisition of important early reading skills rather than providing more generalized workshops that teachers have to figure out how and when to apply to their practice. At the lesson level, this concrete application includes (1) explicit teaching in the context of real words and connected text; (2) a consistent structure and sufficient pacing to address multiple objectives; (3) students' incentive to "do the work" by engaging them in productive struggle; and (4) explicit teaching of skills to support students' development as independent readers (Aiken et al., 2021). As one teacher noted:

> "She grew. I mean, she was reading those multisyllabic words like boom, boom, boom. So the students grew up. I feel I grew as a teacher, as well. I had another little student . . . she made such great progress and she was blossoming so well and she knew those short vowels and she knew her long vowels and Spanish was the only language spoken in the home. So for her to make that much progress within six weeks' time—it's like it was a gift from heaven."

More specifically, as highlighted earlier, the TRI PL process focuses teachers' attention on building necessary specific foundational skills, such as decoding and oral language comprehension, and on how to improve each. Ensuring that all students acquire these vital literacy skills helps establish a frame for equity and social justice (Greene, 2008). However, in addition to foundational skills, teachers learn to provide instruction in which these skills are applied in concert with other skills such as vocabulary knowledge or comprehension strategies, as demonstrated through significant comprehension gains in prior research studies (e.g., Amendum et al., 2011). Supporting teachers through PL in how to build individual students' skills by matching instructional strategies to individual students' needs helps children acquire proficient reading with comprehension over time. This is an important issue related to social justice.

Supporting Teachers to Help Students They May Have Struggled to Assist in the Past

The TRI PL process encourages teachers to focus on students with specific reading needs, students whom they may not have known how to help in the past. Through their initial interactions with teachers, TRI coaches often hear anecdotal evidence from teachers who express doubts about individual learners' abilities. After engaging in the TRI process, these same teachers often quickly realize that any child can read. One teacher captured this view:

> "Because [of] the way the lessons are broken down . . . It just helped guide me on to where I could help those learners, because I think I struggled before. . . . the TRI just kind of helped me determine what point I should start with them or where I should pick up with them and help them improve."

Teachers often note that the structure of TRI lessons and the materials supported their own learning and helped them match their instruction to their students' needs. In one case study, researchers showed how a first-grade multilingual learner made significant progress in her reading development across her first-grade year (Amendum et al., 2013). She began the year labeled a "nonreader" based on her school's assessments, with very limited letter/sound knowledge and a few print concepts. During the course of the school year, the student learned key early reading skills, including blending skills, orthographic patterns, and processing chunks of visual information; locating known and unknown words; and monitoring her own understanding. She ended first grade "on level" by meeting the required reading performance benchmarks for her school district.

The following section contains a report of a case study that depicts the path taken by one teacher, Ms. Green, as she progressed through the

TRI PL process. Her experiences highlight the ways TRI provides teachers with sustainable and equitable PL opportunities.

A Case Study of TRI PL

In the fall, TRI partnered with Kennedy County School District (KCSD; all names are pseudonyms) to provide professional development to all K–2 teachers in the district. KCSD served approximately 2,200 students in four elementary schools, one middle school, and two high schools. This two-year commitment included supporting 24 teachers across the four elementary schools as they implemented TRI with students in their classrooms.

Ms. Green was a third-year teacher at East Melton School, a Title I school with 258 students. Eighty-nine percent of students at the school were Black, and 99% qualified for free and reduced lunch. Less than half of third- through fifth-grade students at the school scored proficient on the state reading exam. Although she identified 8 of her 17 second-grade students as potential students for TRI implementation, Ms. Green worked with three students during the school year.

Ms. Green had strong community ties. She grew up in Kennedy County and currently lived in the East Melton attendance zone. She was an active member of her church community, which also served many of the students attending East Melton. Her undergraduate work was in elementary education with a reading endorsement, so she began TRI with what should have been a strong background in reading instruction. The TRI coach, Kelly, noted that Ms. Green was eager to learn and obviously wanted to do her best for her students.

During her second week implementing TRI, Ms. Green participated in a TRI coaching session with Coach Kelly. During the lesson, it seemed that Ms. Green was planning "on the fly." She grabbed letter tiles from her box to use for each word rather than having materials prepared ahead of time and ready for the lesson. Additionally, the Word Work portion of the lesson focused on four-sound words (Blue level), but the book selected for Connected Text Reading was from the Pink level and was clearly too easy for her student, Alexa. Ms. Green appeared to have grasped the basic TRI routines, but she often stopped during the lesson to check in with Coach Kelly, asking, "Is that okay?" or "What should I do next?" At the end of the lesson, Ms. Green and Coach Kelly discussed the lesson for a few minutes. During this time, Ms. Green continued to focus on correct implementation of TRI activities, expressing concern about whether she was "saying it right." It was also clear during their conversation that Ms. Green was unfamiliar with the difference between digraphs (more than one consonant that combines to make a single sound, e.g., /th/ or /sh/) and blends (two or more consonants that are pronounced together but still make individual sounds, e.g., /bl/ or /fr/). When asked to identify potential next steps for Alexa, Ms. Green was unable to make any suggestions.

During the initial implementation weeks, Ms. Green was a willing implementer of TRI instruction but did not seem to fully commit to the TRI process. She appeared to be going through the motions, implementing two or three TRI lessons per week and planning her lessons as she did them. There were several instances during coaching sessions when she scrambled to gather materials or struggled to come up with the next word for Alexa to work with. She lacked the intentionality that is the hallmark of a strong TRI lesson, but she genuinely seemed to want her students to learn. This somewhat laissez-faire approach to implementation slowly began to change as she continued to work with Coach Kelly.

During week six, Ms. Green guided Alexa through another lesson and debriefed with Coach Kelly. Several notable changes took place around this time. First, Ms. Green confidently applied the vocabulary with which she had been so tentative during her earlier lessons, accurately describing specific instances when Alexa successfully worked with blends versus digraphs. Ms. Green also demonstrated her understanding of the TRI strategies, guiding Alexa through *Blend as You Go* (a TRI strategy that promotes the use of progressive blending) when she was stuck on a word. Perhaps most notably, Ms. Green was able to explain her rationale for word selection within the lesson, focusing on patterns that were challenging for Alexa and determining next steps to ensure continued growth. From this point forward, Ms. Green became more intentional with her instruction and more regular with her implementation. She reported implementing four or five TRI lessons per week; even her coaching sessions fell into a regular routine—occurring on the same day and same time every week. Ms. Green had settled into the TRI process.

For the second implementation period, Ms. Green worked with a new student, Raheem. Raheem was a slightly more advanced reader, beginning his TRI experience at approximately the same level as Alexa finished. During coaching sessions, Ms. Green no longer looked to Coach Kelly for guidance on basic TRI implementation. Instead, Coach Kelly offered support regarding vocabulary, providing examples and sentences, and offering guidance on next steps for Raheem. These next steps included two separate occasions during which Coach Kelly was instrumental in encouraging Ms. Green to move Raheem into the next higher level of TRI activities. During their first session, Coach Kelly noticed that Raheem fluently read the text during Rereading for Fluency. Before the lesson moved into Word Work, she and Ms. Green discussed the possibility of moving

Raheem into Green, the next TRI level. At the end of the lesson, the two focused on how to implement a shift to the Green level, with Coach Kelly providing logistical support for the structure of the transitional lesson. Several weeks later, this interaction was repeated as Raheem moved into the Purple level of TRI. Overall, the interactions between coach and teacher were more reciprocal, as the two shared ideas and built on the other's thoughts. Coach Kelly was still influential in Ms. Green's instructional decision making, but Ms. Green demonstrated greater confidence in her own ideas and a willingness to express her opinions about Raheem's needs.

By the end of the school year, Coach Kelly, in collaboration with the school principal, invited Ms. Green to become a TRI Facilitator. TRI Facilitators, selected on the basis of their frequency of implementation, mastery of TRI, and leadership ability, would complete the TRI certification process and assume the role of TRI literacy coach within their school buildings for the following school year (Aiken et al., 2020). Within this context, Ms. Green truly blossomed. She described why she became a TRI Facilitator, expressing her desire to share the knowledge and confidence she had gained from implementing TRI with other teachers. Ms. Green worked hard with the teachers she supported, conducting weekly coaching sessions and offering to meet after school to plan TRI lessons. She spent time encouraging the other teachers, intentionally monitoring the feedback she provided, and naming three positives about each lesson along with one wish or activity to work on. One of her teachers was brand new to both teaching and TRI, and by the end of the year this teacher credited Ms. Green with providing the knowledge and learning support that enabled her to proficiently implement TRI for her students.

During her time as a TRI Facilitator, Ms. Green continued to work with her own students and meet weekly with Coach Kelly. The conversations during these lessons were markedly different from those in the first year. Ms. Green had a new aura of confidence as she discussed her students and their progress. She was less likely to seek permission for a course of action, instead providing a description of her rationale for selecting an activity, text, or word. In the words of Coach Kelly, "Teaching TRI to others seemed to make it click" for Ms. Green.

Ms. Green's increased knowledge about the mechanics of teaching reading was perhaps best demonstrated on the survey administered at the beginning and end of the first year. The survey included two classroom scenarios with a series of questions. Each of the scenarios described a student and problem of practice, followed by a series of scaled questions (ranging from 1 (strongly disagree) to 4 (strongly agree) and three open-ended questions ("What were the lesson strengths?"; "What would you change in the lesson?"; and "Is there anything else you'd like to say about the lesson?). Initially, Ms. Green only answered two of the open-ended questions, listing "activating prior knowledge" as a strength and suggesting "the child should do the work" as something to change. At the end of that year, Ms. Green expanded the areas for improvement to include limiting the number of letters presented to the child at one time, utilizing *Blend as You Go* specifically, and including comprehension questions within the lesson. She also added a response to the final question, which read:

> "With a struggling reader, it is important not to overwhelm them any more than what they already may be. I would suggest to the teacher to let the student do the work but provide modeling and support as needed. When a teacher quickly tells a student an answer, sometimes that can make them feel even more frustrated."

Before she became fully certified and began supporting teachers herself, Ms. Green already applied what she had learned from TRI to additional instructional settings, suggesting evidence of instructional transfer.

Conclusion

PL in literacy frequently takes one of two paths: (1) training teachers to implement highly scripted instruction in the classroom, or (2) building knowledge about reading content and pedagogy that teachers are expected to independently apply to their teaching. In this chapter we detailed an innovative PL process—the Targeted Reading Instruction—which provides a bridge between these two methods, building classroom teacher knowledge and capacity through the PL process while simultaneously enhancing teachers' practice through the use of TRI lessons and activities. Through the TRI model, equitable and sustainable PL is provided as teachers learn within the situated context of providing reading instruction to students, focusing on matching diagnostic strategies to individual students' needs. Using innovative models such as the TRI can provide sustainable PL to teachers that supports equitable outcomes for all.

REFERENCES

Aiken, H. H., Bratsch-Hines, M., Amendum, S. J., & Vernon-Feagans, L. (2021). Targeted Reading Instruction: Four guiding principles. *The Reading Teacher, 74*(5), 505–515.

Aiken, H. H., Varghese, C., Pedonti, S., Bratsch-Hines, M., & Vernon-Feagans, L. (2020). Targeted Reading Intervention teacher certification: An approach to building and sustaining teacher expertise in rural schools. *Literacy Research and Instruction, 59*(4), 346–369.

Allington, R. L. (2013). What really matters when working with struggling readers. *The Reading Teacher, 66*(7), 520–530.

Amendum, S. J., Amendum, E., & Almond, P. (2013). One dy I kud not red a book bot naw I can: One English learner's progress. *The Reading Teacher, 67*(1), 59–69.

Amendum, S. J., Bratsch-Hines, M., & Vernon-Feagans, L. (2018). Investigating the efficacy of a web-based early reading and professional development intervention for young English learners. *Reading Research Quarterly, 53*(2), 155–174.

Amendum, S. J., Vernon-Feagans, L., & Ginsberg, M. C. (2011). The effectiveness of a technologically-facilitated classroom-based early reading intervention: The Targeted Reading Intervention. *Elementary School Journal, 112*(1), 107–131.

Austin, C. R., & Vaughn, S. (2019). Reading interventions for young learners with reading difficulties and disabilities: The role of word reading and word meaning. In F. E. Obiakor & J. P. Bakken (Eds.), *Special education for young learners with disabilities* (Vol. 34, pp. 15–37). Emerald.

Bear, D. R., Invernizzi, M., Templeton, S., & Johnson, F. (2012). *Words their way: Word study for phonics, vocabulary, and spelling instruction* (5th ed.). Pearson/Prentice Hall.

Bratsch-Hines, M., Vernon-Feagans, L., Pedonti, S., & Varghese, C. (2020). Differential effects of the Targeted Reading Intervention for students with low phonological awareness and/or vocabulary. *Learning Disability Quarterly, 43*(4), 214–226.

Brown, J. S., Collins, A., & Duguid, P. (1989). Situated cognition and the culture of learning. *Educational Researcher, 18*, 32–42.

Cheatham, J. P., & Allor, J. H. (2012). The influence of decodability in early reading text on reading achievement: A review of the evidence. *Reading and Writing, 25*, 2223–2246.

Cohen, L., Krustedt, R. L., & May, M. (2009). Fluency, text structure, and retelling: A complex relationship. *Reading Horizons: A Journal of Literacy and Language Arts, 49*(2), 101–124.

Desimone, L. M., & Garet, M. S. (2015). Best practices in teachers' professional development in the United States. *Psychology, Society, and Education, 7*, 252–263.

Foorman, B. R., Beyler, N., Borradaile, K., Coyne, M., Denton, C. A., Dimino, J., . . . Wissel, S. (2016). *Foundational skills to support reading for understanding in kindergarten through 3rd grade.* National Center for Education Evaluation and Regional Assistance (NCEE), Institute of Education Sciences, U.S. Department of Education. Retrieved from the NCEE website: *http://whatworks.ed.gov.*

Fuchs, D., Fuchs, L. S., & Vaughn, S. (2014). What is intensive instruction and why is it important? *Teaching Exceptional Children, 46*(4), 13–18.

Gärdenfors, P. (2017). Semantic knowledge, domains of meaning and conceptual spaces. In P. Meusburger, B. Werlen, & L. Suarsana (Eds.), *Knowledge and Action* (pp. 203–219). Springer International.

Garet, M. S., Cronen, S., Eaton, M., Kurki, A., Ludwig, M., Jones, W., . . . Silverberg, M. (2008). *The impact of two professional development interventions on early reading instruction and achievement.* National Center for Education Evaluation and Regional Assistance 2008-4034, U.S. Department of Education, Institute of Education Sciences.

Goldhaber, D., Lavery, L., & Theobold, R. (2015). Uneven playing field?: Assessing the teacher quality gap between advantaged and disadvantaged students. *Educational Researcher, 44*, 293–307.

Greene, S. (2008). Introduction: Teaching for social justice. *Counterpoints, 316,* 1–25.

Grimm, R. P., Solari, E. J., McIntyre, N. S., & Denton, C. A. (2018). Early reading skill profiles in typically developing and at-risk first grade readers to inform targeted early reading instruction. *Journal of School Psychology, 69,* 111–126.

Guskey, T. R. (2002). Professional development and teacher change. *Teachers and Teaching, 8*(3), 381–391.

Hanushek, E. A. (2016). What matters for student achievement. *Education Next, 16*(2). Retrieved from *www.educationnext.org/what-matters-for-student-achievement.*

Hernandez, D. J. (2011). *Double jeopardy: How third-grade reading skills and poverty influence high school graduation.* Annie E. Casey Foundation.

Institute of Education Sciences. (2008). *Reading First impact study final report.* Institute of Education Sciences, NCEE 2009-4038. U.S. Department of Education.

Kainz, K., & Vernon-Feagans, L. (2007). The ecology of early reading development for children in poverty. *The Elementary School Journal, 107,* 407–427.

Korthagen, F. A. J. (2010). Situated learning theory and the pedagogy of teacher education: Towards an integrative view of teacher behavior and teacher learning. *Teaching and Teacher Education, 26,* 98–106.

Langer, P. (2009). Situated learning: What ever happened to educational psychology? *Educational Psychology Review, 21,* 181–192.

Language and Reading Research Consortium. (2015). The dimensionality of language ability in young children. *Child Development, 86*(6), 1948–1965.

López, F. A., Thompson, S. S., & Walker-Dalhouse, D. (2011). Examining the trajectory of differentially skilled first graders' reading fluency of words in isolation and in context. *Reading & Writing Quarterly, 27*(4), 281–305.

McIntyre, E., Kyle, D. W., & Moore, G. H. (2006). A primary-grade teacher's guidance toward small-group dialogue. *Reading Research Quarterly, 41*(1), 36–66.

National Center for Education Statistics. (2020). *Nation's report card: 2019 NAEP reading: National student group scores and score gaps.* Retrieved from *www.nationsreportcard.gov/reading/nation/groups?grade=4.*

No Child Left Behind Act of 2001. (2001). Public Law 107-110. Retrieved from *www.ed.gov/nclb/landing.jhtml.*

Pearson, P. D., & Gallagher, M. C. (1983). The instruction of reading comprehension. *Contemporary Educational Psychology, 8,* 317–344.

Piasta, S. B., & Wagner, R. K. (2010). Developing early literacy skills: A meta-analysis of alphabet learning and instruction. *Reading Research Quarterly, 45*(1), 8–38.

Porche, M. V., Pallante, D., & Snow, C. E. (2012). Professional development for reading achievement. Results from the Collaborative Language and Literacy Project (CLLIP). *The Elementary School Journal, 112,* 649–671.

Rasinski, T. V. (2003). *The fluent reader.* Scholastic Professional Books.

Rasinski, T. V. (2006). Reading fluency instruction: Moving beyond accuracy, automaticity, and prosody. *The Reading Teacher, 59*(7), 704–706.

Risko, V. J., Roller, C. M., Cummins, C., Bean, R. M., Block, C. C., Anders, P. L., & Flood, J. (2008). A critical analysis of research on reading teacher education. *Reading Research Quarterly, 43,* 252–288.

Shanahan, T. (2020). What constitutes a science of reading instruction? *Reading Research Quarterly, 55*(S1), S235–S247.

Shanahan, T., Callison, K., Carriere, C., Duke, N. K., Pearson, P. D., Schatschneider, C., & Torgesen, J. K. (2010). *Improving reading comprehension in kindergarten through 3rd grade: IES practice guide. NCEE 2010–4038.* What Works Clearinghouse. Retrieved from *https://ies.ed.gov/ncee/wwc/PracticeGuide/14.*

Solari, E. J., Denton, C. A., Petscher, Y., & Haring, C. (2018). Examining the effects and feasibility of a teacher-implemented tier 1 and tier 2 intervention in word reading, fluency, and comprehension. *Journal of Research on Educational Effectiveness, 11*(2), 163–191.

Strom, C. H., & Neuman, S. B. (2016). Seizing the sounds: Considering phonological awareness in the context of vocabulary instruction. In R. Schiff & R. M. Joshi (Eds.), *Interventions in learning disabilities: A handbook on systematic training programs for individuals with learning disabilities* (pp. 105–118). Springer International.

Vernon-Feagans, L., Bratsch-Hines, M., Varghese, C., Bean, A., & Hedrick, A. (2015). The Targeted Reading Intervention: Face-to-face vs. webcam literacy coaching of classroom teachers. *Learning Disabilities Research and Practice, 30*(3), 135–147.

Vernon-Feagans, L., Bratsch-Hines, M., Varghese, C., Cutrer, E. A., & Garwood, J. D. (2018). Improving struggling readers' early literacy skills through a tier 2 professional development program for rural classroom teachers: The Targeted Reading Intervention. *The Elementary School Journal, 118*(4), 525–548.

Vernon-Feagans, L., Kainz, K., Hedrick, A., Ginsberg, M., & Amendum, S. J. (2013). Live webcam coaching to help early elementary classroom teachers provide effective literacy instruction for struggling readers: The Targeted Reading Intervention. *Journal of Educational Psychology, 105*(4), 1175–1187.

What Works Clearinghouse. (2017). WWC review of the report "Live Webcam coaching to help early elementary classroom teachers provide effective literacy instruction for struggling readers: The targeted reading intervention." Retrieved from *https://ies.ed.gov/ncee/wwc/study/81447.*

Yoon, K. S., Duncan, T., Lee, S. W.-Y., Scarloss, B., & Shapley, K. (2007). *Reviewing the evidence on how teacher professional development affects student achievement.* U.S. Department of Education, Institute of Education Sciences, National Center for Education Evaluation and Regional Assistance, Regional Educational Laboratory Southwest.

CHAPTER 6

Teacher Agency and Sustainable Learning through Literacy Coaching with Teachers of Adolescents Who Are Emergent Bi- and Multilingual Students

Jennifer Sharples Reichenberg

Watch a related video from the author at this link.

At a time when educators debate which programs and approaches will address the growing linguistic, cultural, racial, and economic complexity of American schools, one thing remains clear—teachers' knowledge and skills are at the core of creating effective student learning opportunities (Darling-Hammond, 2000). Effective teachers are flexible, and their decisions are informed by students' needs and learning goals (Hammerness et al., 2005). In these teachers' classrooms, you will see a variety of approaches employed, and these approaches are tailored to their unique classroom contexts.

Therefore, when students experience extraordinary challenges, such as simultaneously learning English while also learning disciplinary content, the need for teacher expertise is evident. Not only is student achievement at stake, so, too, are equity and the opportunity to succeed after secondary school. For many adolescent students who are also emergent bi- and multilingual (EBM), this may be just a year or two away. That is why, in these complex environments, teachers must exercise agency, drawing upon their expertise to make decisions informed by their unique contexts. This process will not only create more equitable learning experiences for students, but it will also support teachers to engage in sustained professional learning (PL).

In this chapter, I describe a seven-step reflective framework that guides one-on-one literacy coaching interactions with teachers. The framework is anchored in co-viewing video of teachers' instruction with a coach. This process favors teachers' agency and context-informed decision making and has the potential to support sustainable PL.

This chapter highlights how Patrick, a teacher of students who are EBM in an urban high school, and I used the framework together during one school year. First, I discuss related literature highlighting the opportunities and challenges associated with coaching secondary-level teachers of students who are EBM, teacher agency, and contextually informed decision making. Next, I explain the study context and framework. Then, I show how Patrick and I engaged with each step in the framework, highlight the rationale for each step, and unpack those interactions. Finally, I discuss Patrick's thoughts about his use of this approach and why it supports teacher agency, context-informed decision making, and sustainable PL, including when a literacy coach is no longer available.

Related Literature on Literacy Coaching with Secondary-Level Teachers of Students Who Are EBM

Opportunities and Challenges

Literacy coaching is a job-embedded, collaborative, and sustained approach to PL that involves cycles of observation of and feedback on instruction (Bean, 2008; International Literacy Association, 2015). Commonly, coaches first meet with teachers to plan, then observe, co-teach, or model during classroom instruction, and finally meet again to discuss the experience. Although less frequently researched than elementary-level coaching (International Reading Association [IRA], 2006; Rush, 2013), secondary-level literacy coaching is especially useful to support the integration of literacy learning with advanced study of the disciplines such as social studies, science, and English language arts (Davis et al., 2018; Di Domenico et al., 2018; Rush, 2013; Snow et al., 2006) and also to support teachers of adolescents who are EBM (Reichenberg, 2020). Secondary-level literacy coaching has been associated with positive changes in teachers' instructional practices (Fisher et al., 2011; Reichenberg, 2020). Coaching has also been linked to changes in teachers' reflective practices (Reichenberg, 2020), self-efficacy regarding literacy teaching (Cantrell & Hughes, 2008), and willingness to collaborate (Cantrell et al., 2009).

Despite this potential, literacy coaching at the secondary level presents unique challenges. Teachers often express concern about pressure to cover required content within the available time (Bean, 2008). In addition, secondary teachers possess deep disciplinary knowledge that is not likely shared by literacy coaches, making it more challenging for coaches to support them (Bean, 2008). Relatedly, these teachers may not see the utility of literacy instructional practices to their disciplines (Bean, 2008). Finally, coaching is effective, in part, because it is time-intensive and individualized (Steinbacher-Reed & Powers, 2012). However, these attributes may render coaching difficult to maintain. Therefore, it is important to identify coaching principles and practices that make efficient use of teachers' time, allow for the distribution of expertise between teachers and coaches, and gradually replace intensive individual coaching with self-sustainable PL.

Coaching teachers of linguistically diverse students presents additional complexity and opportunity (Ortlieb & Cheek, 2017). These students are tasked with learning English alongside academic content. They encounter texts that require knowledge of content-specific vocabulary and deep background and cultural knowledge, while engaging in complex reading and writing tasks (Cho & Reich, 2008). Research has pointed to promising practices for these students. Scaffolding, such as building background knowledge with experiences and images, can support students' capacity to read complex text (Kibler et al., 2015). Students' first languages are important linguistic resources that teachers can use to increase access to content and to learn English (García, 2009; Lin, 2013). Despite this growing body of knowledge, best practices for supporting the PL of teachers of students who are EBM toward these goals remain elusive, and there is a paucity of research on literacy coaching for these teachers. However, preliminary findings suggest that the PL of teachers of adolescent students who are EBM can be effectively supported by a coach (Reichenberg, 2018; Reichenberg & Boyd, 2019; Russell, 2015, 2017).

An additional challenge is that coaches, often viewed by teachers as quasi-administrators, may be expected to help teachers achieve fidelity to a program or an instructional approach (Kraft et al., 2018; Sailors & Hoffman, 2018). Since effective instruction is characterized by teachers' ability to exercise adaptive expertise—the capability of teachers to respond effectively to unexpected occurrences while teaching students in their classrooms (Bransford et al., 2005; Hayden et al., 2013)—coaching must be driven by contextually informed decision making and guided by teachers' own concerns and insights about their students' needs. In other words, teacher agency is foundational.

Teacher Agency in Literacy Coaching

Agency to transform one's situation by initiating "purposeful action" (Lipponen & Kumpulainen, 2011, p. 813) is supported when one's ideas are valued (Philpott & Oates, 2017). This is especially important in a relationship with potential for the perception that authority rests with one individual, such as a coach (Hunt, 2016, 2018; Robertson et al., 2020). For example, Robertson et al. (2020) found that teachers often viewed coaches as authorities even when coaches sought to position teachers as agentive. However, vulnerability and the sharing of knowledge and expertise were more common when teachers were content area specialists (Robertson et al., 2020), such as at the secondary level (Di Domenico et al., 2018). Therefore, the challenge of coaching secondary-level teachers is also an opportunity to capitalize on bidirectional learning and to foreground teacher agency. While secondary teachers may be disciplinary experts and/or experts on teaching students who are EBM, literacy coaches offer support in integrating literacy across the disciplines or in adopting new instructional approaches for literacy integration with language instruction (IRA, 2012). However, teachers need to exercise agency to make those approaches their own in light of their expertise and unique context. As this occurs, coaches, in turn, learn from the expertise of teachers and are able to offer more contextually informed support.

Contextually Informed Decision Making

Whereas individual agency is important, we can only understand agency in the context of the social world (Wenger, 2008). All activity is embedded in some sort of social context (Rogoff, 1990). Rather than a static construct, however, context is dynamic and continuously reshaped through social interactions in classrooms. These social interactions involve, primarily, the teachers and students in those rooms. They are also shaped by policies, mandates, and the curriculum. Therefore, teachers are experts on the unique classroom contexts in which they teach.

For example, I observed a teacher of a secondary social studies class containing students with ten different first languages spend 20 minutes of class time learning how to say the word "mountain" in each language from her students as they all laughed together at her attempts. They were learning about the geographical features that led to China's relative isolation and unique cultural development. While an observer may consider 20 minutes an inordinate amount of time for this exercise, the teacher mindfully drew upon her students' rich language backgrounds and her rapport with the class to create a memorable experience around a key concept—the impact of geography on cultural development. However, Hunt (2016) found that context was often deemed less important in coaching interactions than implementing particular practices with fidelity. This led to teachers experiencing emotions such as fear, shame, and guilt associated with straying from those practices, which limited deep PL. Therefore, contextually informed decision making, which positions teachers as experts, is a critical aspect of PL driven by teachers' agency.

When teachers are empowered to use context to inform their long- and short-term planning as well as moment-to-moment decisions, they are able to use and develop adaptive expertise. Adaptive expertise is the "gold standard for becoming a professional" (Hammerness et al., 2005, p. 360) because "adaptive experts are much more likely to change their core competencies and continually expand the breadth and depth of their expertise" (Bransford et al., 2005, p. 49). In other words, these teachers are able to be continually and thoughtfully responsive to changes in individual students, community and school events, and curriculum, which is especially important in complex contexts.

Reflective Frameworks and Video: Mediation of PL through Tools

As humans and teachers, we use many different tools to accomplish our goals (Wertsch, 1998). Preservice teachers use lesson plan templates to learn to plan instruction, teachers use running reading records to analyze students' reading strategies, and administrators use virtual platforms to communicate with teachers and families. When new tools are added to our metaphorical toolbelt, our thinking and actions often change as a result. Wertsch (1998) asserts that these changes frequently include the way power and authority are enacted in relationships. For example, if a school begins to employ an app that facilitates faster teacher/family communication, then teachers and families have greater potential to partner for students' success in real time. Rather than being recipients of reports from teachers at the end of the school day, families can become increasingly active participants in supporting their children's success through more frequent, timely communication. This same principle has powerful implications for teacher PL.

Tools used by literacy coaches and teachers can foreground contextually informed decision making and teachers' agency in their own PL. One such tool is a framework to guide the reflective process. Often employed with teacher candidates, reflective frameworks have been associated with candidates' ability to notice more details about student learning (Hayden & Chiu, 2009) and to interrogate their own instruction through comparison and critique of their practice (Jay & Johnson, 2002). Inservice teachers have also used reflective frameworks to make sustainable changes to their thinking and instruction (Reichenberg, 2018, 2020; Reichenberg & Boyd, 2019).

Another such tool is video. Teaching is fast-paced, with little time to engage in retrospective reflection. Viewing video allows teachers time to revisit decisions, contemplate students' responses, and formulate future plans. As it provides time for deeper reflection, it also contextualizes that reflection in the time and space in which the teaching occurred. Another benefit of video is the way in which it favors teachers' agency. Discussion of teaching with coaches often relies on coaches' notes and recollections of events. In contrast, video allows the teacher to comment directly on the action in the classroom, highlighting the teacher's expertise as the instructor. Studies of teachers reflecting with video have shown that these teachers make changes in their own classroom practices that positively impact student learning experiences (McVee et al., 2015; Ortlieb et al., 2015; Reichenberg, 2018). In this chapter, I show how a reflective framework used with video during literacy coaching has the potential to create a teacher-driven, context-informed sustainable approach to teachers' PL.

School Context and PD-CASE-R Framework

The literacy coaching described in this chapter took place in an urban middle and high school with approximately 700 students. Over 40 languages and language variations were represented in the building in which almost 70% of students spoke a first language or two other than English and 80% were considered economically disadvantaged. I participated as a literacy coach in the school for 3 years, first as part of a PL grant and later as a researcher, coaching four to five teachers each year.

Most coaches and coached teachers are familiar with the common three-part recursive coaching cycle, which includes a prelesson conversation, observation, and postlesson conversation. I decided to integrate a routine into the postlesson conversation using video of the teachers' instruction that I hoped would position teachers as drivers of the conversation rather than me as the coach. To do so, I built upon the ideas of John Dewey (1933), who wrote about reflective thinking. I formed his ideas about the reflective process into the seven steps of the PD-CASE-R framework (see also Reichenberg, 2019, 2020). The name of the framework is an acronym formed from the first letter of an important word in each step.

- *P/Step 1: Identify Perplexity*—Identify a portion of the lesson you find to be perplexing or intriguing. This may be a challenge, problem, dilemma, or something that went well.
- *D/Step 2: Describe*—Describe that portion of the lesson and your thinking in detail while viewing the video.

- *C/Step 3: Create a Central Challenge Question*—Create a focus question to articulate the challenge present in the situation.
- *A/Step 4: Generate Alternatives*—Generate alternative ways to address the challenge.
- *S/Step 5: Select Alternative(s)*—Select one or a combination of the alternatives.
- *E/Step 6: Enact*—Enact.
- *R/Step 7: Reflect again*—Revisit the situation to reflect again (Reichenberg, 2020, p. 59).

The framework is intended to guide the postlesson conversation, beginning with teachers' own perplexity. Since one important characteristic of effective teaching is adaptability to unanticipated student responses (Taylor & Pearson, 2002), the framework begins with the unexpected. Dewey (1933) referred to these surprises as "forked-road" situations (p. 14). These situations may include unexpected challenges, but we may also analyze unanticipated success. Therefore, I explained sources of perplexity to teachers as *challenges* or *things that went well*. Each subsequent step built upon that initial perplexity and favored either teacher direction or collaboration between the teacher and coach with the goal of building teacher agency, employing context-informed decision making, and creating sustainable PL.

During each 30-minute one-on-one coaching session, teachers and I used the PD-CASE-R framework with video of their lesson. As part of that process, we planned for future instruction. In this chapter, two coaching cycles with Patrick and his students are explored. Patrick is a veteran teacher of English as a new language (ENL). His 12th-grade ENL class was reading *The Autobiography of Malcolm X* (X & Haley, 1965/1992) as part of the mandated English language arts curriculum. The language proficiency level of most of these students was *emerging* or *transitioning*—levels two or three of five English proficiency designations ranging from beginning (level one) to commanding (level five). At these levels, these students still depended on supports to engage with the academic language and content of their grade level (emerging) or were beginning to experience some independence (transitioning). Like many ENL teachers, Patrick was tasked with helping students new to the English language construct meaning from text that was challenging because of its concepts and themes, historical context, and unfamiliar vocabulary. In this chapter I highlight Patrick's use of the framework and video during coaching sessions to support his students to exercise greater autonomy in unpacking the language and ideas in the book.

I selected Patrick's work for this chapter because it shows how the framework supported his agency to make pedagogical adjustments based on context across two lessons and coaching sessions. I first show how Patrick engaged with each step in the framework, after which I explain and unpack that step, focusing on how it supported Patrick's agency and contextually informed decision making. Finally, I share Patrick's thoughts on the process and his own sustainable PL.

PD-CASE-R Framework in Action: Patrick Reflects on English Language Arts Instruction with Students Who Are EBM

After 20 years as an ENL teacher, Patrick was experienced in teaching vocabulary, academic language, and grammar to adolescent students who were EBM. However, the recent implementation of new learning standards in Patrick's state, newly mandated curricular materials, and the increase in the adolescent refugee population in his district posed new challenges for him.

In early fall, Patrick's students were reading *The Autobiography of Malcolm X* (X & Haley, 1965/1992) as part of the English curriculum. Patrick supplemented English instruction each day during an ENL period with these students. One learning objective he established to help students succeed in English class was for them to determine the author's central ideas or meaningful main points. Patrick spent a good deal of time helping his students establish the historical context of the events in the book. He explained that, at this point in mid-September, students were able to read the words in the text and understand the action of the story with support, but they needed a great deal of help to identify central ideas.

Therefore, during our first coaching session of the year at the end of September, we created a thinking guide to scaffold students' understanding of the literal and inferential meanings in short passages of text (see Figure 6.1). The thinking guide prompted students to read a question and a designated passage from the text, reread the question and passage, write notes to put the passage in their own words, talk to a partner about the literal meaning and possible central ideas, and then write an answer to the question.

The following week, Patrick implemented the thinking guide for the first time with the questions: "What does Malcolm X tell the readers about the ideas of Mr. Muhammad? What central idea does this support?" Through a think-aloud, Patrick modeled reading the question and corresponding passage, rereading the question and passage, putting the passage into his own words, and thinking about the broader meaning in the passage. He then presented students with a second question and passage and led the class in discussion using the same steps. The following week,

READAND REREAD 

Read the question.
Read the text.
Read the question AGAIN.
Read the text AGAIN.

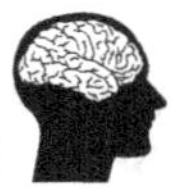

THINK AND NOTE

Text Says	My Own Words
"Most whites don't give a Negro credit for having sense enough to fool them—or nerve enough" (p. 106).	

TALK 

FIGURE 6.1. Thinking guide.

we met to discuss this lesson using the PD-CASE-R framework and video of the lesson.

Ideally, coaching sessions would occur immediately after a lesson so that details would be fresh in the teacher's and coach's minds. However, due to schedule constraints, there were usually a few days between the taught lesson and our coaching session. Therefore, before we met, I made a brief list of the major events in the lesson video and times they occurred as a reminder to teachers and to help us quickly find specific points.

Step 1: Patrick Identifies Perplexity (P)

At the beginning of Patrick's coaching session, I shared the list of major events from his last lesson with him. He said, "They all needed some sort of guidance, generally, but one mistake I think I made was I didn't preteach the vocabulary when we did it." When I asked which portion of the video he would like to watch, he quickly responded: "Trying to make the connection with the central idea."

Patrick chose to focus on the challenge of helping students infer central ideas from the literal meaning of the text. Therefore, we began watching the video at the part of the lesson in which Patrick and the students discussed the deeper meaning of the second passage in the lesson. In the focal passage, Malcolm X described his horror when he began reading and learning about the enslavement of Africans on American soil (X & Haley, 1965/1992).

Step 1/P Explained

Imagine a hiker navigating a wooded trail to a desired destination. As the hiker advances, the ground becomes uneven, cluttered with rocks and crisscrossed by roots. Her eyes are drawn downward to help navigate the terrain. This adjustment meets the immediate challenge of maintaining the hiker's footing. However, ahead, the trail forks. If the hiker, now preoccupied with maintaining her footing, never looks up, she may miss the fork and indiscriminately continue down a less than ideal path, leading her further away from her destination.

Dewey (1933) suggested that reflective thinking begins with perplexity, which he likened to noticing and engaging a fork in the road. Like the hiker, teachers may develop a strong focus on immediate challenges, which sometimes makes it difficult to lift their eyes to see forks that arise. Noticing these forks is engaging perplexity, which can help teachers more readily reach their pedagogical and learning goals with students.

Since teacher agency is supported when teachers focus their PL on areas they deem important, the first step in the PD-CASE-R framework is for teachers to identify their own perplexity about the lesson. This could be a moment that presented a challenge, something intriguing, or something that exceeded their initial expectations. This determined which part of the video we watched.

Patrick's experience using the PD-CASE-R framework with me during the previous year may have supported his quick identification of two sources of perplexity: knowing academic vocabulary and identifying the deeper meaning in the passage. This is an indication of how distributed expertise between a secondary-level teacher and a literacy coach can support reflective development.

Patrick's 20 years of experience teaching students who were EBM meant that he quickly recognized the problem of students not understanding the passage, the likely cause being unfamiliar vocabulary and a potential solution being pre-teaching academic vocabulary. Patrick was familiar with a variety of ways to teach academic vocabulary. In contrast, Patrick recognized that he needed more support with his second source of perplexity, students having difficulty identifying the deeper significance in the text. Here, a literacy coach possesses expertise that could be helpful. For this reason, he chose to focus our reflective viewing on his second challenge.

Step 2: Patrick Describes (D)

Sliding my laptop computer in front of Patrick, I said: "Make this is as loud as you want." As we watched the video, Patrick commented that it was "hard for them . . . to make the jump from this horrible thing . . . that slavery existed in the United States, to make the connection to . . . the central [idea]—the oppression by the white man against the black man is still prevalent in his society." He added that it was important for students to see the parallels between the oppression of slavery and the oppression described by Malcolm X in the book.

I also described what I, as the coach, noticed. I emphasized Patrick's use of academic language: "I noticed in your modeling that when you are trying to come up with the central idea, . . . you said, 'He's not just talking about history.'"

Step 2/D Explained

When faced with perplexity, Dewey (1933) contended that a reflective practitioner is "willing to sustain and protract that state of doubt" by seeking additional evidence (p. 16). Therefore, Step 2 in the framework prompts teachers to describe that part of the lesson they find perplexing, with the goal of noticing more than was possible while teaching. Watching between 2 and 6 minutes of video, teachers were encouraged to pause the video to describe action and thinking, while withholding judgment. Unlike traditional coaching, which relies on coaches' notes and teachers' recollections, use of the framework and video positioned teachers as experts and contextualized the conversation in their knowledge of the content and their students.

By placing the laptop computer in front of Patrick, my goal was to emphasize Patrick's agency in the coaching session. Control of the tools of reflection places teachers in the lead. As he described, Patrick pointed out the difficulty his students had connecting the events of the book with central ideas such as the link between the oppression of enslavement with the oppression of black people Malcolm X experienced at the hands of white people. These comments reinforced Patrick's expertise on the content of his lesson and his students. While Patrick controlled the video and took the lead when describing, my participation allowed me to model describing without judgment or to point out effective teaching moves or unexpected student responses. My goal in pointing out the specific academic language Patrick used was to draw attention to some of the different ways he explained the concept of central idea to his students.

Step 3: Patrick Creates a Central Challenge Question (C)

Patrick's initial perplexity focused on students' identification of central ideas in the text. However, revisiting this initial perplexity about students "making the jump" to the central idea in light of new insights from description helped Patrick to add specificity to his question. Patrick's initial perplexity about "trying to make the connection with the central [idea]" developed further after viewing the video. When asked to state the central challenge he would like to explore, Patrick responded: "the connection from the text to the central . . . idea." To help Patrick focus his question, I suggested adding the phrases "help" and "break it down." Patrick's final central challenge question became: "How can we help students break down the process of making the connection from the text to the central . . . idea?"

Step 3/C Explained

Whereas teachers' initial perplexity is often vague or difficult to articulate, in Step 3, teachers transform that vague notion into a highly focused question to guide the rest of the coaching session. As Dewey noted (1933), a "question well put is half answered" (p. 108). This question is like the fulcrum of a lever, carefully placed to amplify the power of the teacher's reflective thought. Schön (1983, p. 42) calls this process "naming and framing." The central challenge question *names* that to which the teacher and coach will attend and *frames*, or intentionally includes, the information most useful to the inquiry.

This step is an opportunity for the literacy coach to support refinement in the trajectory of the path ahead, which includes generating alternatives in Step 4. In this coaching session, I *reconceptualized* Patrick's question (Cazden, 2001). Reconceptualizing occurs when one conversational partner slightly alters the trajectory of the other person's statement in meaning or focus. My suggestion to add the phrases "help" and "break it down" focused Patrick's initial question ("the connection from the text to the central idea") more tightly on breaking down the process of determining the central idea into smaller steps.

Patrick's new question was "How can we help students break down the process of making the connection from the text to the central . . . idea?" This reconceptualized question focused our attention more tightly on two aspects of his initial perplexity: breaking down the process and possible scaffolds (i.e., "help"). This reconceptualized question would point us toward identifying incremental supports on the way to student independence.

Step 4: Patrick Generates Alternatives (A)

Patrick and I then discussed a variety of ways to scaffold students' understanding of the deeper meanings in the text, often building on one another's suggestions. First, I suggested matching central ideas to short passages as a scaffold to employ before asking students to independently identify them. Patrick liked this idea and suggested some common central ideas in the text he could use. He also envisioned eventually having students do quick-writes about evidence in the short passages in support of the corresponding central ideas.

Patrick suggested using a wordless, animated short video to illustrate the concept of the central idea. To build on this idea, I mentioned continuing to model academic language with the video through carefully chosen phrases to scaffold students' understanding of the central idea. Patrick agreed that modeling his "metacognition" would be critical and suggested phrases such as "What does this [show] about the meaning of life?" and "What is he trying to say about society in general?"

We discussed adapting the thinking guide to prompt students to talk *before* taking notes, instead of after, and to include a section for students to write notes about the central idea before being asked to write out complete sentences to explain it. Finally, we collaboratively identified specific academic vocabulary that would be important to understand these passages, a challenge Patrick identified in Step 1.

Step 4/A Explained

With renewed focus achieved by formulating the central challenge question in Step 3, teachers and coaches generate alternatives together in Step 4. Although generating alternative courses of action is a familiar process for teachers, Dewey (1933) emphasized thinking through the consequences of each action and suspending final judgment until considering multiple ideas. This requires the attitude of open-mindedness, as the teacher entertains various possibilities, and foresight, which is the ability to visualize the consequences of an action (Dewey, 1933).

This step serves three purposes important to agency, contextually informed decision making, and sustainability: (1) the conversation emphasizes teachers' agency in the brainstorming process by creating the expectation for teachers and coaches to contribute their expertise, (2) the conversation allows coaches to help teachers slow down to consider contextual factors and multiple options before taking action, and (3) the collaboration encourages risk taking, including designing learning experiences that afford students who are EBM greater responsibility for their own learning. This, in turn, supports sustainability because teachers are more likely to continue a new practice when they see it work successfully in their own classrooms (Guskey, 2002).

During this step, Patrick and I each suggested and built upon one another's ideas, showcasing the differing expertise of the teacher and coach. For example, Patrick suggested using a wordless, animated short video to illustrate the concept of the central idea, an effective approach for students who are EBM. I built upon this idea, drawing on my expertise in literacy instruction, by suggesting that we select specific academic language to scaffold students' understanding of the central idea while viewing.

Step 5: Patrick Selects Alternatives (S)

Patrick decided to pre-teach the vocabulary in the focal passages more deliberately, although he opted to decide exactly how to do so later. He also chose to adapt the thinking guide we had created together to include a new section for notes about the central idea right after the section paraphrasing the text. This would serve as a bridge to writing an answer to the question about the central idea at the end of the lesson. Finally, Patrick returned to the matching idea I proposed, saying, "Maybe we give six different passages [with] different [central ideas] and then each group has to categorize" the passage with the central idea.

Step 5/S Explained

Dewey (1933) notes that this process of selecting a course of action can transform initial ideas, at first "remote and wild," into "apt and fruitful" plans (p. 112). In Step 5, teachers choose alternatives to enact, again foregrounding teacher agency. This step may also include planning with the coach and deciding when to enact the plan.

Patrick decided to pre-teach vocabulary, but he said he would determine exactly *how* later. This showcases the flexibility of the framework for Patrick to enact his confidence and expertise with this aspect of teaching students who are EBM. He also decided to adapt the thinking guide, deeming it effective, yet in need of improvement. Again, Patrick took the lead by deciding what would work best in the context of his classroom.

Step 6: Patrick Enacts (E)

Before my next classroom coaching visit, Patrick hung five sheets of chart paper, each with a quotation from the focal passage of *The Autobiography of Malcolm X*, around the classroom. Each passage dealt with the topic of religion. Patrick underlined a key word or phrase in each quotation such as *worship* and *responsibility*. As students entered the room, he assigned them to a group of three or four and asked them to visit each quotation. Together, the students read the quotation, talked, and used context to try to put the underlined word or phrase into their own words, recording their ideas on sticky notes and leaving them with each passage. After the students visited each quotation, Patrick engaged the whole class in a discussion of the meaning of the words, phrases, and quotations. This introductory activity addressed Patrick's observation that students would have benefited from the pre-teaching of academic vocabulary.

Next, Patrick introduced the focal passage by explaining that every quotation they just read dealt with religion, but that they should now think about the central ideas in the passage as a whole. Choosing specific academic language to express the concept of central idea in a variety of ways, he said, "I'm going to ask you to read deeper than just religion. What is he trying to say about religion? What is he trying to teach readers in this book? What is his main point?"

Patrick then projected a revised thinking guide (see Figure 6.2) and reminded students about the steps they would use together to think

READ AND REREAD 

Read the question.
Read the text.
Read the question AGAIN.
Read the text AGAIN.

TALK 

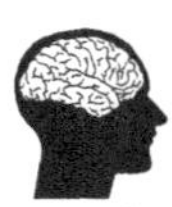

THINK AND NOTE

Text Says	My Own Words	Central Idea
"Most whites don't give a Negro credit for having sense enough to fool them—or nerve enough" (p. 106).		

FIGURE 6.2. Adapted thinking guide with additional column for notes about the central idea.

through the passage. After reading the question and passage aloud to the students once, he invited them to engage in the process with a partner. As the students worked together, Patrick circulated the room to assist and provide feedback. Although, during our coaching session, Patrick had indicated his plan to have students match text with central ideas, he did not enact that plan during this lesson.

Step 6/E Explained

Enactment of decisions takes place in Step 6. Dewey (1933) and Freire (1993) emphasized the importance of action in the reflective process. This is because new developments during enactment, or putting one's "working hypothesis" into action, may lead to further adjustments (Dewey, 1933, p. 110). Enactment provides yet another opportunity to revise thinking. Rather than representing definitive decisions made in Step 5, enactment is dynamic and responsive to new input.

Patrick's decision to have students collaboratively determine the meanings of specific academic vocabulary from context showcases his expertise as an ENL teacher and a move toward greater student autonomy, a concern addressed during our first coaching session. Patrick's enacted lesson also included using specific academic language to express the concept of the central idea in a variety of ways (i.e., "I'm going to ask you to read deeper than just religion. What is he trying to say about religion? . . . What is his main point?"). This mindful employment of academic language addressed another of Patrick's concerns that arose during our coaching session, scaffolding students' understanding of how to determine a central idea. He took up our conversation about using a variety of specifically chosen phrases to show students what he would ask himself to determine a central idea in a text.

Step 7: Patrick Reflects Again (R)

During the next coaching session, Patrick deepened his exploration of his students' progress with reading for central ideas, again using the PD-CASE-R framework. While he noticed students were becoming more proficient with paraphrasing the literal meaning, perhaps due to deliberately pre-teaching the vocabulary, generating a central idea continued to pose a challenge. Patrick explained that students "could put it (the text) in their own words, but they . . . weren't sure what to write" for the central idea in the new portion of the thinking guide we created for them to jot notes.

This observation led Patrick to revisit the ideas mentioned during our previous coaching session. These ideas included building the concept of the central idea through a short, animated video, students matching six short passages with two different central ideas provided, and displaying a poster with academic language associated with the central idea. Patrick implemented all of these ideas in his next lesson (see Reichenberg, 2019, for further description).

Step 7/R Explained

Dewey (1933) noted that a return to reflection after enactment often helps to "define and clarify" the initial challenge (p. 114). In Step 7, teachers repeat the reflective process, creating an opportunity to reflect with increased depth due to new information gained during enactment. Enactment allows teachers to explore initial thoughts with greater sophistication and may highlight additional sources of perplexity.

This step showcases the centrality of teacher agency in the process of reflecting and enacting. Some ideas discussed during our first coaching session were not implemented in the lesson. These included matching passages with central ideas, using an animated short video, and creating a poster of central ideas. Although Patrick decided not to implement these ideas in the first lesson, the experience of enacting some of them likely supported Patrick's readiness to thoughtfully integrate these additional ideas during the next lesson. Patrick led this process, making contextually informed decisions according to his own timeline and based on his expertise with my input, rather than having changes thrust upon him.

Sustainable PL through Agency, Distributed Expertise, and Context-Informed Decision Making

Teacher Agency

When teachers begin their PL with their own concerns, challenges, and celebrations, learning becomes more powerful and meaningful. This also lays a foundation for teachers to exercise agency throughout the coaching process. The PD-CASE-R framework, employed in the context of literacy coaching with video analysis, helped position Patrick as an agent of his PL because it began with his perplexity (Step 1) and continued to favor his agency with each step. At the end of the study, Patrick commented on his sense of agency: "I liked that I was always given the option to make that choice of . . . what I thought was important to look at." He added that it "gave me more ownership of reflection." During the events highlighted in this chapter, Patrick exercised his agency to consider, select, enact, and revisit ideas discussed during coaching sessions and classroom visits according to his timeline. If the teacher–coach dyad is imbued with a power differential based on traditional notions of coaching, then introducing a tool such as the PD-CASE-R framework can help to disrupt that perception and forge a new path, enacting distributed expertise.

Distributed Expertise

The structure of the framework afforded Patrick and me opportunities to share our expertise in pursuit of improved student learning. Coaching practices that emphasize distributed expertise are associated with teachers' positive response to coaching (Robertson et al., 2020). While foregrounding teacher agency, the framework simultaneously presented opportunities for me, as the coach, to provide strategic input. This built a structure and routine that encouraged enacting distributed expertise. One obvious example is Generating Alternatives (Step 4, A), when I made specific suggestions for instruction. I also provided strategic input while Describing (Step 2, D) to point out the strength of Patrick's academic language. Another key moment for coach input is creating the Central Challenge Question (Step 3, C), when I slightly recontextualized Patrick's initial question to focus more specifically on breaking down the process of determining a central idea and using scaffolds. The coach must thoughtfully choose when to provide consonance and when to introduce productive dissonance into coaching conversations. (For a detailed discussion of the role of consonance and dissonance in literacy coaching, see Reichenberg, 2018, and Reichenberg & Boyd, 2019.) While the framework does not guarantee that this distribution of expertise will be enacted, it provides a structure that encourages the coach and teacher to do so.

Context-Informed Pedagogy

Patrick deliberately adapted his pedagogy in the two lessons described here in response to students' learning. He rooted these adaptations in his experience teaching the lesson and his observations and recollection while viewing the video. Patrick's decisions were incremental and based on cumulative knowledge gained through successive lessons. In other words, his decision making was contextually informed. Patrick contrasted this approach with some previous PL experiences: "I find most districts don't have in-service training opportunities embedded within the day or within their school year." Patrick preferred PL that occurred within his classroom context.

Many of the ideas Patrick eventually implemented were discussed during our first coaching session but were not implemented until after our second coaching session (e.g., matching passages of text with central ideas, introducing central idea using an animated wordless video). We worked according to Patrick's timeline, not mine.

Sustainability

At the conclusion of the study, Patrick referred to the PD-CASE-R framework as a structure that created a "habit" and "routine" for his reflective thinking about teaching and learning. He noted that systematic reflection had become "more of a regular part of my teaching" that is really necessary "throughout your entire career. It's not just for new or inexperienced teachers that need opportunities to learn and develop their skills. I think now it's more ingrained in how I work and prepare." He also communicated his intent to continue to reflect as part of his routine: "going forward from this point in time trying to see how I have adapted . . . so I can, in going forward next year, improve the instruction." These comments indicate Patrick's intention to sustain his own PL using the thinking routine established by the PD-CASE-R framework. In contrast to top-down professional development, beginning with teachers' concerns may increase teacher investment in both the process and the results.

Conclusion

In an era of scripted programs, some may find an approach rooted so deeply in teacher-direction uncomfortable. Whereas the PD-CASE-R framework encourages teachers to make many decisions about *how* to reach their destination, the destination remains clear—equity and the opportunity for success for all students. Research has already shown that top-down approaches to PL do not work well (Porter et al., 2000). Coupled with the growing complexity of schools, an approach that foregrounds teachers' expertise and adaptive decision making holds great potential for sustainable and responsive PL.

Coaching with the PD-CASE-R framework has the added benefit of being adaptable to various situations, including peer-coaching and teacher preparation. I have used this approach with preservice literacy clinicians in their culminating practicum to gain experience coaching their peers. It could be used by in-service teachers in the same way. In uncertain fiscal times, the availability of literacy coaches may be limited. Therefore, coaches could dedicate time to a few teachers at a time, who can, in turn, use the approach with their peers as part of a community of professional learners.

College supervisors of student teachers and mentor teachers in pre-student teaching field-based courses could use the framework with teacher candidates. In this way, the formative experiences of teacher candidates would include the message that teachers must exercise agency in their own PL. For those who prefer not to video record or find the logistics of video recording challenging, the PD-CASE-R framework can be used to examine student work, which is also a powerful impetus for teacher reflection (Finkelstein, 2019). In these varying circumstances, different amounts of guidance and input would be warranted by the individual acting as the coach. This is an area that requires further study. As teachers take ownership for their PL, in collaboration with coaches, administrators, and colleagues, the PD-CASE-R framework provides one process for literacy coaches and teachers to engage in teacher-led contextually informed decision making that emphasizes distributed expertise in pursuit of self-sustaining PL.

REFERENCES

Bean, R. (2008). Literacy coaching and the middle school/high school levels. In S. Lenski & J. Lewis (Eds.), *Reading success for struggling adolescent learners* (pp. 265–287). Guilford Press.

Bransford, J., Darling-Hammond, L., & LePage, P. (2005). Introduction. In L. Darling-Hammond & J. Bransford (Eds.), *Preparing teachers for a changing world* (pp. 1–39). Jossey-Bass.

Bransford, J., Derry, S., Berliner, D., Hammerness, K. (with Beckett, K. L.). (2005). Theories of learning and their roles in teaching. In L. Darling-Hammond & J. Bransford (Eds.), *Preparing teachers for a changing world* (pp. 1–39). Jossey-Bass.

Cantrell, S. C., Burns, L. D., & Callaway, P. (2009). Middle- and high-school content area teachers' perceptions about literacy teaching and learning. *Literacy Research and Instruction, 48,* 76–94.

Cantrell, S. C., & Hughes, H. K. (2008). Teacher efficacy and content literacy implementation: An exploration of the effects of extended professional development with coaching. *Journal of Literacy Research, 40,* 95–127.

Cazden, C. B. (2001). *Classroom discourse: The language of teaching and learning* (2nd ed.). Heinemann.

Cho, S., & Reich, G. A. (2008). New immigrants, new challenges: High school social studies teachers and English language learner instruction. *The Social Studies, 99*(6), 235–242.

Darling-Hammond, L. (2000). Teacher quality and student achievement: A review of state policy evidence. *Education Policy Analysis Archives, 8*(1), 1–44.

Davis, M. H., McPartland, J. M., Pryseski, C., & Kim, E. (2018) The effects of coaching on English teachers' reading instruction practices and adolescent students' reading comprehension. *Literacy Research and Instruction, 57*(3), 255–275.

Dewey, J. (1933). *How we think: A restatement of the relation of reflective thinking to the educative process.* D. C. Heath.

Di Domenico, P. M., Elish-Piper, L., Manderino, M., & L'Allier, S. K. (2018). Coaching to support disciplinary literacy instruction: Navigating complexity and challenges for sustained teacher change. *Literacy Research and Instruction, 57*(2), 81–99.

Finkelstein, C. (2019). Doing our part: Trust and relational dynamics in literacy coaching, *Literacy Research and Instruction, 58*(4), 317–337.

Fisher, D., Frey, N., & Lapp, D. (2011). Coaching middle-level teachers to think aloud improves comprehension instruction and student reading achievement. *The Teacher Educator, 46,* 231–243.

Freire, P. (1993). *Pedagogy of the oppressed* (rev. 20th anniversary ed.; M. B. Ramos, Trans.). Penguin.

García, O. (2009). Emergent bilinguals and TESOL: What's in a name? *TESOL Quarterly, 43*(2), 322–326.

Guskey, T. R. (2002). Professional development and teacher change. *Teachers and Teaching: Theory and Practice, 8*(3/4), 381–391.

Hammerness, K., Darling-Hammond, L., Bransford, J., Berliner, D., Cochran-Smith, M., McDonald, M., & Zeichner, K. (2005). How teachers learn and develop. In L. Darling-Hammond & J. Bransford (Eds.), *Preparing teachers for a changing world* (pp. 358–389). Jossey-Bass.

Hayden, H. E., & Chiu, M. M. (2009). Lessons learned: Supporting the development of reflective practice and adaptive expertise. *Literacy Research Association Yearbook, 62,* 279–296.

Hayden, H. E., Rundell, T. D., & Smyntek-Gworek, S. (2013). Adaptive expertise: A view from the top and the ascent. *Teaching Education, 24,* 395–414.

Hunt, C. S. (2016). Getting to the heart of the matter: Discursive negotiations of emotions within literacy coaching interactions. *Teaching and Teacher Education, 60,* 331–343.

Hunt, C. S. (2018). Toward dialogic professional learning: Negotiating authoritative discourses within literacy coaching interaction. *Research in the Teaching of English, 52*(3), 262–287.

International Literacy Association. (2015). *The multiple roles of school-based specialized literacy professionals* (Report No. 9414). Author.

International Reading Association. (2006). *Standards for middle and high school literacy coaches.* Author.

Jay, J. K., & Johnson, K. L. (2002). Capturing complexity: A typology of reflective practice for teacher education. *Teaching and Teacher Education, 18,* 72–85.

Kibler, A. K., Walqui, A., & Bunch, G. C. (2015). Transformational opportunities: Language and literacy instruction for English language learners in the Common Core era in the United States. *TESOL Journal, 6*(1), 9–35.

Kraft, M. A., Blazar, D., & Hogan, D. (2018). The effect of teacher coaching on instruction and achievement: A meta-analysis of the causal evidence. *Review of Educational Research, 88*(4), 547–588.

Lin, A. (2013). Toward paradigmatic change in TESOL methodologies: Building plurilingual pedagogies from the ground up. *TESOL Quarterly, 47*(3), 521–545.

Lipponen, L., & Kumpulainen, K. (2011). Acting as accountable authors: Creating interactional spaces for agency work in teacher education. *Teaching and Teacher Education, 27*(5), 812–819.

McVee, M. B., Shanahan, L. E., Pearson, P. D., & Rinker, T. W. (2015). Using the Gradual Release of Responsibility model to support video reflection with preservice and inservice teachers. In E. Ortlieb, M. B. McVee, & L. E. Shanahan (Eds.), *Video reflection in literacy teacher education and development: Lessons from research and practice* (pp. 59–80). Emerald.

Ortlieb, E., & Cheek, E. H. (2017). *Addressing diversity in literacy instruction* (Vol. 8). Emerald.

Ortlieb, E., Shanahan, L. E., & McVee, M. B. (Eds.). (2015). *Video research in disciplinary literacies* (Vol. 6). Emerald.

Philpott, C., & Oates, C. (2017). Teacher agency and professional learning communities: What can Learning Rounds in Scotland teach us? *Professional Development in Education, 43*(3), 318–333.

Porter, A. C., Garet, M. S., Desimone, L., Yoon, K. S., & Birman, B. F. (2000). *Does professional development change teaching practice?: Results from a three-year study.* U.S. Department of Education.

Reichenberg, J. S. (2018). A model of joint action for literacy coaching: The intersection of consonance and dissonance with responsive and directive approaches. *Literacy Research: Theory, Method, and Practice, 67,* 109–130.

Reichenberg, J. S. (2019). Literacy coaching for agentive and sustainable teacher reflection: Joint action within a gradual release of responsibility as apprenticeship. In M. B. McVee, E. Ortlieb, J. S. Reichenberg, & P. D. Pearson (Eds.), *The gradual release of responsibility in literacy research and practice* (pp. 169–187). Emerald.

Reichenberg, J. S. (2020). Literacy coaching with teachers of adolescent English learners: Agency, sustainability, and transformation for equity. *Journal of Adolescent and Adult Literacy, 64*(1), 57–66.

Reichenberg, J. S., & Boyd, F. B. (2019). The functions of consonance and dissonance in secondary level literacy coaching. *Teacher Development, 23*(1), 83–100.

Robertson, D. A., Padesky, L. B., Ford-Connors, E., & Paratore, J. R. (2020). What does it mean to say coaching is relational? *Journal of Literacy Research, 52*(1), 55–78.

Rogoff, B. (1990). *Apprenticeship in thinking: Cognitive development in social context.* Oxford University Press.

Rush, L. S. (2013). Literacy coaching in Wyoming secondary schools: A situational analysis of roles in context. *Journal of Literacy Research, 45*(3), 267–294.

Russell, F. A. (2015). Learning to teach English learners: Instructional coaching and developing novice high school teacher capacity. *Teacher Education Quarterly, 42*(1), 27–47.

Russell, F. A. (2017). The role of the English learner facilitator in developing teacher capacity for the instruction of English learners. *Teachers and Teaching, 23*(3), 312–331.

Sailors, M., & Hoffman, J. V. (2018). *Literacy coaching for change: Choices matter* [Literacy leadership brief]. International Literacy Association. Retrieved from *https://literacyworldwide.org/docs/default-source/where-we-stand/ila-literacy-coaching-for-change-choices-matter.pdf.*

Schön, D. A. (1983). *The reflective practitioner: How professionals think in action.* Basic Books.

Snow, C., Ippolito, J., & Schwartz, R. (2006). What we know and what we need to know about literacy coaches in middle and high schools: A research synthesis and proposed research agenda. In International Reading Association, *Standards for middle and high school literacy coaches* (pp. 35–49). International Reading Association.

Steinbacher-Reed, C., & Powers, E. A. (2012). Coaching without a coach. *Educational Leadership, 69*(4), 68–72.

Taylor, B. M., & Pearson, P. D. (Eds.). (2002). *Teaching reading: Effective schools, accomplished teachers.* Erlbaum.

Wenger, E. (2008). *Communities of practice: Learning, meaning, and identity.* Cambridge University Press.

Wertsch, J. V. (1998). *Mind as action.* Oxford University Press.

X, M., & Haley, A. (1965/1992). *The autobiography of Malcolm X: As told to Alex Haley.* Ballantine Books.

PART II

PROFESSIONAL LEARNING IN/THROUGH/WITH SOCIAL NETWORKS AND COMMUNITIES

CHAPTER 7

Equitable, Accessible, and Sustainable Professional Learning That Makes a Difference

The Case of the Aboriginal Reading Project

Pauline Harris

Watch a related video from the author at this link.

As it is our custom in Australia to begin meetings and events with "Acknowledgment of Country" to honor First Peoples in Australia, I start this chapter thus:

> I acknowledge the traditional custodians of the lands on which the professional learning reported here occurred and all Aboriginal groups for whom these lands hold significance; and pay my respect to elders past, present, and emerging. I value and respect these nations' respective cultural heritages, beliefs, and relationship with the land and their continuing importance to their respective nations today.

In 2017, the South Australia Department for Education developed a historic professional learning (PL) project for early years educators working with Aboriginal children. Called the Aboriginal Reading Project (ARP), the project saw the incubation of an idea that began on a small scale and delivered PL to four small regional hubs across South Australia. The project came about in response to South Australia's imperative to meet the Australian Council of Australian Government's "Closing the Gap" target of halving the achievement gap between Aboriginal children and other children in Year 3 (third grade) on Australia's National Assessment Program for Literacy and Numeracy by 2018.

In offering a detailed account of ARP, this chapter first provides *a description of the layered contexts in which the ARP was undertaken*, followed by an account of *ARP's sites and participants*. Next, the chapter describes *ARP's approach to professional learning*, which provided ongoing input on the "why" and "what" of early years reading development, contexts, pedagogy, and assessment, supported by dialogic processes that gave educators time and space to think through some of the implications ("how"). The Department's ARP project officers worked alongside educators in their sites to help them translate the PL content into teaching actions that were contextual, sustainable, and effective for children. In these ways, the equity, accessibility, and sustainability of the PL were optimized. This account is followed by an exploration of changes to educators that saw translations of *theory into practice vis-à-vis small shifts in educators' practices for big impact*. ARP's *impact on children in participating educators' preschools* is then described in some detail, before the chapter closes with a consideration of *key lessons for equitable, accessible, and sustainable PL*.

Contexts of the ARP

The Commonwealth of Australia

Australia is an ancient land and is home to the most ancient surviving cultures on earth (Arthur & Morphy, 2018). Aboriginal people as First Nations People have inhabited Australia for 65,000 years. Aboriginal people first arrived in Australia as they migrated from Asia during the Pleistocene epoch and dispersed across the island continent. Today, many distinct language and cultural groups—nations—make up Aboriginal Australia, with each nation having its own culture, customs, language, and laws. These Aboriginal cultures continue to be expressed in dynamic ways.

At the core of Aboriginal cultures and spirituality is their relationship with the land, including designated sacred grounds. This relationship is enshrined in the Dreaming, which comprises stories passed through millennia of Aboriginal generations that explain how the land and universe came to be, how humans and animals were created, and how the Creator intends for humans to behave in their world. Aboriginal people always were and continue to be readers and symbolic representers of their worlds—a reality strongly upheld throughout the ARP. The Dreaming is believed to have no end—it is a continuum of past, present, and future.

The continuum of Aboriginal lives was sorely disrupted following British colonization in 1788. Coastal Aboriginal populations were absorbed, killed, depleted, or forced from their lands; traditional aspects of Aboriginal lives and nations prevailed most strongly in areas where

European settlement was sparse. At the time of colonization, around 250 Aboriginal languages were spoken, along with many dialects within each language group. Today, 120 Aboriginal languages are spoken, although many of these languages are now described as "endangered" (Marmion et al., 2014) or by some Aboriginal people as "sleeping." There are rich and complex linguistic environments in remote communities, with various language codes, including traditional languages, nonstandard varieties of English such as Kriols or Aboriginal English, and Standard Australian English (Wigglesworth et al., 2011).

As a sovereign country and member of the Commonwealth of Nations, Australia comprises the mainland of the Australian island continent, the island of Tasmania, and numerous smaller islands. It is organized into six states and three mainland territories—including the Australian Capital Territory where the nation's capital, Canberra, is located; and the state of South Australia where the ARP reported in this chapter was conducted. Australia is the largest country in Oceania and the world's sixth-largest country by total area—comparable in land mass to the United States. Its population of nearly 26 million is highly urbanized and heavily concentrated on the eastern seaboard where its two most populous cities, Sydney and Melbourne, are located. The country's other major metropolitan areas are Brisbane, Perth, and Adelaide—the last-named being the capital of South Australia where the ARP was undertaken. Otherwise, Australia's population density on average is 3.4 persons/kilometer and is one of the most sparsely populated countries in the world owing to its large interior expanse of semiarid and desert country.

In years all too recent, moves have been made to effect reconciliation between Aboriginal peoples and all Australians. In 1976, the Australian Government passed the Aboriginal Land Rights (Northern Territory) Act, which reinstated ownership of traditional Aboriginal land in the Northern Territory to some Aboriginal people. This act was the first law in Australia to recognize the Aboriginal system of land ownership, legislate the concept of inalienable freehold title, and establish native title—traditional occupation of land—as a legal basis for Aboriginal people to claim land rights. However, it remains a difficult and contentious process.

Another initiative is National Sorry Day, which marks the tabling of the Australian Human Rights Commission's "Bringing Them Home" Report (1997) in the Australian Parliament. This report documented the forcible seizure of children from their homes and their subsequent placement in institutions so as to assimilate them into White Australian culture. These children became known as the "Stolen Generations" and their traumas still reverberate today—as do Aboriginal people's ongoing advocacy and activism for sovereignty, justice, and the sustenance of rich lifeways.

The State of South Australia

South Australia (SA), where the ARP was conducted, is located on the southern central coast of Australia. With its land mass of 983,482 square kilometers (around 379,724 square miles),

> [SA is] similar in size to Egypt, the Canadian province of Ontario, or the combined areas of France and Germany. It shares borders with all other mainland states and the Northern Territory. Its landscape varies from rugged outback wilderness and desert . . . to scenic mountain ranges and a coastline that stretches more than 3,700 kilometres. (South Australia Government, 2021)

SA covers some of Australia's most arid parts. and so it is sparsely populated: 77% of SA's 1.76 million people live in its capital city, Adelaide, and surrounding metropolitan areas. Large regional population areas include Mount Gambier in the state's southeast and Whyalla, Port Lincoln, and Port Augusta on the Eyre Peninsula. In all of these areas, educators participated in the ARP.

"Closing the Gap"

In 2006, the Council of Australian Governments (COAG) committed itself to closing the gap between Aboriginal and Torres Strait Islander people and non-Indigenous Australians in terms of learning, well-being, health, and safety. With regard to education, the core stated outcome was that "Aboriginal and Torres Strait Islander people achieve their learning potential and flourish." In 2018, Australia's Prime Minister released his report on the "Closing the Gap" initiative, affirming:

> For Indigenous engagement to be most effective, it needs to be based on the aspirations and priorities of Aboriginal and Torres Strait Islander people and conducted within an Indigenous-driven process. (Commonwealth of Australia, 2018, p. 16)

As previously noted, the South Australia Department for Education established the ARP in response to COAG's "Closing the Gap" target of halving the achievement gap between Aboriginal children and other children in Year 3 (third grade) on Australia's National Assessment Program for Literacy and Numeracy (NAPLAN) by 2018. In Australia overall, the 24% difference between Indigenous and non-Indigenous Australians on NAPLAN reading scores in 2014 was reduced to an 18% difference in 2017. The South Australia Department for Education was committed to reducing the gap in their own jurisdiction and therefore approved the Aboriginal Reading Project to address this complex issue.

Sites and Participants in the ARP

Over 100 participants took part in the ARP, including preschool and schoolteachers, leaders, school support officers, Aboriginal education teachers, Aboriginal community education officers, Aboriginal education staff, local education team members, speech pathologists, and project officers from the Department's state office. Aboriginal Elders were also involved and contributed to participants' learning.

Seventeen preschools participated. These preschools had the highest enrollment numbers of early-entry (3-year-old) Aboriginal children in the state. Each preschool's main destination school was invited to engage in the project and was included for cohort tracking. Schools were not required to engage in ARP activities, although some schools did choose to do so. Indeed, collaborations between some preschools and schools continued in 2019 even after ARP's intensive input had ceased—indicating high commitment to closing the achievement gap through collaborative action.

Educators engaged in PL and collaboration in face-to-face workshops in four small regional hub groups in South Australia (a hub being a cluster of preschools and schools and regional leaders in the same locality). The hubs eased isolation issues and the logistics of delivering ARP across South Australia's vast and sparsely populated expanse. The hubs were located in:

- *Metropolitan Adelaide*—Eight sites, with preschools and schools either co-located on the same site or combined as a birth–high school children's center, took part in Adelaide. The Adelaide Plains are the traditional lands of the Kaurna people, stretching from Port Broughton down to Cape Jervis.

- *Mount Gambier in southeastern South Australia*—Two sites took part, a preschool and a school located next to each other. The entire school staff elected to participate after the program began. The Bunganditj or Boandik people are the First Nations and sovereign peoples of this region.

- *Port Augusta and Whyalla, situated on Eyre Peninsula*—Six preschools took part, along with some adjoining schools. The Eyre Peninsula is the traditional home to the Barngarla (Port Lincoln area), Nauo on the southern side, and Wirangu peoples further up the far west coast, including Ceduna.

- *Ceduna, located in South Australia's far west region, and Port Lincoln, located on the western side of the Eyre Peninsula*—Two preschools took part, with some involvement from their feeder schools. Because of the geographic distance between them, ARP meetings alternated between these two locations. As already noted, the Eyre Peninsula is the traditional home to the Barngarla (Port Lincoln area), Nauo on the southern side, and Wirangu peoples further up the far west coast, including Ceduna.

Approach to PL in the ARP

ARP's stated objectives were clear as it set out to achieve "higher numbers of Aboriginal children achieving at or above the level of non-Aboriginal students in measures of reading; and educators' increased knowledge, capabilities, collaboration and confidence in implementing evidence-based approaches to improving reading for Aboriginal children" (South Australia Department for Education, 2019, p. 1).

ARP had a unique asset that was a product of its time: the opportunity to work intensively with the de Lissa Chair (this chapter's author), which was an endowed professorial appointment shared between the University of South Australia and the South Australia Department for Education. How this partnership worked in the ARP is described in a later section of this chapter, "Partnership Approach."

ARP's vision, shown in Figure 7.1, was to grow its initial, small-scale implementation for immediate and sustained improvement (described later in this chapter) across South Australia over time. This goal was to be

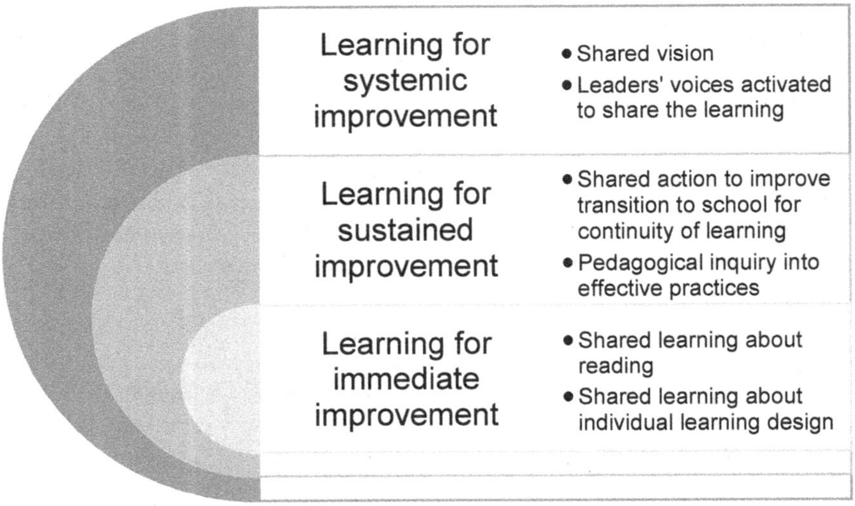

FIGURE 7.1. Vision for growing ARP across South Australia.

achieved with the support of an online resource that the work of the ARP would (and in fact did) inform and shape—which could ultimately lead to systemic change. The driving question behind this vision was, "What effective practices acknowledge, enable, and grow every Aboriginal child as a capable and competent reader?"

Framed by this vision, how ARP's approach optimized equity, accessibility and sustainability of PL is explained below in terms of ARP's:

- Strengths-based view of Aboriginal children as capable and competent readers
- Partnership approach
- Culturally relevant and sustaining pedagogy
- Co-designed participatory action research processes.

Strengths-Based View of Aboriginal Children as Capable and Competent Readers

ARP adopted a strengths-based approach that placed emphasis on Aboriginal children's rights to culture, language, and education for success; and Aboriginal children's rights to access a literacy curriculum that would respect them as Aboriginal children and readers. These considerations are all matters of justice and are seen to be crucial to "closing the gap." Indeed, recognizing all children's cultural rights, combined with their academic success, constitutes a shift from a deficit view to an approach that identifies and builds upon all children's strengths.

Partnership Approach

Critical to ARP's equity, accessibility, and sustainability was its partnership between an early years literacy researcher and scholar (the de Lissa Chair); project officers with specialist skills and knowledge of early years; Aboriginal education and preschool leaders and teachers committed to improving their practice; and Aboriginal children and their families. Together, these partners achieved immediate and sustained improvement (envisaged in Figure 7.1), which resulted in an evidence-informed, field-tested teaching resource for systemic improvement (discussed later in this chapter under "Key Lessons for Equitable, Accessible, and Sustainable PL").

This work was supported by partnerships within each ARP hub, among the hub's preschool and schoolteachers, leaders, School Support Officers, Aboriginal Education Teachers, Aboriginal community education officers, Aboriginal Education staff, Aboriginal Elders, local education team members, speech pathologists, and Department for Education project officers.

ARP's partnerships saw the coming together of minds that enabled (1) discussion and negotiation of participants' diverse perspectives and experiences and what the PL was offering them; (2) continuity of PL processes across participants and sites in a hub; and (3) local leadership, support, and advocacy.

Culturally Relevant and Sustaining Pedagogy

Aligned with culturally relevant or responsive pedagogy (CRP; Ladson-Billings, 1995), ARP foregrounded high expectations for all Aboriginal children to succeed in its subtitle, "Every Aboriginal child a capable and competent reader." This was not simply an aspiration for what children in the ARP would become, but a recognition, too, of what each Aboriginal child knows, understands, and can do. ARP explored practices for building on children's cultural strengths to democratize their formal education spaces and foster reading development; explicitly valued Aboriginal knowledges and practices; foregrounded Aboriginal ways of knowing; and ensured educational practices being promoted were authentic and built bridges between children's home/community and preschool/school experiences.

The introduction of the third-space concept (Levy, 2008) to educators in workshops in order to democratize education spaces by finding common ground with children's homes and communities proved particularly influential. It challenged educators to think deeply about the learning environments they were providing for Aboriginal children. ARP's project officers connected third space back to Australia's *Early Years Learning Framework* (EYLF) and referred to it as "the sweet spot where children's learning could accelerate."

ARP also drew on culturally sustaining pedagogy (CSP), which comprises practices that support communities' lifeways disrupted by external forces (McCarty & Lee, 2014; Paris & Alim, 2014), such as experienced by Aboriginal Australians. CSP has four central tenets (Paris & Alim, 2014, 2017) that were enacted in the ARP.

First, CSP demands culturally pluralist outcomes that are inclusive of diverse ways of knowing and learning (Paris & Alim, 2014). Thus, children's Aboriginal ways of knowing, learning, and being literate were recognized, honored, and foregrounded—as reflected in the following proposition by Karen, an Aboriginal participant in dialogue about literacy learning across cultures:

> There is an Aboriginal system of literacy we don't think about. Our children are always judged by a non-Aboriginal system of knowledge. Our children know how to talk, know how to listen . . . for Western people, reading is

> about books and libraries. For Aboriginal people, it is in our head. You can't see it, the library is in our heads . . . . Teachers must build upon, rather than replace, the libraries in their heads. (Quoted in Fleer, 2001, p. 25)

Second, CSP attends to communities' practices and knowledge in ways that resist "static, unidirectional notions of culture and race" (Paris & Alim, 2014, p. 95). ARP promoted practices based on understanding how literacies are lived and experienced in children's life worlds; and engagement in dialogue with children, families and communities in "yarning spaces" in which educators yarn (talk) up, not down, with Aboriginal families and communities in reciprocal, respectful exchanges, as explored in the ARP (Fluckiger et al., 2012).

Third, CSP recognizes young people's significant role in evolving cultural traditions and supports children in this role. ARP was approached with an awareness of Aboriginal children as members of dynamic cultures, with Aboriginal Elders and community members supporting and growing educators' understanding of their local community. As Early Childhood Australia (2008, p. 3) states:

> All children have rights to their cultural strengths and identities and a right to the knowledge, skills and capabilities that will enable them to participate fully in mainstream society . . . the power lies in enabling children to use different cultural resources in different circumstances and to continually construct "identities" that give them the best chance to live constructive and fulfilling lives.

Fourth and finally, CSP asks members of cultural and linguistic groups to critically reflect on the efficacy of the cultural practices of their own communities in promoting the greater good. Thus, as educators of Aboriginal children, participants were encouraged to critically reflect on the efficacy of their practices not only for fostering children's literacies but also for sustaining the children's and communities' cultural and linguistic heritages—what in fact were called "assets" in the ARP to counter the deficit or "exotic othering" sometimes encountered.

In applying these CSP tenets to ARP, the languages and cultural identities of children and their families and communities were privileged and validated. ARP advocated for continuance of children's access to their home languages that, when denied, result in the oppression of children's home languages and identities, and silence the social, cultural, and historic contexts in which languages and language learning are situated (Garcia & Kleifgen, 2018; International Literacy Association, 2019a, 2019b; Wiley & Garcia, 2016). As Aboriginal elder William Tilmouth, chair and co-founder of Children's Ground, has said, "Without language you don't have culture, without language you don't have land, without language you don't have law, without language you don't have kinship. All these things are held together and glued together by language" (Tilmouth, 2017).

It was important to pay heed to how to secure participants' buy-in to these CRP and CSP principles for, as ARP's Project Officers explained, "as soon as we add a culture badge, educators often think it's not for them, it's for other folks, and it is something exotic." Thus, this CRP/CSP work was grounded in Australia's mandatory EYLF (Department of Education, Employment and Workplace Relations [DEEWR], 2009), so that CRP and CSP would and, in fact, did become part of educators' everyday work because it is part and parcel of EYLF's national mandate. For example, the following EYLF statement was linked to CSP's first tenet on pluralist outcomes:

> There are many ways of living, being and knowing. Children are born belonging to a culture, which is not only influenced by traditional practices, heritage and ancestral knowledge, but also by the experiences, values and beliefs of individual families and communities. (DEEWR, 2009, p. 13)

Co-Designed Participatory Action Research Processes

Critical participatory action research (CPAR) framed ARP's PL processes and is defined as inquiry undertaken with and by practitioners to collaboratively build knowledge for understanding and transforming practice (Kemmis et al., 2014). CPAR supported ARP's equity, accessibility, and sustainability through:

- providing knowledge input in a series of workshops that seeded educators' new knowledge and inquiries (these workshops are described in the next section)
- mobilizing educators' agency as reflective inquirers into their reading pedagogic knowledge and practices to meet the needs of their children and circumstances
- creating conditions for educators to understand and transform their reading pedagogic practices from within the contexts of their preschools and communities that shaped and informed these practices
- engaging continuously as individuals and as collective groups in co-constructing experiential, propositional, and practical ways of knowing related to effective reading pedagogic practices for young Aboriginal children
- developing shared language grounded in ARP's shared context that is accessible and inclusive for all involved.

These processes were implemented through three key components of delivery: participatory workshops; dialogic encounters embedded in the workshops; and educators' action inquiries supported by site visits.

Participatory Workshops

Educators in each hub engaged in a series of six 3-hour, module-based face-to-face workshops in each hub over the course of 2 years. This chapter's author was asked to lead the development and facilitation of these workshops in collaboration with the Department for Education's project officers. Content was informed by evidence garnered from a range of rigorous research studies and approaches that captured the diversity and complexities of children's worlds and contexts in which educators engage with young children. The co-construction of these workshops was predicated on developing and sustaining a community of learners within each hub (Lave & Wenger, 1999).

The workshop modules aligned with Australia's mandatory EYLF (DEEWR, 2009), as shown in Figure 7.2, and with the *Australian*

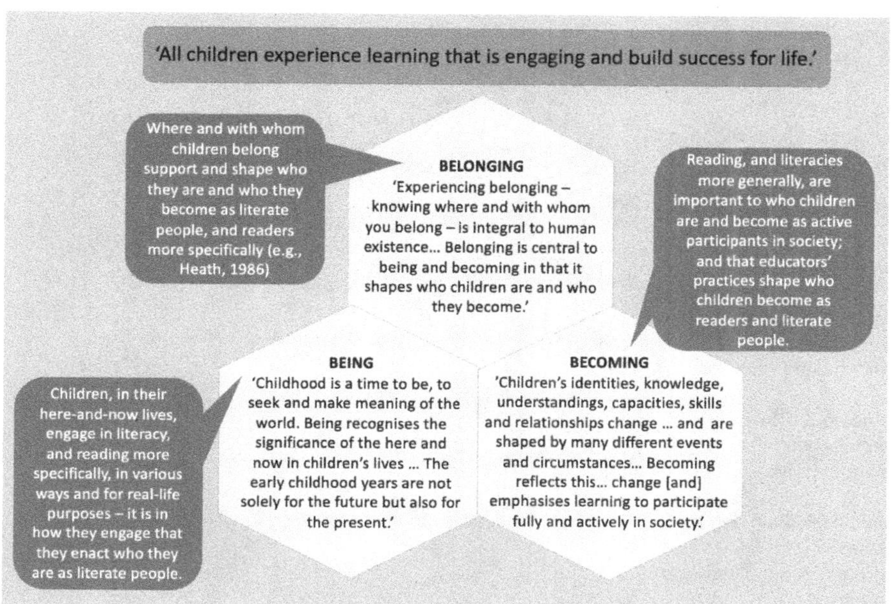

FIGURE 7.2. Belonging, being, and becoming in Australia's *Early Years Learning Framework*. All text quoted directly from DEEWR (2009, p. 7).

Curriculum: English (ACARA, 2010), to facilitate continuity of knowledge and practices between preschool and school years.

As seen in Figure 7.3, "Seeing and understanding the Aboriginal literate child" was at the heart of the ARP. It was the first module to be delivered, and it framed the other modules that followed. In keeping with CRP and CSP, this module established sociocultural views of literacies (Gee, 2015) that support educators to acknowledge Aboriginal children's cultural and linguistic resources; it also established that early years literacies pedagogies must embrace multimodal literacies, along with social practices that honor diverse identities of children and their families (Brock & Harris, 2019). Differences between Western and Indigenous literacies were seen *not* to indicate deficit in children's literacies capabilities (Hanlen, 2007). Rather, disadvantage is created when educators fail to recognize and build on the capabilities and resources that children bring to literacies education programs.

Reading was framed comprehensively as decoding, making meaning, using texts for social purposes, and critically reflecting on texts (Freebody & Luke, 2003), situated in and shaped by children's life worlds

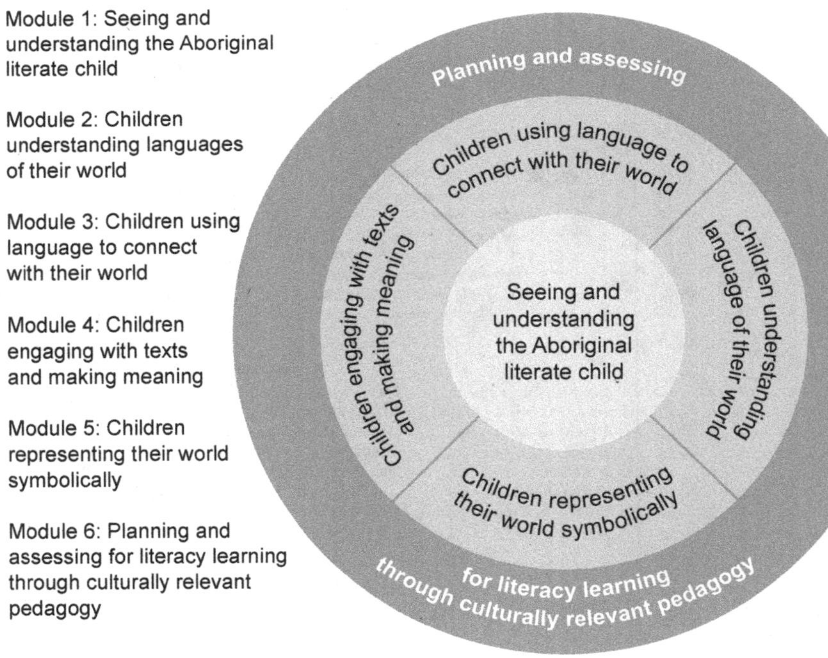

FIGURE 7.3. Overview of the ARP's six workshop modules.

and broader cultural and linguistic settings. This reading model provided a lens through which to understand capable and competent readers. The stage was thus set for educators to recognize and acknowledge Aboriginal children as capable early readers; and to open their minds to what they were not previously noticing as children's competent reading practices.

Modules 2–5 deepened explorations of these ideas and their pedagogic applications with Aboriginal children in preschools. Each of these modules focused on one of four preschool literacy indicators devised by the South Australia Department for Education (2015); each was explored in detail in relation to reading. Key messages in these modules included:

- Drawing on Aboriginal children's funds of knowledge to see and understand and what children know as readers and to create new learning pathways (González et al., 2005)
- Designing reading environments as third spaces with children's homes and communities that encourage children's engagement and growth as readers (Levy, 2008)
- Using the power of story as windows into land, cultures, and languages, through which Indigenous peoples have kept their histories and cultures alive, to build bridges between Aboriginal children's home languages and cultures (Ewing et al., 2016)
- Fostering oral language in the context of reading through strategies such as building bridges and seeding discussions (Bremmer & Scull, 2016)
- Engaging in intentional, child-voice-oriented interactions with children that promote reader engagement and foster specific reading capabilities, including dialogic or conversational reading that ARP's project officers found to be highly influential on educators
- Enriching children's play with literacies and literacies with play (Harris, 2009), including the concept of text as playground, leading to an exploration of young children's picture books that afford children space to play as agentic readers (Williams, 1991)

The sixth and final module concerned planning and assessment for learning, and it wrapped around the other five modules as it pulled their threads together. Planning and assessment practices for learning were viewed within a framework of culturally relevant and sustaining pedagogy and assessment that validates children's linguistic identities, supports first languages, acknowledges children's language resources, and establishes cultural and language connections with homes that build on Aboriginal children's prior knowledge, social practices, and literacy experiences.

As it was important that this workshop series be responsive to educators' circumstances and contexts, the series was run separately for and tailored to each of the four hubs. So doing further contributed to the equity, accessibility, and sustainability of educators' PL.

Dialogic Encounters

Dialogic encounters with and among educators were embedded in the workshops. Defined as encounters among people in which participants name and problematize aspects of their world and what they wish to transform (Freire, 1983), dialogic encounters provided the means for educators to reflect and act on their evolving learning for supporting Aboriginal children as readers and what they wished to change.

Conducted in small groups two or three times during each workshop, these encounters afforded opportunities for participants to speak, listen deeply to one another, and reflect assumptions and implications of what was being said back to the speaker and the rest of the group (Bohm et al., 1991). As such, dialogic encounters endowed workshops with generative processes of thought and action (praxis); and transformed PL from "stand and deliver" approaches to acts of co-created learning and change (Freire, 1983). In these ways, dialogic encounters enhanced:

- Equity by providing opportunities for all educators to bring their reflections and conundrums to ARP's collective tables where all had agency and voice.
- Accessibility by scaffolding connections between workshops and educators' own settings and inquiries.
- Sustainability by supporting educators' action inquiries that saw the continuance of educators' PL in meaningful, relevant, and viable ways.

Educators' Action Learning Inquiries

Through action inquiries in their own settings, educators translated ARP's key messages into effective, everyday practices. Through these inquiries, too, accessible opportunities for equitable and sustainable PL were deeply situated in educators' professional contexts and histories and, most importantly, in terms of the children, families, and communities with whom the educators were working.

To support these action inquiries, project officers undertook regular site visits. These visits enabled further deep connections to be made between workshops, inquiries, and educators' own local priorities and concerns vis-à-vis children, families, and communities with whom they worked and the circumstances in which they worked. These connections saw educators critically reflect on teaching practice for improvement.

These visits also helped inform how to meet the challenge of embedding change from one year to the next in the ARP. This was a recurring challenge for site leaders due to various factors, including high staff turnovers. In 2018–2019, site leaders and educators integrated their action inquiries into everyday preschool business and enacted one significant change through a whole-team approach. Here are some examples of how this worked in 2019:

- Project officers designed workshops, site visits, and a change-story framework for leaders and teachers to scaffold manageable improvements.
- Site leaders attended ARP PL and other project activities to ensure alignment with site priorities and support them to share with staff back at their sites.
- Site leaders integrated the reading focus into existing site projects, priorities, and PL programs.
- Site leaders ensured that ARP inquiry work was a standing agenda item at staff meetings.
- Teachers actively involved Aboriginal children's family and community in their improvement work.

From Theory into Practice: Small Shifts in Educators' Practices for Big Impact

From educators' ARP participation, documented changes reported to the South Australia Department for Education's Senior Management Group included educators' increased capacity to identify and improve Aboriginal children's reading capabilities; and clearer understanding of how Aboriginal children's language competencies enable their reading growth. Aboriginal children's reader identities were enhanced, including confidence to engage purposefully and meaningfully with a range of texts. More effective reading transitions between preschool and school partner sites also were evidenced, due to partner sites coming together in the workshops' dialogic encounters.[1]

Educators found that three strategies had the most impact for reading, as identified in ARP's final report (South Australia Department for Education, 2019). Through these strategies, as listed in the following, educators make connections, recognize strengths, and provide stretch with and for children.

---

[1] From personal correspondence with Claire Jenkins (September 23, 2018).

- Everyday talk as back-and-forth exchanges between adults and children or among children throughout daily routines as part of the curriculum.
- Symbolic play of a text that involves exploring and representing the meaning and characteristics of a text in a range of ways.
- Conversational reading as reading with (rather than to) children that involves responsive and reciprocal talk, back-and-forth exchanges between adults and children.

As the report also documents, educators found that these strategies were most effective when they aligned them with belonging, being, and becoming in Australia's EYLF (DEEWR, 2009). That is, educators:

- made a connection with what was meaningful to the lives and interests of the children—**belonging**
- recognized and built on children's language and social strengths for reading enjoyment—**being**
- planned for and scaffolded the stretch for each individual child as a reader—**becoming.** (South Australia Department for Education, 2019, p. 7)

Every preschool provided a report on their action inquiries annually through ARP. These reports detailed the steps taken at each site to identify the highest priority for change and strategic actions for improvement. At ARP's close, sites developed "change stories" in which participants reflected on changes in their knowledge and practices that came from their ARP involvement. ARP's project officers provided a pro forma for developing these change stories, as shown in Figure 7.4. Educators were asked to note and reflect upon one key change they had put in place.

Project officers thematized and categorized changes noted by educators, such as seen in Figure 7.4. These pro forma figures revealed educators' reframed perspectives, informed by a deeper understanding of reading that helped them see the literacy learning processes that children were and were not using as readers, and to see 3-year-old Aboriginal children as capable and competent readers.

This reframing also derived from educators transforming their practices. As educators made changes, their perceptions shifted, enabling them to see and understand the young literate child in their many guises, as noted in ARP's final report (South Australia Department for Education, 2019). Moreover, reframing educators' inquiry reports as stories of change assisted educators in seeing the impact that even a small change to their practices could make.

Educators used to think . . .	So educators made these changes . . .	Now educators understand . . .
Aboriginal children are not interested in reading books.	Rostered staff to read daily to children, individually and in small groups.	Aboriginal children are very interested in books and remain engaged when the reading experiences connect in personal and meaningful ways.

FIGURE 7.4. Pro forma and an example of ARP's "Change Stories."

Together, these reports and change stories, triangulated with site visits, provided evidence on ARP's impact on educators' work in supporting preschool Aboriginal children as capable and competent readers. For example, prior to their ARP participation, some educators had been narrowly focusing on improving children's oral language skills. This focus had been underpinned by deficit views of what Aboriginal children could not or did not choose to do. However, as educators' learning evolved in the ARP, their expectations and understanding of what each Aboriginal child knows, can do, understands, and feels about reading expanded.

These and other changes in educators' practices and thinking throughout ARP's life had an immense impact on the learning opportunities they made available to Aboriginal children. For example, educators perceived that parents did not read to children at home. However, once educators made literacy packs available for children to share at home or set up a borrowing library or baskets of books for families to keep or exchange, educators' perceptions shifted. Educators now recognized that Aboriginal families were important partners in promoting children's reading enjoyment and capabilities, and powerfully contributed to and affirmed children's identities as readers.

Connecting with Aboriginal Children's Dispositions to Reading

Before ARP, several educators had perceived that many Aboriginal children in their sites were neither interested nor engaged in reading books. These educators perceived that children's interests were related to outdoor activity and that educators needed to change their stories and songs frequently if they were to hold children's interest. However, after educators engaged in ARP, *they decided to change their practices* to enhance children's reading interest and engagement. For example, as documented in their change stories:

> - Rostered staff to read daily to children, individually and in small groups.
> - Created accessible and inviting reading spaces for children at preschool and school.
> - Placed books in all learning areas, particularly where the children chose to play.
> - Engaged children with the same text but in many different ways, such as at story tables and through songs and chants, role plays, and arts and crafts. (South Australia Department for Education, 2019, p. 5)

Having made these changes, educators now saw that the children in fact did have interest in reading. By their own reports, educators found that

> the children remained engaged when the reading experiences connected in personal and meaningful ways; and purposefully used books that connected with their lives and their play; and saw that revisiting a text built familiarity [that] could lead to increased enjoyment, creativity and mastery of concepts and language. (South Australia Department for Education, 2019, p. 5)

Where Literacy Learning Happens

Many educators came to ARP with an implicit sense that literacy learning happens inside rather than outdoors. For example, educators thought the following:

> - Books and story tables belong inside where teachers can ensure they are looked after.
> - Intentional teaching of literacy is teacher directed and explicit. This happens at group time when a book is read to children.
> - Intentional teaching happened only at mat time. (South Australia Department for Education, 2019, p. 6)

This thinking was turned on its head when these educators made changes that:

> - Extended the print-rich environment to outdoor areas, with signs, maps, and writing materials.
> - Planned regular reading experiences in the community, such as at the local or school library, and with Aboriginal student buddy readers.
> - Set up story tables inside and outdoors and modeled how to use them. [These tables] included sensory materials.
> - Placed the book on the floor to read with a small group of children.

- Used open questions, active listening, and "I wonder" to invite children to talk more than the educator in small groups about what is being read. (South Australia Department for Education, 2019, p. 6)

Making these changes revealed to the educators that the children "can and do engage with books and writing for real purposes; and that Aboriginal children's literacy skills and dispositions improve when an interested adult or older child is present to guide and scaffold learning and be a role model" (South Australia Department for Education, 2019, p. 6).

Educators also concluded that intentional teaching of literacy is confined to neither time nor place. Rather, intentional teaching can and should happen in regular, meaningful, social contexts throughout the day, such as at mealtimes, on the bus, during social play, as well as in small, literacy-focused group times.

Play and Literacy

Some educators focused on changing their approaches to children's play to render play a vehicle for prompting children's reader engagement. For example, educators used story tables and other play situations to model new words. Educators also shifted their interaction patterns from being distant observers of children's play to entering into play with children. For example, educators reported that they "interacted alongside at child's level; used a more indirect communication style, modelling, commenting and gesturing; and followed the child's lead in a back-and-forth way" (South Australia Department for Education, 2019, p. 6).

Educators making these changes had come to ARP believing that children would "just learn by playing"—not realizing the impact of their intentional efforts as educators. Some educators were also concerned that children are deterred by their educators moving in on their play: "children move away or go quiet if I try to join their play, so I just watch over them" (South Australia Department for Education, 2019, p. 6).

In consequence of these changes in practices and perceptions, educators, by their own accounts, came to value play as an approach to literacy learning. For example:

- Books can be used to playfully invite and respond to children's ideas—they can spark deep thinking and talking with other
- Language becomes more complex when children are engaged in extended periods of play with peers and adults
- Aboriginal children express their thoughts and feelings when given appropriate time, space, and in some instances, the words or "script" to engage purposefully with others. (South Australia Department for Education, 2019, p. 6)

ARP's Impact on Children in Participating Educators' Preschools

At ARP's close, a formal, independent evaluation of ARP's impact on children was conducted. As the evaluation report explained,

> Data to inform the evaluation of impact on children's reading were available for 178 children from 16 centers. Criteria for children's inclusion in the evaluation were that the child should have attended a center for at least four terms and that educators had sufficient evidence to make an informed judgment of the child's progress against five criteria. (Curtis, 2019, p. iii)

Evaluation criteria were drawn from Australia's EYLF (DEEWR, 2009) and South Australia's *Indicators of Preschool Numeracy and Literacy* (IPNL; South Australia Department for Education, 2015). The criteria were:

- Demonstrate a knowledgeable and confident identity as a reader.
- Demonstrate dispositions for learning as a reader.
- Use increasingly complex language to connect and communicate.
- Choose and use texts purposefully to make meaning and represent thinking.
- Demonstrate an understanding that print conveys meaning. (Curtis, 2019, pp. iii–iv)

Given possible indicators of each of these criteria as some suggestions, educators were asked to judge each child's individual progress as:

- High progress—more than 1 year of growth for a year of preschool input
- Moderate progress—1 year of growth for a year of preschool input
- Low progress—less than 1 year of growth for a year of preschool input
- N/A—insufficient evidence to provide fair assessment of growth. (Curtis, 2019, p. iv)

Criteria were elaborated in instructions for educators to support educators in making consistent judgments about children's progress as learners and readers. A template for recording progress judgments for children also was provided to educators. The evaluation report that followed made clear that since

> children commence their journey through formal education starting at very different levels . . . comparison with a standard is antithetical to understanding children's different starting points and crafting individual programs to build from those points. In order to acknowledge the individual contexts, identities and interests of children, educators were asked to make judgments

> of progress from those diverse foundations. Thus, educators were asked to judge progress, not achievement against an absolute standard. Again, this approach will not satisfy those who are seeking evidence of achievement against a standard. The approach used, however, is compatible with the educational philosophies that are characteristic of early years education. (Curtis, 2019, p. 3)

Educators' sources of evidence varied across sites but involved at least five of the following: individual learning plans (used by 70% of educators); speech or language screening tools (60%); observations (50%); One Plan (South Australia Department for Education pro forma) (48%); portfolios of children's work (44%); and interactions with children's families (37%).

Results of the evaluation of children's reading progress are shown in Figure 7.5. In summary:

> A substantial majority of children achieved one year's progress for a year of preschool input, and most exceeded this goal . . . 97 children (62%) achieved more than a year's progress over a year's preschool input, a further 39 children (25%) made a year's progress, while 20 children (13%) recorded less than one year's progress. Factors associated with the variation in progress are discussed in the report, but the number of terms enrolled and attendance are strong predictors of progress. Of the children who made little progress, a variety of family and community factors external to the preschool context were identified in qualitative comments made by educators. These include trauma, illness, and some behavioral challenges. (Curtis, 2019, pp. iv–v)

Criterion	Low Progress	Moderate Progress	High Progress	Total
Demonstrate a knowledgeable and confident identity as a reader	9.6%	35.9%	54.5%	100.0%
Demonstrate dispositions for learning as a reader	10.2%	29.9%	59.9%	100.0%
Use increasingly complex language to connect and communicate	8.3%	31.2%	60.5%	100.0%
Choose and use texts purposefully to make meaning and represent thinking	15.3%	36.9%	47.8%	100.0%
Demonstrate an understanding that print conveys meaning	17.2%	35.7%	47.1%	100.0%

FIGURE 7.5. Overview of findings on ARP children's reading progress.

The evaluation report further established that

> the majority of children (120 or 76%) in the ARP have made at least one year's growth for a year of preschool input on all five criteria and that 51 children (31%) achieved high progress on all five criteria. Only eight children were judged to have made less than one year's growth on all five criteria. (Curtis, 2019, p. 7)

The ARP project officers observed and concluded that the changes described here ultimately came about because

> the educators were willing to honestly examine their practices and assumptions about Aboriginal children as readers. They worked with families and other educators to implement the 3 research-based strategies from the PL program. They observed, designed, planned and assessed for learning with each Aboriginal child's belonging, being and becoming in mind. This was the sweet spot of learning acceleration. (South Australia Department for Education, 2019, p. 10)

Key Lessons for Equitable, Accessible, and Sustainable PL

Clearly, changes in educators' practices and thinking arising from ARP had an immense impact on the learning outcomes of Aboriginal children—ARP did make a positive difference. Every educator who chose to participate had voice and agency at their PL table where they brought their experiences, wonderings, and challenges to consider and transform their practices. This voice and agency contributed to ARP's equity, accessibility, and sustainability, as did:

- Using a strengths-based view of Aboriginal children
- Mobilizing a partnership approach to grow collective efficacy
- Providing participatory workshops with culturally relevant and sustaining content
- Connecting with mandatory documents
- Tailoring the PL to local hubs and sites
- Engaging educators' praxis through their own action inquires
- Engaging in dialogic encounters within and across sites.

As critically, when educators understood the "why" behind a pedagogic reading practice, they were more consistent, confident, and intentional. Transformed practices thus became embedded practices rather than a passing fad. The challenge for educators to continuously think about their assumptions and practices, and the clearly evidenced impact on Aboriginal children as readers, also supported ARP's sustainability. Such challenge, ARP's project officers concluded, was "cultural competency and culturally responsive pedagogy in action, without anyone doing a special course—it was normal, expected teacher's work to foster each child's belonging, being and becoming" (South Australia Department for Education, 2019, p. 10).

To support and grow the equity, access, and sustainability of the ARP PL and its consequences for strengthening the reading capabilities of young Aboriginal children, an online PL resource called *Talk, Play, Read* was developed and disseminated to educators and leaders throughout South Australia at the end of 2020. The collective learning from the ARP informed the development of this resource. The resource requires commitment to a dialogic, reflective way of working as enacted throughout the ARP and consistent with requirements in Australia's EYLF (DEEWR, 2009). The resource provides input on the strategies for reading improvement that were effective in the ARP; describes how to design learning in a way that is connected and meaningful for each child by building on their literacy and language strengths for reading; and provides challenge that is timely, well targeted, and personally satisfying for Aboriginal learners. This resource has been disseminated to educators and leaders throughout the state of South Australia.

While ARP and its subsequent resource realized its first two phases of immediate and sustained learning improvement (as seen in Figure 7.1), the third phase of systemic learning improvement is emerging as the state engages with *Talk, Play, Read* and as ARP participants share their learning at state and national levels. ARP as described here ultimately is seen as an incubation phase, endorsed by the Department for Education, for further supporting embedded practices and broader applications of the learning undertaken. Such consideration is worthy of further investigation as an education system in South Australia.

As to what happens next, the key message closing this chapter concerns shared, dialogic learning that lies at the heart of equitable, accessible, sustainable PL. In the words of Freire (1983, p. X), who inspired the ARP's dialogic encounters, in such encounters:

> The teacher is no longer merely the one-who-teaches, but one who is [herself or] himself taught in dialogue with the students, who in turn, while being taught, also teach. They become jointly responsible for a process in which all grow.

So it was for all in the ARP, which grew a community of learners among us all in the name of working with and strengthening young Aboriginal children as capable, competent readers.

ACKNOWLEDGMENT

I acknowledge the South Australia Department for Education, for leading the development and implementation of the Aboriginal Reading Project, and the staff, children, and families in the preschools who were key drivers. Without everyone's expertise, drive, and vision, the ARP and the rich benefits it reaped would not have seen the light of day.

REFERENCES

ACARA. (2010). *Australian curriculum: English.* Australian Curriculum and Reporting Authority.

Arthur, B., & Morphy, F. (2018). *Macquarie atlas of Indigenous Australia* (2nd ed.). Macquarie.

Australian Human Rights Commission. (1997). Bringing them home: The "Stolen Children" report. Retrieved from *https://humanrights.gov.au/our-work/aboriginal-and-torres-strait-islander-social-justice/publications/bringing-them-home.*

Bohm, D., Factor, D., & Garrett, P. (1991). Dialogue: A proposal. Retrieved August 9, 2015, from *www.dialogue-associates.com/files/files/Dialogue%20A%20Proposal.pdf.*

Bremmer, P., & Scull, J. (2016). Teaching young Indigenous literacy learners: Language for literacy. In J. Scull & B. Raban (Eds.), *Growing up literate: Australian literacy research for practice* (pp. 195–212). Eleanor Curtain.

Brock, C., & Harris, P. (2019). Using multiliteracies as a lens to explore young children's engagement with multimodal texts. In B. Exley & A. Woods (Eds.), *Literacies in early childhood: Foundations of equity and quality* (pp. 225–241). Oxford University Press.

Commonwealth of Australia. (2018). *Closing the gap: Prime Minister's report 2018.* Author.

Curtis, D. (2019). *Aboriginal Reading Project evaluation report.* Author.

Department of Education, Employment and Workplace Relations. (2009). *Belonging, being and becoming: The early years learning framework for Australia.* Author.

Early Childhood Australia. (2008). *Early Years Learning Framework—Early Childhood Australia Submission.* Author.

Ewing, R., Callow, J., & Rushton, K. (2016). *Language and literacy development in early childhood.* Cambridge University Press.

Fleer, M. (2001). Literacy learning across cultures. *Every Child, 7*(1), 24–25.

Fluckiger, B., Diamond, P., & Jones, W. (2012). Yarning space: Leading literacy learning through family-school partnerships. *Australasian Journal of Early Childhood, 37*(3), 53–59.

Freebody, P., & Luke, A. (2003). Literacy as engaging with new forms of life: The "Four Roles Model." In G. Bull & M. Anstey (Eds.), *The literacy lexicon* (2nd ed., pp. 1–2). Pearson.

Freire, P. (1983). *Pedagogy of the oppressed*. Continuum.

García, O., & Kleifgen, J. A. (2018). *Educating emergent bilinguals: Policies, programs, and practices for English learners* (2nd ed.). Teachers College Press.

Gee, J. (2015). *Social linguistics and literacies* (5th ed.). Routledge.

González, N., Moll, L., & Amanti, C. (2005). *Funds of knowledge: Theorizing practices in households, communities, and classrooms*. Erlbaum.

Harris, P. (2009). *Language learning in the baby and toddler years*. David Barlow.

International Literacy Association. (2019a). Right to policies that ensure equitable literacy instruction. Retrieved November 23, 2020, from *www.literacyworldwide.org/docs/default-source/where-we-stand/9460_right_to_policies_final.pdf.*

International Literacy Association. (2019b). The role of bilingualism in improving literacy achievement. Retrieved November 23, 2020, from *www.literacyworldwide.org/docs/default-source/where-we-stand/ila-role-bilingualism-improving-literacy-achievement.pdf.*

Kemmis, S., McTaggart, R., & Nixon, R. (2014). *The action research planner: Doing critical participatory action research*. Springer.

Ladson-Billings, G. (1995). Toward a theory of culturally relevant pedagogy. *American Educational Research Journal, 32*(3), 465–491.

Lave, J., & Wenger, E. (1999). *Situated learning: Legitimate peripheral participation*. Cambridge University Press.

Levy, R. (2008). "Third spaces" are interesting places: Applying "third space theory" to nursery-aged children's constructions of themselves as readers. *Journal of Early Childhood Literacy, 8*(1), 43–66.

Marmion, D., Obata, K., & Troy, J. (2014). *Community, identity, wellbeing: The report of the Second National Indigenous Languages Survey*. Australian Institute of Aboriginal and Torres Strait Islander Studies.

McCarty, T., & Lee, T. (2014). Critical culturally sustaining/revitalizing pedagogy and Indigenous education sovereignty. *Harvard Educational Review, 84*(1), 101–124.

Paris, D., & Alim, S. (2014). What are we seeking to sustain through culturally sustaining pedagogy?: A loving critique forward. *Harvard Education Review 81*(1), 85–100.

Paris, D., & Alim, S. (Eds.). (2017). *Culturally sustaining pedagogies: Teaching and learning for justice in a changing world*. Teachers College Press.

South Australia Department for Education. (2015). *Implementation guidelines for indicators of preschool numeracy and literacy*. Author.

South Australia Department for Education. (2019). *Accelerating achievement in Year 3 reading for Aboriginal learners 2016–17 report*. Author.

South Australia Government. (2021). Living in South Australia. Retrieved from *www.sa.gov.au/topics/about-sa/living-in-sa*.

Tilmouth, W. (2017). Our languages matter. Retrieved July 11, 2017, from *#NAIDOC2017. #OurLanguagesMatter #QandA*.

Wigglesworth, G., Simpson, A. C., & Resnick, L. B. (2011). NAPLAN language assessments for Indigenous children in remote communities: Issues and problems. *Australian Review of Applied Linguistics, 34*, 3.

Wiley, T. G., & García, O. (2016). Language policy and planning in language education. *The Modern Language Journal, 100*(S1), 48–63.

Williams, G. (1991). Space to play: The use of analyses of narrative structure in classroom work with children's literature. In M. Saxby & G. Winch (Eds.), *Give them wings: The experience of children's literature* (2nd ed., pp. 355–368). Macmillan.

CHAPTER 8

Whole-Community Early Literacy Improvement

K–3 Academic Vocabulary Instruction

Susan V. Piazza, Sarah Summy, and Robert Herrera

Watch a related video from the authors at this link.

"The most helpful part of today's [professional development] was learning and practicing effective ways to teach word concepts . . . and realizing that making even one change at a time is important." —SECOND-GRADE TEACHER

The chapter-opening quote is a reflection that was voiced after the first summer institute of our professional learning (PL) initiative in which teachers, administrators, and researchers across three schools in a rural community collaborated to examine current and recommended early literacy practices. Our PL project—funded by our State Department of Education—focused specifically on improving K–3 students' use of academic vocabulary. Our work took place in a midwestern state, one of many states that has adopted the Read by Grade Three Law (2016), which mandates retention of readers deemed to be below proficiency by the end of third grade.

Longitudinal research has demonstrated strong relationships between third-grade reading proficiency and high school achievement, graduation, and college attendance (Lesnick et al., 2010). However, policy that mandates retention for students who are underperforming in third grade disproportionately disadvantages low-income and economically marginalized students, as well as racially, ethnically, and linguistically diverse learners and male students (Tavassolie & Winsler, 2019). In addition, policy that mandates retention contributes to deficit models that frame economic, racial, social, and linguistic differences as problems to be fixed (Bonilla-Silva, 2006). As a result, many school districts in our midwestern state are making concerted efforts to implement change processes that meet the demands of the new reading law. This law requires PL that supports educators to set high expectations and to design challenging learning experiences that are socially, culturally, and linguistically responsive to students' needs.

Regardless of the high stakes and stress attached to third-grade reading laws, there is little agreement on how to design effective whole-school change efforts that show evidence of improved curriculum, student-centered instruction, and student learning (Shen, 2020). For example, Duke (2019) describes the complexities that districts face when attempting to improve early literacy instruction, which can be undermined by either weak PL content, weak PL processes, or both. Weak content with solid processes or vice versa will compromise schools' efforts to improve instruction. Whereas there are no formulas or quick fixes to improve early literacy at the whole-school or community level, the project we describe here is intended to help others design strengths-based PL to improve equitable early literacy outcomes.

In this chapter, we describe our project context and the design and implementation of the PL that took place over an 18-month period, and we explain *why* our work created accessible opportunities for equitable and sustainable PL. We also explain *how* we successfully navigated the complexities of PL.

Project Context, Description, and Implementation

The rural community in which we worked is highly segregated; moreover, 75% of students in the community experience low-income and economic marginalization. Less than 50% of K–3 students in this community demonstrate literacy proficiency on state and school-based assessments. The student population in this community is 63% White, 17% Hispanic, 13% Black, 6% multiracial, 1% Native American, and 1% Asian.

Our project served one public school district containing two elementary schools and one local private school. A total of 39 educators participated in our PL initiative, including 33 K–3 teachers, three principals, two instructional coaches, and one curriculum coordinator. There were between seven and nine teachers in each K–3 grade level. The project was implemented over 18 months; each participant engaged in approximately

90 hours of PL during this time. Student–teacher ratios in these schools were typically 18 to 1.

Figure 8.1 demonstrates the integrated nature of the leadership team and the school-based project team as we engaged with each other and with the community. An important feature of the project was our intentional early effort to connect with and include voices from different parts of the community to honor the funds of knowledge (FoK) specific to this setting (Moll et al., 1992). FoK typically include "historically-accumulated and culturally-developed bodies of knowledge and skills essential for household or individual functioning or wellbeing" (Moll et al., 1992, p. 133). Seeking out community-based FoK allowed us to build reciprocity among participants (Valdés, 1996) in the project design process. Our approach was different from traditional notions of PL that position knowledge as fixed and transmissible (Currin, 2019). Instead, we approached PL and new knowledge as shared and co-constructed.

We served on the leadership team for this communitywide collaborative project. Susan, a literacy professor, was the lead principal investigator and director of the research project funded by the U.S. Department of Education Title II Part A (3) Improving Teacher Quality grant. Sarah, a special education professor, served as co-principal investigator and lead evaluator. Finally, Robert, the former superintendent in the participating school district, collaborated on this publication to document and member-check the PL processes and outcomes. The six-member leadership team

FIGURE 8.1. Project leadership and engagement.

consisted of the three authors along with three principals, each from participating schools in the project.

The six-member leadership team recruited teacher leaders across grade levels from each school. These teacher leaders made up the school-based project team and helped to implement the PL work between leadership team meetings. As well, teacher leaders on the school-based project team facilitated book clubs and provided ongoing constructive feedback and embedded leadership in the schools throughout the project.

The community steering committee included members of a local reading council, the public library, a parent resource center, the city's diversity coalition, and religious leaders from two local churches. Conveniently, the public library representative was also a city council member, which provided greater insight regarding local issues, politics, and resources. The librarian on the steering committee had insider knowledge of lived experiences in this African American community and was well connected in the community. She also had first-hand experience with racism and segregation that she and her neighbors experienced. As a council member, she was active in the diversity coalition, which advocated for antiracist and equity-focused partnerships in schools and community. She recruited stakeholders from local businesses and organizations, as well as parents, during the initial stages of the project. Working with leaders in the community demonstrated that we valued the significant contributions of residents, their FoK, and their desire to make improvements within their schools (Moll, 2019; Suarez-Balcazar, 2020).

PL Process

This process was formative; we adjusted our plans based on feedback and requests along the way so that students' needs informed PL plans. Figure 8.2 displays the five components of the inquiry, design, ownership, leverage, and sustain (IDOLS) framework we developed. To be clear, these five components are not linear or mutually exclusive, but they do represent the general focus of our work across the 18-month project. There were times when we moved back and forth between the components to revisit earlier work, enacting a formative feedback loop to continuously improve PL and students' learning experiences. We discuss each component of the IDOLS framework in turn.

Inquiry Stance toward PL

We assumed a participatory action research (PAR) stance (Bergmark, 2020), which prioritizes an inquiry focus intended to achieve more "horizontal relationships among professionals, colleges of education, public

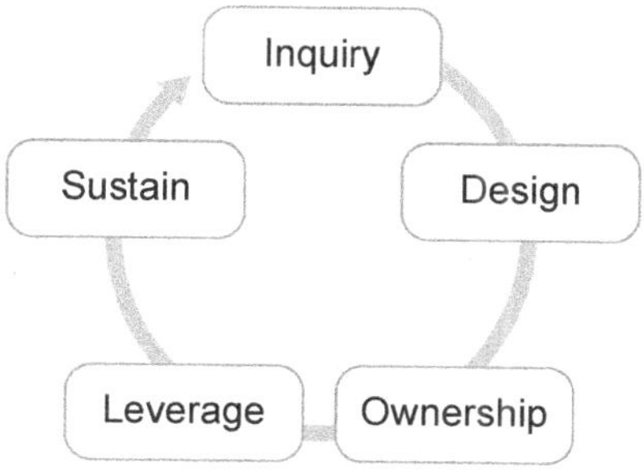

FIGURE 8.2. IDOLS PL process.

schools, and low-income communities" (Anderson, 2017, p. 432). Moreover, an inquiry stance toward PL encourages educators to engage in systematic and intentional learning about their pedagogies of practice directly related to communities of learning (Cochran-Smith & Lytle, 1993).

Our first major task was to "inquire" about the participating teachers' early literacy knowledge and instructional needs. Consequently, the leadership team implemented an electronic needs assessment survey to all K–3 educators during the first month of the project. Survey results were shared with teachers, school leaders, stakeholders, and educators. Survey results identified academic vocabulary development for K–3 learners as the top content priority. When the leadership team compared teachers' perceived PL needs with student achievement, it appeared that the greatest potential for growth was in building students' academic vocabulary.

Design Process for PL

At the beginning of the project, all stakeholders were brought together to discuss students' needs, educators' needs, and the community's needs as they related to early literacy. The university partners served as facilitators, took minutes, and reported back to the group. Suggestions for practice led us to project design features that included engaging families of underrepresented groups, having community partners host early literacy PD events, and inviting guest speakers from the community to increase engagement with schools and families. All partners indicated a willingness to collaborate and work together on ways that the schools and teachers might become more responsive to students' racial, cultural, social, and linguistic backgrounds.

After the wider community and school stakeholder input, we began to work with the school-based project team and K–3 teachers to evaluate the effectiveness of teachers' current instructional strategies and materials.

Our work together promoted flexible mindsets to select, adapt, and use resources in culturally responsive ways that meet students' unique and individual needs. The school-based project team led the examination of programs and materials. The PL schedule included time and space for teachers to check for accessibility and appropriate supports found in their existing instructional approaches and materials. The evaluation of curriculum focused on meeting the needs of learners with exceptionalities, multilingual learners, and socioculturally and racially diverse learners (Piazza et al., 2015).

The design of PL across three schools was negotiated to accommodate schedules, materials, and interests. The leadership and project team, with input from teachers, determined that 90 hours of PL would consist of summer institutes, half-days of released time during the academic year, PL meetings that were part of teachers' scheduled working hours, and peer-coaching within and across grade levels. After choosing the PL focus, designing the PL schedule, and evaluating resources, teachers began taking ownership of instructional and assessment practices within the IDOLS PL process. Figure 8.3 represents the timeline of PL benchmarks across an 18-month period.

Ownership of PL

Ownership is the next phase of the IDOLS PL process as described in Figure 8.2. The individuals engaged in the PL process began to assume

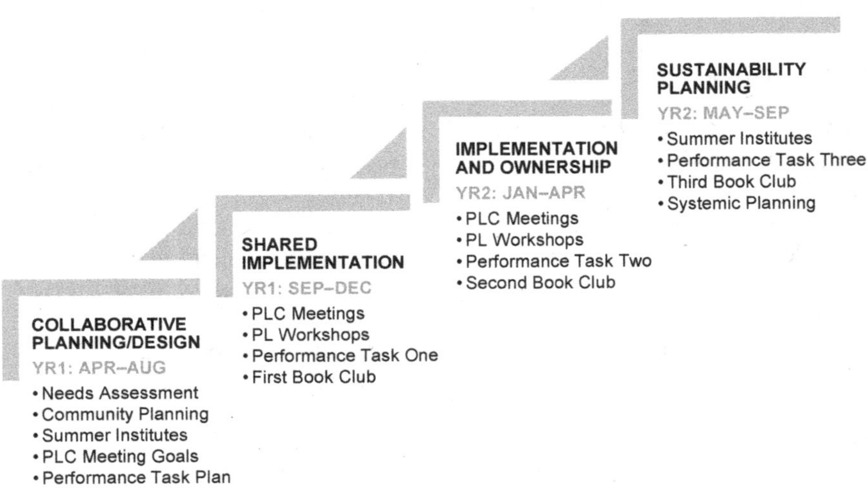

FIGURE 8.3. Timeline of PL across 18 months.

ownership as they played a role in making decisions about materials and content. For example, based on identified needs, the school-based project team, representing all K–3 teachers, identified three relevant professional readings aligned with the pedagogical and equity-focused goals of the project. Three professional books were selected to increase shared understandings and dialogue around building academic vocabulary while strengthening family and community engagement to support early literacy. Grade-level teams met once per week as part of their teaching contract, and teachers elected to incorporate book studies into their grade-level team meeting times.

The first professional book study focused on a practical guide titled *Your UDL Lesson Planner: The Step-by-Step Guide for Teaching All Learners* (Ralabate, 2016), highlighting inclusive practices for learner variability and diversity. Universal Design for Learning (UDL) helped educators coordinate instructional planning with the need to increase culturally responsive pedagogies, including ways to increase engagement with families and the local community (Kieran & Anderson, 2019). In fact, the chapter-opening quote was in response to discussions around the use of UDL to increase culturally responsive practices.

The second professional book study examined *No More "Look Up the List" Vocabulary Instruction* (Cobb & Blachowicz, 2014), which offers practical and research-based vocabulary approaches. We used this resource to negotiate and critique the schools' adopted commercially packaged program, *Journeys* (Houghton Mifflin Harcourt, 2009). Drawing on our knowledge from reading this book and the state standards, we made curricular and instructional decisions together about best ways to foster academic vocabulary learning.

The third professional book study, *New Ways to Engage Parents: Strategies and Tools for Teachers and Leaders, K–12* (Edwards, 2016), helped raise educators' awareness about race, economics, and language differences in their community.

As teachers met weekly in PL groups and engaged in book study work, they also identified end-of-year student learning outcomes (SLOs) for each grade level related to building academic vocabulary. This SLO work in conjunction with the book studies allowed teachers to customize their use of materials, learning strategies, instructional supports, and assessments to fit the unique context of their community.

Curricular materials were used as resources, but each grade-level identified strengths and weaknesses within those materials. For example, one building used a basal reading program that included little linguistic, cultural, or racial diversity in reading or visual materials. Teachers identified ways to supplement the basal program to ensure a more inclusive and bias-free curriculum. Grade-level teams began implementing new approaches and reported back during PL meetings. Thus, through our collaborative work across time, teachers and administrators assumed ownership of the critical evaluation of materials and approaches, which laid the groundwork for more equitable student learning.

Leverage Practices for PL

Leveraging practices to support and assess student learning is the next phase of the IDOLS PL process as described in Figure 8.2. To foster culturally responsive instruction and assessments, we implemented three rounds of teacher-created performance-based assessments to analyze student learning over the 18-month project. The academic vocabulary content priorities were identified early, but teachers still needed to explicitly identify their student learning outcomes (SLOs) within a content area before constructing performance tasks that might best capture knowledge and skill while attending to equity and inclusion. Figure 8.4 displays two examples of artifacts from kindergarten and third-grade teachers' SLO planning before they began designing performance tasks. Third-grade teachers eventually determined that they would focus on the development of academic vocabulary use within a mathematics context and through written language use for SLOs, as indicated in Figure 8.4.

Working in grade-level teams, teachers created a formative process for determining beginning, middle, and end-of-year measures for students' learning outcomes related to academic vocabulary. Together, we agreed that a feasible plan included analyzing student learning outcomes at the beginning, middle, and end of the year on one consistent authentic measure of how students used academic vocabulary. In addition, while the three schools relied on state standardized assessments, teachers agreed on the need to examine how students were authentically using academic vocabulary within their unique contexts and over time.

When SLOs and authentic assessments are used in a recursive process to analyze student learning over time, educators are afforded opportunities to participate in a self-reflective, adaptive, self-corrective, and a self-renewal process with local control (Darling-Hammond, 1994). In addition, when teachers customize assessments to students' backgrounds and prior learning, it provides a more valid measure of their understandings and use of vocabulary both in and out of school (Quyên, 2019).

Sustaining PL over Time

Sustaining PL over time is a crucial component of the IDOLS PL process as indicated in Figure 8.2. Instructional improvements around academic vocabulary instruction emphasizing equity and inclusion evolved across

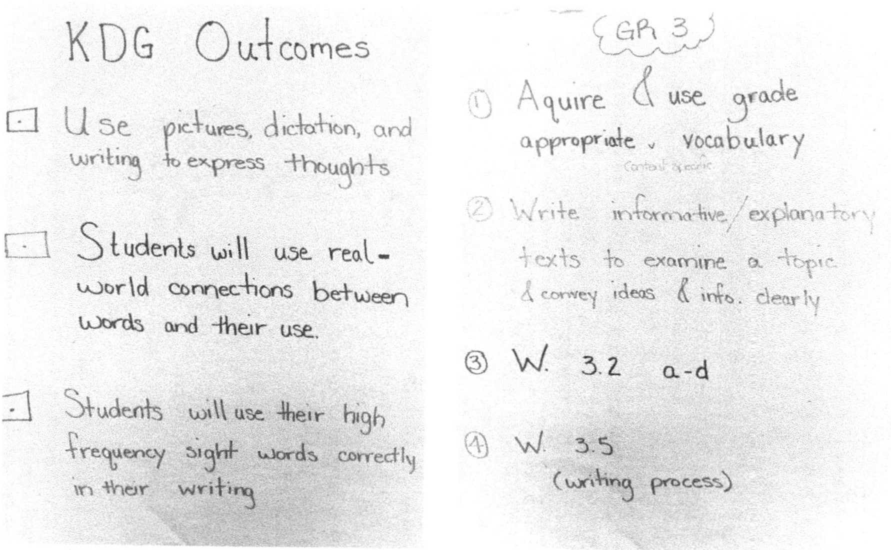

FIGURE 8.4. Kindergarten (left) and third-grade (right) student learning outcomes (SLOs).

formal and informal PL meetings. Teachers found their first round of creating performance tasks to be complex and messy. In short, the process of developing performance-based classroom assessments was unfamiliar to teachers. (See Table 8.1 for an example of a third-grade performance task.) Teachers were more familiar with being asked to use commercially packaged assessments provided in curricular materials.

Discussion about designing tasks with high expectations became a priority. After the pilot and the first round of implementation, we observed a great deal of peer feedback that encouraged revision to include more complex tasks, UDL approaches, and instructional supports. As part of this process, we designed a peer review form that teachers used after each implementation. Figure 8.5 provides a peer review example. It shows how teachers helped each other with suggestions for more instructional support and variations for students to express their understandings differently, such as "acting out new words," as found in this example.

The SLOs remained the same for each implementation cycle across three times per academic year (beginning, middle, and end), with opportunities to strengthen instructional practice, scaffolds, and use of diverse materials and resources. While the SLOs remained the same each round, the topic or content changed during each implementation at different

TABLE 8.1. Third-Grade Performance Task

Student learning outcome: Students will be able to explain their strategic thinking to solve word problems while using appropriate academic vocabulary related to mathematical content standards.

The teacher will . . .	The students will . . .	UDL strategies	Accommodations/ modifications
Hook: • display/read multiple word problems. This will include story problems with Tier Two vocabulary words (*explain, demonstrate, solve*, etc.).	• choose the correct operation and move to appropriate symbol corner using the Four Corners strategy.	• Four Corners—Action and Expression. • Names, topics, and visuals will be culturally sustaining. Students may answer with movement, orally, or written responses.	• Preteach vocabulary words; small-group instruction; dual language dictionaries; word walls; and visuals. Students may use first language as needed.
Present content: • introduce Tier Two academic vocabulary words related to math lesson. • provide word problems, including students' names, as well as roles (director, sleuth, recorder, reporter) for small-group work. • model think-aloud on how to solve problems.	• complete the graphic organizers using the words found within story problems. • solve and act out word problems, complete with a written response that will be presented to the class. Demonstrations should include the appropriate use of academic vocabulary.	• Act out a word, peer discussion, use of visuals, multiple forms of expression. • Visuals and word walls to support new vocabulary. • Peer reading partners for increased engagement and support with reading. • Options for story problems to be read individually, in small groups, or with adult support.	• Premade vocabulary boxes. • Access to word bank for questions. • Teacher scribe if needed. • Students may use first language as needed.
Independent practice and assessment: • performance task story problem.	• demonstrate understanding of multiplication by explaining. • create a word problem.	• Create a word problem. • Expression—oral, textual, visual.	• Scribe if needed. • Model additional problems as necessary.
Closing: • confer with students, observe. • provide exit slip/checklist.	• complete the problem-solving checklist/exit slip.	• Action and written expression. • Oral communication as needed.	• Teacher can read and scribe for students as needed.

points in the school year. The same performance task was adapted across multiple topics and disciplines, but the rubric remained consistent; it focused on student learning of academic vocabulary.

Teachers demonstrated increased ownership after creating SLOs, authentic performance tasks, and rubrics, and after analyzing multiple rounds of implementation across the academic year. Although round one was a steep learning curve for most educators, rounds two and three revealed an increasingly in-depth professional knowledge about the teaching and learning process. We observed that educators were much more adept at connecting research, theory, and practice to the academic vocabulary student learning outcomes. Teachers developed shared understandings about the continuous improvement process, and after round two,

Lesson/Task Characteristics	Strongly Disagree	Disagree	Undecided	Agree	Strongly Agree
1. Hook will motivate/engage students to actively participate in the lesson.	o	o	o	(o)	o
2. Introduces word meanings during reading and/or content instruction using child-friendly explanations.	o	(o)	o	o	o
3. Provides opportunities for children to pronounce new words and be able to see the spelling of new words.	o	(o)	o	o	o
4. Allows students to use new words in meaningful contexts and to address multiple or nuanced meanings of words.	o	o	o	(o)	o
5. Encourages talk, particularly during content area learning around print or digital texts.	o	o	o	(o)	o
6. Teaches morphology (i.e., menaing of word parts), including common word roots, inflections, prefixes, and affixes.	o	o	(o)	o	o
7. Includes UDL strategies that allow for variations in the ways that teachers *represent* new words/information.	o	o	o	(o)	o
8. Includes UDL strategies that allow for variations in the ways that students *express* their understandings of new words/information.	o	o	o	(o)	o
9. Includes UDL strategies that allow for variations in the ways that teachers *engage* students during learning and practicing new words/information.	o	o	o	(o)	o
10. Includes opportunities for student self-assessment.	o	o	o	(o)	o
11. The lesson includes measurable goals/outcomes demonstrated by the student artifact.	o	o	o	(o)	o
12. Rubric criteria are clearly aligned with the student performance/artifacts.	o	o	(o)	o	o
13. Will this lesson/task and rubric uncover the areas of instruction that need further development?	o	o	(o)	o	o

Handwritten comments: row 2: need intro to words "I do"; row 3: display words; row 4: real world can be acted out; row 6: depends on words, etc.; row 11: homework; row 12: it's probably "great"; row 13: see above.

Please provide suggestions and/or question that may help to strengthen this lesson/task (use the back of this sheet if you need more space). Add a rubric, introduce words early on, display them, etc.

FIGURE 8.5. Peer review for third-grade performance task.

they began expressing an appreciation for the recursive PL process. Table 8.2 presents a range of feedback from teachers' survey responses after the beginning, middle, and last PL session focused on performance task implementation.

After each round of task implementation, teachers brought a class set of student data in the form of artifacts to their grade-level meetings. They were asked to evaluate student work with the rubric first and then share the class set with colleagues to complete peer reviews for rater agreement using the rubric. This process helped teachers validate and ensure reliability for their tasks and rubrics, and it also contributed to a shared understanding of student learning objectives, instructional supports, and rubric criteria.

In addition, our project facilitated the creation of a communitywide, electronic repository housed in the schools as shared electronic files. These files were shared across all participants in this project. The data accumulated in these shared files became valuable resources and reference points for teachers to leverage as they developed future performance tasks. Student artifacts were also housed in this electronic repository. They included details such as (1) clarifying expectations for students, (2) improving demonstration and scaffolding techniques during instruction, (3) creating meaningful opportunities for students to apply and use academic vocabulary, (4) suggested teacher or student resources/materials, and (5) differentiating instruction for diverse student needs.

As PL facilitators, we have experienced this cycle of thinking over multiple rounds of implementation and revisions. We have observed familiar patterns of thinking by educators. During the pilot and first rounds of implementation, many teachers tend to worry more about appearing incapable of supporting their students or they worry that student performance will reflect poorly on them as teachers. During the second round of implementation, teachers tend to shift their attention to student learning processes and are willing to take a closer look at opportunities to improve instructional practices that better support learners. Finally,

TABLE 8.2. Teachers' Feedback after Implementation

Round One: "I'm confused about this performance-task work and worry about my students not doing well."

Round Two: "This is messy, but I think I am beginning to get the point of this. I am trusting that the next round will be much clearer."

Round Three: "This is *making* sense, and I love how this tool lets us look at a detailed analysis of our teaching and how students understand the concepts."

clarity and confidence are most often observed during round three when teachers see direct connections between the task, instructional supports, and the rubric that measures SLOs. This is when we recognized how the PL process created accessible opportunities for equitable and sustainable PL among educators.

Equitable and Sustainable PL

Whether students are racially, culturally, or linguistically diverse, whether they lack access to technology or food, or whether they are differently abled, literacy learning needs are complex and require knowledgeable educators who understand how to address inequities within their educational roles. Thus, our entire project is grounded in the belief that PL should be inclusive, equity-focused, and centered on an inquiry stance. Moreover, an equitable, inclusive, inquiry stance can contribute to long-term and sustainable PL (McNair, Bensimon, & Malcom-Piqueux, 2020).

Research supporting effective PL primarily focuses on how it results in improved student achievement (Desimone, 2009), yet we knew our team valued instructional equity alongside academic achievement. We needed to contextualize PL with respect to the students' needs and FoK within our community. For example, scholars of effective vocabulary instruction recommend (1) providing rich and varied language experiences, (2) teaching words through rigorous instruction and regular reviews, (3) scaffolding word-learning strategies, and (4) expanding concept development and awareness of learning about words (Cobb & Blachowicz, 2014; Graves, 2006; Graves et al., 2012; Neuman & Wright, 2015; Sprenger, 2017). Notice, however, that the aforementioned list does not include mention of race, culture, or economics. We recognized the need to embed issues of equity and inclusion to support the Black and Indigenous people of color, migrants, the economically marginalized, and English learners in our community.

At the onset of this project, K–3 educators expressed concerns because they had little to no PL experience related to how to best support Spanish-speaking migrant students. When asked about specific initiatives to support their emerging multilingual learners, they only referenced a summer mobile library that visited farms to share bilingual resources. This highlighted the need for future and sustainable PL efforts to focus on increasing the use of academic vocabulary but with particular emphasis on equity for migrant learners.

Also supporting equitable and sustainable PL, teachers extended their knowledge base and connected equity and inclusion to their instructional practices through peer discussions of our three professional books. UDL focused on the diversity of learning needs for all students (Ralabate, 2016). Teachers began engaging parents and community members with curriculum, welcomed them into classrooms, and improved two-way communication (Edwards, 2016), all while remaining focused on increasing academic vocabulary (Cobb & Blachowicz, 2014). These practices and resources were instrumental in supporting PL over time. Next, we explain how our PL approach successfully addresses the complexities that often challenge the success of PL initiatives.

Navigating the Complexities of PL

Effective PL should not be event-based, nor should PL communities operate on volunteerism organized by teachers. A great deal of research confirms that a variation of the following two factors will ensure effective PL that improves student outcomes: (1) strong administrative and organizational leadership, and (2) consistent and ongoing collaborative learning opportunities (Darling-Hammond et al., 2017; Keehne et al., 2018; Epstein, 2018). These key factors influenced the success of our PL project.

We observed strong administrative ownership and collaboration as building principals and literacy coaches actively engaged in 92 hours of PL activities supported by the project. A dedicated instructional leader, such as the principal, in each building is instrumental in modeling the importance of PL in collaborative ways. Teachers appreciated having the opportunity to collaboratively make decisions at the school, district, and community levels. Throughout the project, we observed growing mutual respect between teachers, administrators and the community.

Time is a precious resource in schools, and lack of time may pose great challenges to PL initiatives. There may also be a lack of consistency in schools when planning for PL (Darling-Hammond et al., 2017). Administrators supported a consistent schedule for PL by working with the collective bargaining unit in the two public schools to gain 12 more hours of PL per year in addition to the existing 30 hours of required monthly staff meetings and professional development days. This consistency and dedicated release time allowed grade-level teams, teacher leaders, and principals to address literacy improvement efforts across all three schools.

Across the project, university and school leaders initially established meeting agendas based on identified priorities; however, a formative revision of that process moved the entire PL project toward a more collaborative model that invited teachers to co-plan the embedded PL and the formal meetings. This allowed everyone associated with the PL initiative to make better use of limited time. Teacher-centered collaboration and ownership were vital to the success of this project.

Financial resources are always a concern when planning for PL. Influencing factors include whether a school is unionized, whether teachers are paid to collaborate and learn, or are asked to engage in PL during their free time. This project allowed us to offer stipends for all work time beyond the district-supported PL. Whether districts value or credit teachers for time invested in PL and the amount of time and resources that schools are willing to devote to PL, all need to be considered when planning and implementing PL. In this project, the two public schools were unionized, but the private school was not, which required coordination and compromise when creating the schedule, particularly when planning after-school and summer meeting times.

Educators, principals, instructional coaches, and project team members negotiated a plan for PL that consisted of some district and school-sponsored whole days, half-days, and several days in the summer referred to as summer institutes. We also used at least 50% of the grade-level meeting times during the academic year to support PL through a memorandum of agreement in which school leaders agreed to protect time for project goals. Given these arrangements, the schedule for PL supported by the school district still fell short of the minimum 90 hours required by the funding source for this project. Therefore, the leadership team funded stipends to ensure educators were compensated for PL activities outside their everyday responsibilities.

The resulting IDOLS PL cycle is proving to be recursive and sustainable following project completion. Three years have passed since the conclusion of this project. We are in touch with these K–3 schools. Teachers and administrators are still meeting in grade-level teams to follow student learning over time, still using the electronic repository for sharing resources, and using PL meeting times to focus on analyzing student learning outcomes and artifacts. Meeting the goals of this project was an evolving process that consisted of shared expertise and collaboration across all members of the initiative (e.g., researchers, PL facilitators, administrators, teachers) that enabled the enactment of authentic opportunities to actualize PL through everyday practice.

Summary of PL Outcomes

This project allowed for multiple checkpoints during the IDOLS PL cycle, including individual and group reflections, peer coaching, external coaching, classroom observations by literacy coaches, and video analysis of peer teaching. Analyses of video recordings of lessons followed by instructional coaching and conversations were a key focus of PL meetings whereby educators examined and critiqued instructional practices pertaining to academic vocabulary. In addition, each formal PL workshop or meeting was followed by a survey to collect formative feedback from teachers.

GoReact—a video analysis tool through which observers can tag a video with a timestamped comment about an identified practice—was used for video lesson sharing among peers. GoReact allowed teachers to video record, self-evaluate, and share videos within their grade-level teams for constructive feedback. Teachers tagged others' videos specifically in areas that focused on improving the effectiveness of vocabulary instruction. Analysis of videos confirmed that our project significantly increased the effective use of comprehension and vocabulary strategies during instruction. Upon reflection, we believe this tool would have been more beneficial if we had a baseline video and then an end-of-project video. Unfortunately, we only had one set of video data to analyze toward the end of the project.

As part of the project evaluation process, university researchers/partners conducted classroom observations three times across the 18 months using the Taylor Observation (T-Obs) Tool (Taylor et al., 2002). For this chapter, we are reporting only the vocabulary and comprehension domains assessed by this tool. Results from this data source show positive changes in teacher instructional behavior observed during rounds 2 and 3. This is significant because of the high priority placed on these categories and their relationship to increasing students' acquisition and use of academic vocabulary.

Using data to inform instruction is a common refrain in PL literature (Henderson & Corry, 2021). However, teachers are not often responsible for the planning, design, implementation, analysis, and interpretation of student learning outcomes. This PL initiative positioned educators as knowledgeable professionals capable of analyzing student learning outcomes using tasks and rubrics explicitly customized for their community of learners.

We offer ten guidelines for anyone wishing to engage in a whole-school change process specifically focused on early literacy improvements. The guidelines can be easily adapted across diverse contexts and goals.

Ten Guidelines to Improve Whole-School Early Literacy

Our collaborative partnership between three high-needs schools in a rural community and a local university resulted in increased teacher knowledge and pedagogy in early literacy practices, with a specific focus on academic vocabulary. We recommend these critical ingredients for success when planning PL projects to support whole-school or communitywide improvement in K–3 literacy.

1. *Build communitywide consensus.* Consensus strengthens participation and ownership. A shared vision should be grounded in standards, research, and local stakeholder input.
2. *Set priorities for student achievement in context.* Contextualized data collected from schools and community, often in the form of a comprehensive needs assessment, will strengthen customized PL.
3. *Establish systems for PL.* Equitable and sustainable PL requires administrative and teacher leadership, opportunities to collaborate, timelines with checkpoints, and transparent roles and responsibilities.
4. *Create PL community norms.* Establish consistent meeting times and expectations. PL communities were essential to this initiative. Teachers should be compensated when asked to meet after school.
5. *Favor collaboration and inclusion.* Educators and school leaders must collaborate on agendas, topics, and activities for PL. Teacher leadership, ownership, and collaboration are vital.
6. *Use student data to inform instruction.* Educators should be responsible for collecting, evaluating, and analyzing student learning outcomes to drive PL for instructional improvements.
7. *Encourage instructional conversations and peer coaching.* All learning is social. Teachers need time to interact and observe each other and debrief collaboratively.
8. *Evaluate progress toward goals.* Monitor the progress of PL initiatives in formative ways across time. Multiple data sources are needed to ensure credibility and continuous improvement.
9. *Build a shared repository of evidence and resources.* Systematically and transparently create, store, and share access to PL priorities, goals, assessment data, resources, plans, agendas, and minutes.
10. *Be flexible.* PL is a dynamic process that should shift and change over time based on student and community needs.

Conclusion

Our school–university partnership set goals to improve early literacy achievement in grades K–3 through supporting teachers' PL. Local stakeholders and school personnel from the racially and economically segregated rural community identified issues of equity and academic vocabulary as a top priority for the PL project. This endeavor resulted in positive PL outcomes and increased student achievement across all learners as measured by external state evaluators (e.g., Science and Mathematics Program Improvement, 2017). According to schools' standardized assessment of students' performance in foundational skills and vocabulary across grades K–3, in a comparison of average scores from the first year to the second year after implementing this project, students demonstrated gains ranging from 5 to 20% across grade levels, with the highest gains in first grade (NWEA, 2021).

Educators' professional knowledge related to content and pedagogy of academic vocabulary instruction had a statistically significant increase from the pre-survey to the post-survey (Science and Mathematics Program Improvement, 2017). Finally, after 90+ hours of sustained and embedded PL, we observed a substantial shift in teachers' depth of understanding related to supporting early literacy outcomes, with emphasis on equity and inclusion. It is noteworthy that this project provided more than the typical 30 hours, or 5 days, of professional development per academic year for teachers. We take pride in the fact that at least half of the hours were embedded and directly tied to instructional practice and student learning. Results such as feedback from teacher surveys, increases in student learning outcomes, and the practices sustained in these three school settings lead us to conclude that schools need additional time and resources for successful and equitable PL.

We thank all the educators and collaborators for the opportunity to be part of a process that celebrated local control and collaboration for school improvement and that genuinely centered on issues of instructional equity for underserved students. For the continued work in this community, one teacher summed it up best when she shared that they are "keeping things fresh and reaching all students; continuing to align the curriculum vertically; continuing to work on culturally responsive instruction; and continuing to learn about more ways to differentiate lessons for underperforming and advanced students" (K–3 teacher comment from final program evaluation).

REFERENCES

Anderson, G. (2017). Participatory action research (PAR) as democratic disruption: New public management and educational research in schools and universities. *International Journal of Qualitative Studies in Education, 30*(5), 432–449.

Bergmark, U. (2020). Rethinking researcher–teacher roles and relationships in educational action research through the use of Nel Noddings' ethics of care. *Educational Action Research, 28*(3), 331–344.

Bonilla-Silva, E. (2006). *Racism without racists: Color-blind racism and the persistence of racial inequality in the United States.* Rowman & Littlefield.

Cobb, C., & Blachowicz, C. (2014). *No more "look up the list" vocabulary instruction.* Heinemann.

Cochran-Smith, M., & Lytle, S. L. (Eds.). (1993). *Inside/outside: Teacher research and knowledge.* Teachers College Press.

Currin, E. (2019). From rigor to vigor: The past, present, and potential of inquiry as stance. *Journal of Practitioner Research, 4*(1) Article 2.

Darling-Hammond, L. (1994). Performance-based assessment and educational equity. *Harvard Educational Review, 64*(1), 5–31.

Darling-Hammond, L., Hyler, M. E., & Gardner, M. (2017). *Effective teacher professional development.* Learning Policy Institute.

Desimone, L. M. (2009). Improving impact studies of teachers' professional development: Toward better conceptualizations and measures. *Educational Researcher, 38*(3), 181–199.

Duke, N. K. (2019). Reading by third grade: How policymakers can foster early literacy. *National Association of State Boards of Education, 19*(2), 6–11.

Edwards, P. A. (2016). *New ways to engage parents: Strategies and tools for teachers and leaders, K–12.* Teachers College Press.

Epstein, J. L. (2018). *School, family, and community partnerships: Preparing educators and improving schools.* Routledge.

GoReact. (n.d.). Simply powerful tools for video assessment. Retrieved from *https://get.goreact.com.*

Graves, M. F. (2006). Building a comprehensive vocabulary program. *New England Reading Association Journal, 42*(2), 1–7, 62.

Graves, M. F., August, D., & Mancilla-Martinez, J. (2012). *Teaching vocabulary to English language learners.* Teachers College Press.

Henderson, J., & Corry, M. (2021). Data literacy training and use for educational professionals. *Journal of Research in Innovative Teaching & Learning, 14*(2), 232–244.

Houghton Mifflin Harcourt. (2009). *Journeys.* Author.

Keehne, C. N., Sarsona, M. W., Kawakami, A. J., & Au, K. H. (2018). Culturally responsive instruction and literacy learning. *Journal of Literacy Research, 50*(2), 141–166.

Kieran, L., & Anderson, C. (2019). Connecting universal design for learning with culturally responsive teaching. *Education and Urban Society, 51*(9), 1202–1216.

Lesnick, J., George, R., Smithgall, C., & Gwynne, J. (2010). *Reading on grade level in third grade: How is it related to high school performance and college enrollment.* Chapin Hall at the University of Chicago. Retrieved from *http://citeseerx.ist.psu.edu/viewdoc/download?doi=10.1.1.715.5162&rep=rep1&type=pdf.*

McNair, T. B., Bensimon, E. M., & Malcom-Piqueux, L. (2020). *From equity talk to equity walk: Expanding practitioner knowledge for racial justice in higher education.* Wiley.

Moll, L. C. (2019). Elaborating funds of knowledge: Community-oriented practices in international contexts. *Literacy Research: Theory, Method, and Practice, 68*(1), 130–138.

Moll, L. C., Amanti, C., Neff, D., & Gonzalez, N. (1992). Funds of knowledge for teaching: Using a qualitative approach to connect homes and classrooms. *Theory Into Practice, 31*(2), 132–141.

Neuman, S. B., & Wright, T. S. (2015). *All about words: Increasing vocabulary in the common core classroom, Pre-K–2.* Teachers College Press.

NWEA. (2021). NWEA: Measuring what matters. Retrieved from *www.nwea.org.*

Piazza, S. V., Rao, S., & Protacio, S. M. (2015). Converging recommendations for culturally responsive literacy practices: Students with learning disabilities, English language learners, and socioculturally diverse learners. *International Journal of Multicultural Education 17,* 1–20.

Quyên, V. P. (2019). Performance-based assessment: Implications to English language classrooms. In P. H. Yen & T. V. S. Nguyen (Eds.), *Using alternative assessment to improve EFL learners' learning achievement: From theory to practice* (pp. 63–79). Nova Science.

Ralabate, P. K. (2016). *Your UDL lesson planner: The step-by-step guide for teaching all learners.* Brookes.

Read by Grade Three Law, Michigan Legislature Public Act 306; Section§ 380.1280f (2016). *www.legislature.mi.gov/(S(ag5b2elrpsvpxmukd15zfn5l))/mileg.aspx?page=getObject&objectName=mcl-380–1280f*

Science and Mathematics Program Improvement. (2017). *Title IIA: Improving Teacher Quality Grants Program. Statewide cross-site evaluation: Compilation of teacher pre- and post-survey responses* [unpublished raw data]. Western Michigan University.

Shen, J. (2020). The theory of bifurcated educational system and its implications for school improvement. *International Journal of Leadership in Education,* 1–21.

Sprenger, M. (2017). *101 strategies to make academic vocabulary stick.* ASCD.

Suarez-Balcazar, Y. (2020). Meaningful engagement in research: Community residents as co-creators of knowledge. *American Journal of Community Psychology, 65*(3–4), 261–271.

Tavassolie, T., & Winsler, A. (2019). Predictors of mandatory 3rd grade retention from high-stakes test performance for low-income, ethnically diverse children. *Early Childhood Research Quarterly, 48,* 62–74.

Taylor, B. M., Peterson, D. S., Pearson, P. D., & Rodriguez, M. C. (2002). Looking inside classrooms: Reflecting on the "how" as well as the "what" in effective reading instruction. *The Reading Teacher, 56*(3), 270–279.

U.S. Department of Education. (2018, May 22). Improving Teacher Quality State Grants. Available at *www2.ed.gov/programs/teacherqual/index.html.*

Valdés, G. (1996). *Con respeto: Bridging the distances between culturally diverse parents and schools: An ethnographic portrait.* Teachers College Press.

CHAPTER 9

Using Digital Tools to Promote Teacher Agency and Enhance Teacher Professional Learning

Lauren Breckenridge Padesky, Dana A. Robertson, Alexis Barney, and Noelle Clark

Watch a related video from the authors at this link.

Perhaps one of the greatest advantages of technological inundation in modern society is the increased access to knowledge that was not true of a predigital world. The ability to disseminate information across the globe creates an ease of access and communication that has been profound. Whereas factors such as distance, time, and financial resources can limit PL that relies on in-person coaching, digital tools have created a new era of teacher coaching possibilities, where coaches and teachers can access curated teaching resources, use digital communications to tailor in-person interactions, and engage in iterative cycles of reflectivity (Leighton et al., 2018; Main & Slater, 2022; Stelmach, 2011).

This chapter describes powerful examples of the ways that digital tools bridged face-to-face coaching divides between university-based literacy coaches and elementary educators by relying heavily on a school's existing digital infrastructure. The work was framed within a schoolwide professional learning (PL) goal of vocabulary development at Eagle River Elementary (a pseudonym), a rural PreK–5 school of 277 students and 27 faculty and instructional staff located in a Mountain West state. The school is designated as a Title I school, with 69% of the students receiving free or reduced meals, 10% supplemental English language services, and 15% special education services. According to school reporting, 25% of the families identified as Hispanic/Latino, <1% as Asian, 3% as more than one race, and 71% as White. The faculty worked in looping teams, where classroom teachers looped with the same class of students for two consecutive years. Looping teams were grouped as kindergarten and first grade, second grade and third grade, and fourth grade and fifth grade. Specialist teachers worked across these grade levels to support students within and outside of the classrooms, and one teacher was in charge of a school-based preschool classroom with separate morning and afternoon classes.

First, we briefly review the literature on literacy coaching actions that are important levers for improved teaching. We also consider the potential contributions of digital technologies for increasing the accessibility and responsiveness in teacher PL. We then provide a look into how Noelle, a third-grade teacher (fourth author), and Alexis, a fourth-grade teacher (third author), each used a combination of digital tools and in-person coaching provided by university researchers (Lauren and Dana, first and second authors, along with another colleague), and how these interactions facilitated their agency as decision makers in their own PL and that of their students. Finally, we address possible roadblocks or challenges that the teachers and university partners encountered when engaging in ongoing, digitally mediated PL work across time and space.

Literacy Coaching for Teacher Change

Coaching has been widely recognized as an important lever for improving teacher learning. Studies of literacy coaching have shown that coaches positively impact teachers' knowledge of literacy and beliefs about how literacy instruction is effectively approached (Coburn & Woulfin, 2012; Robertson, Padesky, et al., 2020). Studies also show the important influence of coaches in facilitating teachers' implementation of more effective or new instructional practices across varied levels of teacher experience and instructional contexts (Kraft et al., 2018; Matsumura et al., 2013; Sailors & Price, 2015; Teemant, 2014). Moreover, productive collaborations between coaches and teachers facilitate teacher self-reflection (e.g., Matsumura et al., 2019; Peterson et al., 2009).

Collected findings of literacy coaching research indicate several important patterns of coaching actions that together are important for teacher change. First is that the length of time teachers spend with coaches in various activities matters. There is a strong, positive relationship between more coaching and greater positive outcomes for teachers (Bean et al., 2010; Biancarosa et al., 2010; Sailors & Price, 2015). Second, there is also strong evidence that the frequency of sustained coaching interactions matters. Teachers who engage in more frequent coaching interactions are more likely to demonstrate teaching improvements (Bean et al., 2010; Matsumura et al., 2013; Walpole et al., 2010). Third, the types of groupings used in coaching interactions matter. Specifically, consistently engaging teachers in individual (e.g., co-planning, debriefing) coaching interactions is associated with substantial improvements in teacher practice (Elish-Piper & L'Allier, 2010; Teemant, 2014; Walpole et al., 2010), beyond workshops and grade-level planning and debriefing meetings alone. Finally, even with more frequent one-on-one interactions over a longer period of time, emerging evidence also points to the fundamental importance of teachers exercising agency to fully engage in coaching interactions and shape their own understanding of literacy teaching and learning (Neuman & Wright, 2010; Robertson, Ford-Connors, et al., 2020; Robertson, Padesky, et al., 2020).

Together, these findings show the importance of sustained and intensive opportunities for teachers to engage with coaches. Yet, obviously, these opportunities also require substantial time and effort, and time is a precious commodity in schools with myriad competing demands. One way to address these constraints of time and scheduling is for coaches to use various digital tools to bring more flexibility and accessibility to their interactions with teachers (e.g., see Chapters 5 and 10 in this volume for other examples). Digital tools can increase connections with teachers to maintain more regular interactions across both time and physical space, while also providing opportunities for teachers to take a proactive, agentive role in reflecting upon and shaping their own instructional decision making.

Digital Tools in Professional Learning

With the proliferation of digital tools for communicating, connecting people, and documenting experiences, teachers and PL facilitators—including literacy coaches—have begun to draw on these technologies to facilitate teachers' interactions with content and colleagues in PL (e.g., Glover, 2017; Main & Slater, 2022). For example, teachers have utilized social media (Tomassini, 2013) and e-mentoring through email communication (Smith & Israel, 2010) to forge new peer networks and share content and teaching strategies. Relatedly, in one rural school context, online mentoring through Skype and text messaging was used to expand teachers' access to ongoing PL opportunities (Sawchuk, 2013), while in another context, teachers engaged with avatars to practice new teaching ideas in simulated contexts (Dieker et al., 2015). Teachers' feelings of disconnection and reports of limited access to PL opportunities can be alleviated with the use of digital tools.

Beyond tools for connecting and communicating, video recordings of instruction are one of the most common digital tools used by teachers (Tripp & Rich, 2012) and in coaching conversations (Neuman & Wright, 2010; Robertson, Padesky, Ford-Connors, et al., 2020; Wilkinson et al., 2010) to anchor critical self-reflection and advance teaching expertise (Matsumura et al., 2019). Video streaming and recording—whether used synchronously or asynchronously—has been shown to be a powerful tool for remote coaching opportunities (Kurz et al., 2017). For example, Vernon-Feagans and colleagues (2013) used webcam technologies with their Targeted Reading Instruction intervention to observe live tutoring between teachers and children with reading difficulties, and then to debrief with these teachers in timely ways. Coaching in this way not only increases access to immediate PL, but it also is highly correlated with positive changes in teacher practice and student achievement. Similarly, Leighton et al. (2018) described coaching interactions that flexibly drew on an array of digital communication tools (FaceTime, text messaging, email communications), along with asynchronous viewing of video-recorded instruction, as a second-grade teacher reflectively implemented discussion-based practices in her classroom. Other coaching contexts have combined asynchronous video viewing by coaches and teachers with web-based resources that teachers can draw on to continue to reflect on their teaching practice (e.g., Main & Slater, 2022; Matsumura et al., 2019; Ossa-Parra et al., 2016; Pianta et al., 2008; Powell & Diamond, 2013).

Collectively, digital technologies have expanded teachers' access to colleagues, new content, and PL opportunities, and have created regular opportunities for coaches and teachers to interact in ways that promote more equitable access to PL. Whereas the ever-changing nature of digital tools can be overwhelming, especially for technological novices, these tools can also offer coaches and teachers practical solutions to the limitations of time and access to opportunities within busy school settings. Supplemented with face-to-face interactions, these tools offer coaches flexibility to support more teachers as they work to solve pressing problems of practice (Toll, 2017). In the following sections, we describe how digital technologies were used to mediate literacy coaching and other PL interactions at Eagle River Elementary during one academic year.

Using Digital Tools to Enhance In-Person Coaching

The use of digital technologies in PL facilitated by university-based coaches at Eagle River is first situated within a co-developed, schoolwide PL partnership. Then, we describe how Alexis and Noelle iteratively leveraged the use of digital technologies in concert with in-person coaching to act autonomously and increase their capacity as instructional decision makers using

(1) a digital repository of vocabulary-focused resources and (2) a digital "Communication Link" to document PL activities and facilitate collaboration with peers and the coaches. Throughout the descriptions of the co-constructed PL, sidebar quotes offer additional reflective statements from Alexis and Noelle in relation to their engagement in the process to focus on the teachers' and coaches' use of digital tools to mediate their PL.

Co-Developing an Agentic Approach to PL at Eagle River

The approach to this project placed teacher agency at the forefront of how the teachers engaged with each other and the content (see Robertson et al., 2019, for a fuller description). The university researchers and school faculty strove to co-develop structures and processes where all of the educators in the school had space and voice to act individually and intentionally to promote student learning, yet also to act in interdependent and iterative ways to maintain a collective investment in their shared schoolwide goal (see Figure 9.1). Honoring teachers' voices in their own PL, while also using a combination of in-person and digital communication, provided equitable access to the schoolwide literacy goals for PL. Teachers reported that this sense of autonomy filtered down to the students exercising more agency in their own literacy learning

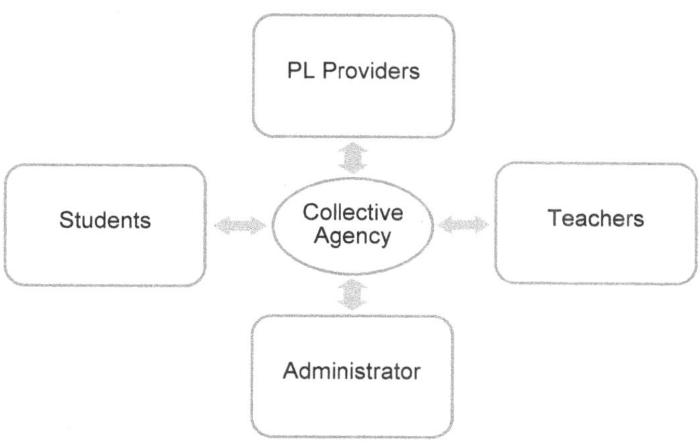

FIGURE 9.1. PL guided by collective agency. From Robertson, D. A., Padesky, L., & Brock, C. H. (2019). Cultivating student agency through teacher professional development. *Theory Into Practice, 59*, 192–201. Copyright © The College of Education and Human Ecology, The Ohio State University. Reprinted by permission of Taylor & Francis Ltd. *http://www.tandfonline.com* on behalf of The College of Education and Human Ecology, The Ohio State University.

Rather than provide a more traditional professional development approach that positions the external partners as experts who come into a school to "fix" teaching, the university-based coaches sought to create a more sustainable culture of PL. The university partners wanted the teachers to feel empowered through autonomous learning within a common, schoolwide goal. Briefly, the approach started with helping all of the educators to refine their understanding of their current reality and engage in visioning (Au et al., 2008; Vaughn & Faircloth, 2013) of a schoolwide goal to advance their literacy teaching and learning. Then, the university partners and school educators co-constructed PL structures to meet their school goal, while also helping them to recognize that each teacher's learning could be individualized within the broader goal. The teachers approached their literacy instruction by building professional knowledge about literacy development, balanced with knowledge of the students in their classrooms. Thus, grade-level or specialist groups followed more individualized pathways while also contributing to the collective sense of agency. As such, the coaches' assumption was that teachers would be more likely to practice what they were experiencing in the PL interactions because of their autonomy to pursue learning goals that were meaningful to their classroom contexts (Bandura, 2001; Deci & Ryan, 1995; Knowles, 1984) while also recognizing the importance of coherence across the school (Harn et al., 2011; Wonder-McDowell et al., 2011).

"As we embarked on this PL experience, I could tell it was going to be different from any other I'd had. Our coaches worked with us to identify our needs, then in partnership, we carefully crafted a plan that was intentional and ongoing. As our needs shifted, we worked together to adapt our learning plan. Instead of focusing on a specific program, or teaching resource, we read articles on teaching strategies, we observed each other, and had reflective discussions. We were empowered as a learning community to tailor our instruction to the unique needs of our students."—NOELLE

Autonomously Driven Learning through Digital Tools and Coaching

Noelle and Alexis were the designated teacher leaders of the English language arts (ELA) Goal Team at their school. The team also included the principal and other grade-level or specialist teacher representatives. The team had analyzed their state assessment data to uncover patterns of performance related to student literacy learning. Noticing a need to strengthen informational text comprehension and vocabulary knowledge, a partnership was established with the university coaches. The school's perceptions of instructional needs were then confirmed and refined through a schoolwide needs assessment process conducted by the university coaches, and the faculty came together around the unifying focus of improving vocabulary instruction schoolwide.

In a structure put forth by the school's ELA Goal Team in consultation with the university coaches, the PL began with a half-day "launch" workshop that provided an overview of a comprehensive approach to vocabulary learning (e.g., Graves, 2016). During the workshop, the school faculty also engaged in self-reflection on their individual PL needs related to vocabulary instruction. This initial session was then followed by cycles of professional discussions of research articles and books within the school's weekly PL community (PLC) meetings (e.g., Westheimer, 2008), cross-grade level sharing at monthly faculty meetings, and monthly liaison meetings between the school leadership team and the university partners via Zoom video conferencing to reflect on PL structures and plan in-person "coaching days."

PLCs and various committees at the school were already in the habit of maintaining common Google Drive folders and documents to facilitate communication and collaboration. Common formative assessments and other teaching tools were readily accessible for shared use, and the PLCs were already in the habit of digitally managing tasks like analyzing student data or co-planning between general education and special education teachers. Alexis and Noelle knew this about their colleagues, and they used this knowledge to propose digital habits to the university coaches that would be familiar and useful to the teachers and thus, minimize steep learning curves for teachers in accessibility and use. Importantly, these digital tools were facilitative of teachers' autonomous engagement with the PL process, allowing PLCs and individual teachers to immediately communicate collective and individual PL needs. This led to a level of individualization that the university coaches had not predicted at the outset of the work.

A Digital Resource Repository for Facilitating Teacher Choice

As one example, Noelle intentionally promoted student-selected vocabulary learning during reading, a goal that she facilitated by flexibly engaging with various digital tools and ongoing coaching support. Always seeking opportunities to expand her teaching repertoire and engage her students, Noelle explored ways her students could self-select vocabulary and foster their own learning experiences in texts that they had selected to read. Noelle envisioned her students engaging in independent reading of informational and narrative texts for varied purposes, and simultaneously being able to autonomously (1) notice when they encountered an unfamiliar vocabulary word, (2) apply word-learning strategies where possible to problem-solve about unknown words, and (3) share their learning with classmates to promote peer-to-peer collaboration. In short, Noelle wanted to find vocabulary teaching practices that also promoted self-regulated learning among her students, a goal that she was able to flexibly pursue within the PL structures that the university faculty coordinated.

In what follows, we describe Noelle self-selecting focus articles from a digital repository and using a digital "Communication Link" to voice her PL needs. We also follow her engagement in a mix of digital and in-person reflective coaching sessions. Through digitally mediated coaching, Noelle had a voice in her own learning trajectory within the schoolwide focus on vocabulary–and ultimately extended learning autonomy to her students in the process.

Noelle had previously seen the benefits of promoting student-selected reading in her classroom, including fostering a shared culture of reading for pleasure and intellectual development. But often in adult learning situations like professional development workshops, readings and resources are predetermined and teachers' fidelity to these resources is measured. Noelle and her teacher–leader partner, Alexis, both suggested to the coaches that a resource collection—rather than a single required reading—would be more beneficial to fit the diversity of teaching needs across the faculty. Just as Noelle assumed that her students were individuals with diverse literacy needs, she also assumed that her colleagues would have similar PL needs. So, the coaches developed a digital resource repository full of curated professional articles and videos, sorted into categories such as "primary grades" and "intermediate grades," "special education and intervention specific." and others related to particular aspects of vocabulary learning (e.g., teaching context clues, read-alouds, rich language environments). Teachers thus had the freedom to access previously vetted research-based materials that were more specific to the particularities of their classroom instructional needs.

As a general education teacher with an inclusive classroom, Noelle was using elements of a reading workshop structure and shared reading practices, within which she was already explicitly teaching specific vocabulary words. She wanted professional resources that focused specifically on helping children develop their own word-learning strategies. Noelle was drawn to Baumann et al.'s (2007) "'Bumping into Spicy, Tasty Words That Catch Your Tongue': A Formative Experiment on Vocabulary Instruction." The article emphasized helping children to become lovers of word learning, describing the process of word awareness development in terms of letting students focus on words that resonated with them as individual readers and writers. The Baumann et al. article was highly aligned with Noelle's specific vision for her classroom, and she refined her own instruction using this article resource along with peer and coach collaborations. Whereas a purely face-to-face PL experience might not be feasibly individualized for all of the teachers in the school, the digital resource repository, curated and vetted by the university partners to ensure research-informed practices, placed the learning trajectory directly into the hands of the teachers and allowed them to converge and diverge as decision makers to meet their students' diverse needs.

Just like Noelle, the other teachers at the school used a wide variety of articles and resources from the digital repository (including several professional books) to inform their classroom vocabulary instruction from the outset of the PL. Whereas the sheer number of different resources could have complicated the university–school partnership, Noelle and her co-teacher-leader, Alexis, developed another digital tool—the "Communication Link"—at their disposal to navigate the complexities of individual teachers or grade levels using varied resources within the shared goal of vocabulary learning.

"Having a wide variety of resources was so beneficial for the teachers in our building. Not only did we have access to relevant evidence-based academic resources, but teachers could differentiate their own professional learning based on their individual needs. While our building was unified under one overarching goal, PLC groups could focus on a sub-goal or strategy that increased their efficacy in meeting the larger goal. As a result, more teachers were invested in professional learning because it was specific to their diverse needs. Additionally, more effective conversations took place within grade-level collaborations as well as within some cross-grade discussions, continuing to unify our building and build our toolbox of instructional strategies."—ALEXIS

Ideas Born in the "Communication Link"

Early on, Alexis and Noelle both shared the importance of being able to compile everyone's PL needs in a single location. At first, their desire seemed fueled by accountability, as in wanting all of the PLCs to document their work on a common forum to ensure they were engaging in the process. From a coaching perspective, however, the university partners' interest in a common forum was about the immediacy of interaction and possibilities for responsiveness to teachers' needs. Previous research (Achinstein & Ogawa, 2006; Bushnell, 2003; Cochran-Smith & Lytle, 2006) has shown that demands for teachers to follow professional development mandates with fidelity might backfire and undermine their willingness to participate fully in a PL context. As such, the coaches saw a forum—herein referred to as the Communication Link (see Figure 9.2)—instead as a possibility for building fast and functional relationships with willing teachers through individualized, timely, and ongoing discussion when they were not present at the school, while also being continuously available for more hesitant teachers to engage with when they were ready.

The language of Communication Link came from Alexis, who had established herself on the ELA team as the notetaker and keeper of the ELA team's Google Drive. The faculty at the school had already been using a Google Drive and shared documents for notetaking during meetings. Based on this history, Alexis suggested, and then nearly instantaneously created, a Google document with bookmarks for each PLC and specialist group. Whereas the original intention of this Communication Link was to be a place where PLCs record the specific vocabulary articles they were reading and report their use of new strategies in the classroom, the e-document quickly evolved into a forum through which engaged teachers could make requests of us as coaches, ask questions about instruction, and otherwise present their classroom needs to help themselves grow.

Importantly, Alexis and Noelle provided the space and flexibility for this evolution in the Communication Link and came to see it as a useful place in which teachers experiencing success with the PD were leaving traces of their work, by which other teachers could be potentially inspired. For example, Alexis and her fourth-grade teaching partner, Ellen (pseudonym), set a goal of creating common formative and summative English language arts assessments that would be better aligned to their standards while meeting both the rigor and developmental needs of their students. Ellen provided context to the university faculty for upcoming classroom observations in her and Alexis's classrooms, and she posed a question for the university coaches to consider as they prepared to meet them (see Figure 9.3). Through use of the Communication Link, they were able to converse with the university coaches, asking questions and providing examples at their own pace during the interim periods when the coaches

RETURN TO TOP

PLC Communication Links

Directions: Once every cycle—visit this document to give us feedback. What are you doing next? How is it going? How can we help?

Kindergarten	First Grade	Second Grade
Third Grade	Fourth Grade	Fifth Grade
AMPE	Specialists (SPED, Tutors, ESL)	Preschool

FIGURE 9.2. Communication Link.

> As Alexis described below we are working on author's viewpoint/perspective, utilizing evidence and reasoning, and doing so with informative and narrative texts during whole group. My small groups are also working on this with the exception that texts are chosen based on their reading ability (which I don't always think is the correct way to group students in small group).
>
> You will be observing me teach two small groups (15 minutes each). Transferring the idea above to small group, we will be looking at a small section of an article to determine the words/phrases that help us to understand the text as a whole. We will also be determining words that convey the key ideas and what they might mean. This is something we discussed earlier as a fifth grade. My intention is to guide them in identifying words or phrases from the text that convey the author's viewpoint and determining what they mean and why the author used them.
>
> Questions I have—Teaching the author's viewpoint connects to so many other conceptual ideas and strategies that can be used to understand what you are reading. This can include using context as a clue to the meaning of words and phrases the author is using to describe things, determining the text structure and why the author chose to use that type of structure to convey their message, interpreting figurative language used in the text, etc. What strategies can you recommend so I can guide them in connecting and using multiple strategies to better understand nonfiction texts at a deeper level?

FIGURE 9.3. A Communication Link post to the university coaches about upcoming coaching.

were not present at the school. These documentations in the Communication Link were embedded into their weekly PLC agendas, and they provided a written record of thinking about their assessments that could be referred back to as often as needed. Thus, true to a PLC structure, the written interactions between the teachers and coaches were relevant, ongoing, and continually improving the teachers' practice.

As these coaching conversations in the Communication Link continued, Alexis and Ellen drew on various articles in the digital resource repository. As they read and discussed articles during their PLC meetings, and then shared questions and insights with the coaches via the Communication Link, their understandings about literacy assessment morphed into application and refinement of how assessment data were captured in their classrooms. These applications (and the e-communications that occurred) then enabled in-person and Zoom coaching conversations that occurred to be focused and efficient because the background understanding of the instructional needs had already been built.

Also in the Communication Link, Noelle began to document her PLC's interactions with the Baumann et al. (2007) article and their desire to watch some modeled teaching around drawing students' attention to "spicy" words in read-alouds. Noelle and her teammates wrote a note requesting modeled teaching for the next in-person PL day with the university coaches, as well as an invitation to watch some of the partner PLC teachers in the second- to third-grade loop as they taught vocabulary lessons. Yet, the coaches also learned from just a few entries on the Communication Link that each PLC had different vocabulary interests, different classroom structures, different pedagogical goals for vocabulary instruction, and different desires regarding what the coaching could "look" like. Noelle, for example, wanted to watch what she termed "expert" modeled teaching before she felt comfortable having her own teaching observed, but her partner teacher, Natalie (pseudonym), wanted to engage in observation-feedback coaching right away. Both had shared the experience of learning about "spicy" words and developing children's awareness of words and language, but the ways they asked for further coaching support in the Communication Link were different based on their individual experiences with teaching vocabulary.

Because the Communication Link existed as an asynchronous space for teachers to inform the coaches and each other of what they wanted and needed from the coaching relationship, it became a tool for easy individualization and informal gathering of information about the personalities and learning styles of the teachers at the school. As mentioned previously, Noelle seemed to be a step-by-step learner—she wanted to digest research, watch new teaching occur, try out and perfect strategies in her classroom alone, and only then invite coach observation of classroom teaching. Natalie, meanwhile, wanted coaching on her teaching from the outset, alongside modeled teaching. Alexis, the school's co-teacher-leader, on the other hand, never requested modeled teaching at all. Alexis and her partner, Ellen, wanted to have collaborative co-planning conversations grounding vocabulary instruction in content-area and discussion-based teaching, as opposed to observation-feedback coaching. The Communication Link made these differences possible and gave coaches the space to tailor coaching days in ways that could reasonably meet these multiple requests from the teachers.

Whereas professional development and coaching literature touts the importance of teacher reflectivity, this has primarily been documented in the context of face-to-face coaching interactions, including observation-feedback cycles (e.g., Peterson et al., 2009). In these face-to-face meetings, reflectivity is often a built expectation (and essential process) of the coaching cycle, perhaps as opposed to teacher reflectivity that is spontaneous and immediate as a routine practice for teachers. The teachers' use of the Communication Link seemed to digitally bypass the need for them to perform reflectivity on demand because they were in a face-to-face coaching interaction, and to engage more routinely in reflection-on-action (Schön, 1987) related to their individual (or team) problems of practice.

> "We were fully immersed in this professional learning, in part because of how customizable it was. We had voice and choice in what we would read, discuss, and implement in our classrooms . . . something we know is best for our students, but is rarely offered to adult learners. Then something quite amazing happened. *As PLC's shared articles they were excited about in the Communication Link and also in faculty meetings, it created a buzz.* PLCs started overlapping in what we were learning about and trying in our classrooms and ideas and strategies spread like wildfire across our school."—NOELLE

Moreover, the rurality of the school meant that the university coaches were not able to engage in the level of face-to-face literacy coaching that would be possible across shorter distances. Consequently, when there were coaching days at the school, the coaches really had to make them count. The agenda for in-person coaching days was co-planned with the school's leadership team via Zoom video-conference meetings. Then, the Communication Link, as mentioned above, was a crucial digital tool for carefully individualizing in-person coaching activities to meet stated teacher and PLC needs, such as determining which teachers wanted to receive lesson observations from a coach, engage in reflective co-planning, or other coach-teacher activities.

As such, the Communication Link also served to tailor in-person coaching by acting as a shared intertextual history (Cairney, 1992) upon which both coaches and teachers could draw when discussing the impact of the PL and resultant instructional change—such as tracking a PLC's evolution from simply discussing a new strategy from an article to watching a coach teach with the new strategy to the teachers implementing and sustaining the practice themselves, all captured in the Communication Link entries. Finally, monthly Zoom video-conference meetings between the university coaches and school's leadership team provided space to debrief the in-person coaching sessions and share successes across grade-level and specialist (e.g., special education, Title I) teaching contexts.

As coaches who were external to the school context, the digital communications that occurred through the Communication Link enabled in-person coaching days with the PLCs that were highly focused. Coaches had a good sense of the background knowledge that teachers had developed through their self-selected articles, as well as a wealth of information about their individual classroom contexts, units of study, focal standards, and other data pieces that could inform the coaching discussions. This provided useful grounding language between the coach and teacher, such as the common vocabulary of "spicy" words from the Baumann et al. (2007) article. With this background, the coaches did not have to spend valuable coaching time acquiring this extra information about why the teachers had done what they had done before co-reflecting on and co-planning next steps. The Communication Link provided a digital way for teachers to share their instructional and personal goals before the coaching, allowing us the preparatory time to hone our coaching toward individual teacher needs.

Noelle, for instance, was following a trajectory toward greater and greater student autonomy in self-selecting words for study and discussion during shared reading and student-selected reading events. The coaches knew that she had already deeply explored word consciousness on her own and with her students, and that she was now using the digital resource repository to locate vocabulary strategies that would graduate her students to more self-directed word-learning experiences. Thus, as Noelle's autonomous desire to try out the Graffiti Wall strategy (Gallagher & Anderson, 2017) emerged, so did her willingness for a coach to observe her vocabulary instruction to support her intentional decisions.

Meanwhile, Alexis and her teaching partner engaged less with practitioner articles about specific vocabulary strategies and sought more "big picture" discussions of what vocabulary teaching could look like in the context of larger content-based reading and writing units. Consequently, Alexis's and Ellen's coaching sessions looked markedly different from those of other teachers, as did their interactions with the Communication Link and the digital resource repository. These teachers requested sessions of reflective co-planning to discuss how specific vocabulary practices could inform other instruction, such as pre-teaching words to support students' informational text comprehension and using keywords repeatedly across a content-area unit to consistently reinforce students' knowledge development. Rather than focusing on single lessons with single strategies, Alexis and Ellen wanted more globalized, curriculum-driven support in embedding vocabulary learning into other literacy instruction.

Although the paths the teachers took in developing their vocabulary instructional skills were divergent, the Communication Link allowed invaluable insights into individual teachers' learning trajectories, needs, and successes. Although the face-to-face coaching was limited by distance, the level of responsivity we could provide was facilitated by the teachers' unique interactions on the Communication Link. Here, the teachers-as-learners at the school left clear digital footprints for the coaches to follow, leading to a coaching relationship that was healthy, successful, and sustainable for all.

> "Teachers, just like our students, have a variety of learning needs. Because the coaches were willing to mold and adapt to the different learning styles of each team and/or teacher, we were able to have more individualized conversations and targeted approaches to learning. It made all the difference in the world pertaining to our learning. It created a sense of trust and an ability to ask any questions that we had without fear or hesitation, whether written or in person. Thus, deepening the conversations and the overall learning. I am so thankful that the coaches took the time to personalize the coaching based on our communication needs."—ALEXIS

Roadblocks and Recommendations

The obstacles Alexis and Noelle faced on this PL journey with their school can be broadly grouped into two categories: relational roadblocks and structural roadblocks. The relational roadblocks are those difficulties that arise from the interpersonal human elements of literacy coaching and teacher development, while the structural are the complications from adapting technological (e.g., regular use of the Communication Link) and organizational infrastructures (e.g., scheduling coaching interactions and debriefs) to meet new PL needs. These challenges also match their unstated roles as co-teacher-leaders. Noelle conducted much of the inter-teacher communication and "checking in" among grade levels throughout the PL process and encountered obstacles that dealt mostly with these interpersonal issues (e.g., varying levels of timeliness with PLCs updating their grade-level sections in the Communication Link), though technological learning was also a factor. Meanwhile, Alexis managed much of the technological infrastructure (remember: she was the source of the Communication Link idea), and her challenges centered on the organizational. Taken together, the following roadblocks and related recommendations further demonstrate that while sustained literacy coaching is undoubtedly a major organizational undertaking, it is also doable for teacher-driven PL.

Relational Roadblocks and Recommendations

Because daily interactions and learning contexts are complex and may take unexpected paths, Noelle grappled with having to adjust her expectations for herself, her PLC, and her other teacher colleagues as they set their PL goals. Initially, PLCs had agreed to a monthly cycle of reading new research articles about vocabulary practices and implementing strategies in the classroom, a timeframe that the groups ultimately found to be unrealistic. The idea of new articles each month was quickly replaced with letting the PLCs flexibly decide how long they wanted to try and discuss new strategies from a single article before deciding to add on new readings. Consequently, the grade levels read a variable number of articles and tried new classroom techniques on separate schedules that matched the needs of the teachers. Noelle suggested that this early adjustment—from expecting uniformity to allowing for autonomy—helped teachers to individually manage their workloads and engage with the PL process within their work balance comfort zones. She acknowledged that her willingness to "scale back," revise, or completely change goals to fit teacher needs was an important leadership move. Iterative reflection on how the PL processes were unfolding was essential. The Communication Link, as well as debriefings that occurred during ELA Goal Team meetings and faculty meetings, were paramount in gauging the PL dispositions of different teacher teams, providing consistent data about realistic pacing for reading new articles, trying new strategies, and reporting interim outcomes.

Relatedly, Noelle was challenged by what she described as "keeping on all the grade levels and interventionists to make sure they were completing work and updating our communication links in a timely manner." Noelle had previously described the initial PL goals as "overambitious," and perhaps this manifested in her experience of having to frequently check in on her different colleagues to ensure they were engaging with the process. Whereas the university coaches envisioned PL and coaching as things that the teachers were actively seeking out, Noelle also had the experience of implementing systems of accountability and the nuanced ways that teachers were engaged (or sometimes not) in the work. These were relational complexities that were a challenge to navigate as both a colleague and a leader; complexities that she tackled by remaining in close contact with each PLC to keep the Communication Link updated, meeting consistently with the ELA Goal Team to receive updates from the grade level representatives, and helping to conduct monthly faculty meetings where verbal updates on professional development progress were expected. She pointed to the benefits of having grade-level representatives on the ELA Goal Team; the representatives were able to communicate between the leadership and the PLCs, leading to better understanding of what was working for the teachers and what were roadblocks to participation (such as the intensity of the initial timeline). This helped to minimize Noelle's responsibility for "ensuring" participation and let the teachers see that there was room for adjustment and reflection in the PL processes.

With all this in mind, we offer the following relational recommendations for facilitating productive PL:

- Use commonly accessible digital structures to facilitate communication and collaboration among teacher teams (e.g., the Communication Link).
- Employ teacher leadership to distribute responsibility across the school, as well as create a trusting environment for all teachers to communicate about PL needs.
- Develop routines and practices that lead to accountability for PL participation (e.g., the Communication Link, monthly faculty meetings).
- Demonstrate willingness to allow teachers to engage autonomously in PL within a specific schoolwide vision (e.g., digital repository of resources related to a common goal, from which teachers self-select learning options).

Structural Roadblocks and Recommendations

The digital platforms used in this work ultimately added to teachers' ability to shape their PL experiences, but the technology itself was not without its own difficulties. This work was conducted pre-COVID, and while the state's rurality necessitated frequent use of Zoom, Google Drive, and other tech-based collaboration tools for university members, these digital mediums were still new for the teachers as a means of accessing PL. Alexis pointed out that while teachers' familiarity and comfort with tech-based teaching and learning have obviously changed dramatically since the pandemic emerged, it would have been beneficial for the university coaches to provide some initial technological training with Zoom, in particular, to help ease its use from month to month. In short, though the world is a digital one, the PL partners and school leaders should not assume that a digital tool is already well known by all participants and spending some preliminary time co-developing some participatory tech skills can ease everyone's (i.e., teachers and coaches) experience with these hybrid coaching cycles.

Surprisingly for the coaches, Alexis also said that information access would be an ongoing problem for the school. Given the Digital Resource Repository the coaches compiled and the amount of freedom teachers had to select their PL materials, the coaches had not fully predicted that access to online resources might be problematic. Yet, Alexis experienced two related difficulties. On the one hand, some teachers found themselves overwhelmed by the sheer volume of resources made available in the Digital Resource Repository and were unsure of where to start. While the university coaches perceived that many teachers had quickly selected their focus articles and asked for related coaching and modeled teaching, there were other teachers who were stymied by the freedom of choice and required more guidance about where to begin. This suggests that initial coaching simply about a good place to start would have been helpful to some teachers, such as conducting an observation of that teacher's existing vocabulary practices and then selecting an article for that teacher specifically related to practices already in place. The choice that the coaches perceived as a positive attribute of the work as coaches was actually a structural roadblock for some of the teachers, pointing back to the never-ending need to monitor the PL progress and adjust accordingly to increase comfortable participation.

On the other hand, though, Alexis also noted that ongoing access to research-based resources has historically been limited for the teachers and that it was problematic that the teachers had to rely on their PL relationship with the university members to access literacy research articles. The only other options for access to recent research of the variety that the coaches used for this project are paid subscriptions and memberships at the school or district level. This presents a lingering roadblock that it will be critical for the educational community to address. Who is really able to access and consume the most recent practice-based research? Is it reliably making it into the hands of teachers seeking professional growth? How much is it to fund a structural roadblock that is perpetuating inequality in teacher growth, and therefore in student experiences? This roadblock, in particular, is one without an easy, actionable response.

With all this in mind, the following are a few structural recommendations for facilitating productive PL and coaching:

- Provide PL opportunities related to productive technology use (e.g., technology shares, IT presentations, demonstrations).
- Provide coaching and support to teachers around the meta-practices of self-directed PL (e.g., how to quickly analyze an article's relevance, read for meaning, apply to the classroom context, and assess interim outcomes).
- For university-based coaches, continuously advocate for research dissemination and translation practices that do not inequitably exclude teachers and schools from accessing critical content in a cost-effective, timely manner (e.g., open-source articles, research-to-practice writings, public blogging, webinars, and other digital outreach methods).

As stated at the outset of this chapter, digital tools have created a new era of teacher coaching possibilities. Despite research noting that geographic location and financial resources of rural communities could pose barriers to fully realizing the potential of digital tools for PL (e.g., Stelmach, 2011), these coaching interactions used a combination of in-person meetings and digital tools, from Zoom meetings and a cloud-based repository of resources to a Google document "Communication Link" and email, allowing for maximum flexibility and responsiveness to teachers' needs. Through experiences like these, coaches and teachers can broaden and deepen their PL experiences in ways that provide equitable access for teachers across varying school contexts, and sustainable opportunities for more frequent coach–teacher interaction among the hustle and bustle of life in schools. Like any new pedagogical practice or tool at coaches' or teachers' disposal, though, the use of these digital technologies for ongoing learning is not as simple as providing access; it requires intentional planning and continual reflection on how the digital tools are extending the learning experiences in ways that would not be realized otherwise.

REFERENCES

Achinstein, B., & Ogawa, R. T. (2006). (In)fidelity: What the resistance of new teachers reveals about professional principles and prescriptive educational policies. *Harvard Educational Review, 76*(1), 30–63.

Au, K. H., Raphael, T. E., & Mooney, K. (2008). Improving reading achievement in elementary schools: Guiding change in a time of standards. In S. B. Wepner & D. S. Strickland (Eds.), *Supervision of reading programs* (4th ed., pp. 71–89). Teachers College Press.

Bandura, A. (2001). Social cognitive theory: An agentic perspective. *Annual Review of Psychology, 52,* 1–26.

Baumann, J. F., Ware, D., & Edwards, E. C. (2007). "Bumping into spicy, tasty words that catch your tongue": A formative experiment on vocabulary instruction. *The Reading Teacher, 61,* 108–122.

Bean, R. M., Draper, J. A., Hall, V., Vandermolen, J., & Zigmond, N. (2010). Coaches and coaching in Reading First schools: A reality check. *The Elementary School Journal, 111,* 87–114.

Biancarosa, G., Bryk, A., & Dexter, E. (2010). Assessing the value-added effects of literacy collaborative professional development on student achievement. *Elementary School Journal, 111,* 7–34.

Bushnell, M. (2003). Teachers in the schoolhouse panopticon: Complicity and resistance. *Education and Urban Society, 35*(3), 251–272.

Cairney, T. H. (1992). Fostering and building students' intertextual histories. *Language Arts, 69*(7), 502–507.

Coburn, C. E., & Woulfin, S. L. (2012). Reading coaches and the relationship between policy and practice. *Reading Research Quarterly, 47,* 5–30.

Cochran-Smith, M., & Lytle, S. L. (2006). Troubling images of teaching in No Child Left Behind. *Harvard Educational Review, 76*(4), 668–726.

Deci, E. L., & Ryan, R. M. (1995). Human autonomy: The basis of true self-esteem.

In M. Kemmis (Ed.), *Efficacy, agency, and self-esteem* (pp. 31–49). Plenum Press.

Dieker, L. A., Hynes, M. C., Hughes, C. E., Hardin, S., & Becht, K. (2015). TLE TeachLivE: Using technology to provide quality professional development in rural schools. *Rural Special Education Quarterly, 34*(3), 11–16.

Elish-Piper, L., & L'Allier, S. K. (2010). Exploring the relationship between literacy coaching and student reading achievement in grades K–1. *Literacy Research and Instruction, 49,* 162–174.

Gallagher, M. A., & Anderson, B. E. (2016). Get all "jazzed up" for vocabulary instruction: Strategies that engage. *The Reading Teacher, 70,* 273–282.

Glover, T. A. (2017). A data-driven coaching model used to promote students' response to early reading intervention. *Theory Into Practice, 56,* 13–20.

Graves, M. F. (2016). *The vocabulary book: Learning and instruction* (2nd ed.). Teachers College Press.

Harn, B. A., Chard, D. J., Biancarosa, G., & Kame'enui, E. J. (2011). Coordinating instructional supports to accelerate at-risk first-grade readers' performance: An essential mechanism for effective RTI. *The Elementary School Journal, 112*(2), 332–355.

Knowles, M. (1984). *The adult learner: The neglected species.* Gulf Publishing.

Kraft, M. A., Blazar, D., & Hogan, D. (2018). The effect of teacher coaching on instruction and achievement: A meta-analysis of the causal evidence. *Review of Educational Research, 88,* 1–42.

Kurz, A., Reddy, L. A., & Glover, T. A. (2017). A multidisciplinary framework of instructional coaching. *Theory Into Practice, 56,* 66–77.

Leighton, C. M., Ford-Connors, E., Robertson, D. A., Wyatt, J., Wagner, C. J., Proctor, C. P., & Paratore, J. R. (2018). "Let's FaceTime tonight": Using digital tools to enhance coaching. *The Reading Teacher, 72*(1), 39–49.

Main, S., & Slater, E. (2022). Online continuous professional learning: A model for improving reading outcomes in regional and remote schools? *Journal of Teacher Education, 73*(2), 201–214.

Matsumura, L. C., Correnti, R., Walsh, M., Bickel, D. D., & Zook-Howell, D. (2019). Online content-focused coaching to improve classroom discussion quality. *Technology, Pedagogy, and Education, 28,* 191–215.

Matsumura, L. C., Garnier, H. E., Correnti, R., Junker, B., & Bickel, D. D. (2010). Investigating the effectiveness of a comprehensive literacy coaching program in schools with high teacher mobility. *The Elementary School Journal, 111,* 35–62.

Matsumura, L. C., Garnier, H. E., & Spybrook, J. (2013). Literacy coaching to improve student reading achievement: A multi-level mediation model. *Learning and Instruction, 25,* 35–48.

Neuman, S. B., & Wright, T. S. (2010). Promoting language and literacy development for early childhood educators: A mixed-methods study of coursework and coaching. *The Elementary School Journal, 111*(1), 63–86.

Ossa-Parra, M., Wagner, C., Proctor, C. P., Leighton, C., Robertson, D. A., Paratore, J. R., & Ford-Connors, E. (2016). Dialogic reasoning: Supporting emergent bilingual students' language and literacy development. In C. P. Proctor, A. Boardman, & E. Hiebert (Eds.), *Teaching emergent bilingual students: Flexible approaches in an era of new standards* (pp. 119–137). Guilford Press.

Peterson, D. S., Taylor, B. M., Burnham, B., & Schock, R. (2009). Reflective coaching conversations: A missing piece. *The Reading Teacher, 62*(6), 500–509.

Pianta, R. C., Mashburn, A. J., Downer, J. T., Hamre, B. K., & Justice, L. (2008). Effects of web-mediated professional development resources on teacher–child interactions in pre-kindergarten classrooms. *Early Childhood Research Quarterly, 23*(4), 431–451.

Powell, D. R., & Diamond, K. E. (2013). Implementation fidelity of a coaching-based professional development program for improving head start teachers' literacy and language instruction. *Journal of Early Intervention, 35*(2), 102–128.

Robertson, D. A., Ford-Connors, E., Frahm, T., Bock, K., & Paratore, J. R. (2020). Unpacking productive coaching interactions: Identifying coaching approaches that supports instructional uptake. *Professional Development in Education, 46*(3), 405–423.

Robertson, D. A., Padesky, L., & Brock, C. H. (2019). Cultivating student agency through teacher professional development. *Theory Into Practice, 59,* 192–201.

Robertson, D. A., Padesky, L. B., Ford-Connors, E., & Paratore, J. R. (2020). What does it mean to say coaching is relational? *Journal of Literacy Research, 52,* 55–78.

Sailors, M., & Price, L. R. (2010). Professional development that supports the teaching of cognitive reading strategy instruction. *The Elementary School Journal, 110*(3), 301–322.

Sailors, M., & Price, L. (2015). Support for the Improvement of Practices through Intensive Coaching (SPIC): A model of coaching for improving reading instruction and reading achievement. *Teaching and Teacher Education, 45,* 115–127.

Sawchuk, S. (2013). For rural teachers, support is a click away. *Education Week, 33*(2), 8–9.

Schön, D. A. (1987). *Educating the reflective practitioner: Toward a new design for teaching and learning in the professions.* Jossey-Bass.

Smith, S. J., & Israel, M. (2010). E-mentoring: Enhancing special education teacher induction. *Journal of Special Education Leadership, 23*(1), 30–40.

Stelmach, B. L. (2011). A synthesis of international rural education issues and responses. *Rural Educator, 32*(2), 32–42.

Teemant, A. (2014). A mixed-methods investigation of instructional coaching for teachers of diverse learners. *Urban Education, 49,* 574–604.

Toll, C. A. (2017). A problem-solving model for literacy coaching practice. *The Reading Teacher, 70*(4), 413–421.

Tomassini, J. (2013). Teachers seek specialized peer networks. *Education Week, 32*(15), 1–19.

Tripp, T. R., & Rich, P. J. (2012). The influence of video analysis on the process of teacher change. *Teaching and Teacher Education, 28*(5), 728–739.

Vaughn, M., & Faircloth, B. (2013). Teaching with a purpose in mind: Cultivating a vision. *Professional Educator, 37*(2), 1–12.

Vernon-Feagans, L., Bratsch-Hines, M., Varghese, C., Bean, A., & Hedrick, A. (2015). The targeted reading intervention: Face-to-face vs. Webcam literacy coaching of classroom teachers. *Learning Disabilities Research and Practice, 30*(3), 135–147. Retrieved from *www.learntechlib.org/p/158845.*

Vernon-Feagans, L., Kainz, K., Hedrick, A., Ginsberg, M., & Amendum, S. (2013). Live webcam coaching to help early elementary classroom teachers provide effective literacy instruction for struggling readers: The targeted reading intervention. *Journal of Educational Psychology, 105*(4), 1175–1187.

Walpole, S., McKenna, M. C., Uribe-Zarain, X., & Lamitina, D. (2010). The relationships between coaching and instruction in the primary grades: Evidence from high-poverty schools. *The Elementary School Journal, 111,* 115–140.

Westheimer, J. (2008). Learning among colleagues: Teacher community and the shared enterprise of education. In M. Cochran-Smith, S. Feiman-Nemser, D. J. McIntyre, & K. E. Demers (Eds.), *Handbook of research on teacher education: Enduring questions in changing contexts* (3rd ed., pp. 756–783). Routledge.

Wilkinson, I. A. G., Reninger, K. B., & Soter, A. O. (2010). Developing a professional development tool for assessing quality talk about text. In R. T. Jimenez, V. J. Risko, M. K. Hundley, & D. W. Rowe (Eds.), *59th Yearbook of the National Reading Conference* (pp. 135–153). National Reading Conference.

Wonder-McDowell, C., Reutzel, D. R., & Smith, J. A. (2011). Does instructional alignment matter?: Effects on struggling second graders' reading achievement. *The Elementary School Journal, 112*(2), 259–279.

CHAPTER 10

Innovations in Elementary Literacy Coaching

Sustaining Coaching Practices in Virtual Spaces

Jacy Ippolito, Rita M. Bean, and Kristine Sacha

Watch a related video from the authors at this link.

The Widescale Shift to Virtual Coaching in 2020

In the United States and around the world, the year 2020 will be forever connected to the global COVID-19 pandemic. In the field of education, and within the larger chronicled history of literacy coaching as a form of job-embedded literacy professional learning (PL) in the United States, the year 2020 will also surely be seen as marking a milestone. While literacy coaches certainly engaged in work with teachers virtually before the year 2020 (Affinito, 2018; Leighton et al., 2018), the global pandemic that swept across the United States in the winter and spring of 2020 suddenly plunged most teachers into virtual teaching and a majority of literacy coaches into the new territory of primarily coaching via computer.

Thus, a natural experiment began in elementary schools across the United States: coaches and literacy leaders suddenly were being asked to support teachers' PL in synchronous and asynchronous modalities using tools that were new to many, if not most, coaches and teachers alike. The in-person coaching that had become the standard operating procedure in so many schools since the Reading First widespread adoption of coaching—the hallway conversations, coaching on the fly, in-depth coaching cycles, small- and large-group PL sessions—all were swept away as schools shut their doors to in-person teaching and learning. In many ways, 2020 marked the beginning of a new era in coaching and literacy PL.

As researchers (Jacy and Rita) and district coaching leaders (Kristi), each of us remained in constant communication with coaches throughout the rise and progression of the pandemic. We three came together and quickly bonded over several simple, but powerful, questions related to this large-scale shift in elementary literacy coaching work:

- What did coaching look like *now*, after shifting to primarily virtual work?
- How were coaches operating similarly or differently from before the pandemic?
- Which new virtual coaching routines and practices were developed?
- In talking with coaches across states, what could we learn and share with others about the potential and the pitfalls of elementary virtual literacy coaching?
- What implications emerged for coaching in the near and distant future?

This chapter provides a glimpse of our collective lessons learned as we sought answers to these questions. The lessons learned shared in this chapter are drawn from an extended case study of the shift to virtual coaching in Akron, Ohio (home to 36 instructional coaches across 43 schools) and from an ongoing study of virtual coaching work across four states, each of which has invested heavily in coaching over time: Florida, Massachusetts, Ohio, and Pennsylvania. Mining these sources for answers to our broad questions, we discovered several ways in which the virtual coaching conducted in 2020 and 2021 illustrates digital and collaborative innovations in literacy PL. We hope that by sharing some of what we learned during the pandemic, we might foster further research and innovations in virtual literacy coaching well after the pandemic is a distant memory.

Virtual coaching was by no means born in 2020; and yet, we would argue that 2020 marks the year that virtual coaching took rapid, unsteady steps into toddlerhood. Elementary schools across the country widely (though perhaps reluctantly) adopted overnight new ways of coaching via Zoom, Google Meet, Sibme, and countless other online tools. And much like the transformation of an infant into a toddler, the results have been messy, exhilarating, and rich with conjecture about what the future will bring. Thus, this chapter serves as a first glimpse of some of the resulting PL innovations, successes, and challenges that arose from that sudden shift to virtual coaching—as communicated by coaches and coaching leaders themselves. The resulting implications are many, for both continued virtual coaching now and well into the future. However, before describing our findings and looking ahead to future implications, let us begin by briefly outlining some of the ways in which coaching has risen to prominence as a critical PL mechanism in U.S. elementary schools. By first looking back, we begin to see the origins of and bedrock upon which current and future elementary virtual coaching is being built.

A Brief History of Coaching as a Critical PL Mechanism

The Rise of Elementary Literacy Coaching

Literacy coaching in the United States has grown, shifted, and thrived for almost 50 years as a job-embedded PL mechanism supporting literacy teaching and learning in the elementary grades. Coaching is often cited in large-scale PL research and policy documents as one of the most effective forms of job-embedded PL available to teachers (Darling-Hammond, Hyler, et al., 2017; Darling-Hammond, Wei, et al., 2009; International Literacy Association [ILA], 2018). Yet, over time, what researchers, policymakers, and educators mean when they say "coaching" has shifted a great deal.

Coaching has evolved dramatically over the decades. It has grown from early peer coaching models forged out of the collaborative teacher-led PL experiments of the 1970s and 1980s (Joyce & Showers, 1996); to cognitive coaching models in the 1980s focused on professional coaches developing teachers' reflective capacities about practice (Costa & Garmston, 2002; Garmston et al., 1993); to the widespread adoption of content and curricular coaching associated with Reading First federal funding in the 1990s (Bean et al., 2010; Deussen et al., 2007); and finally, to myriad differentiated models focused on standards-based and reform-oriented coaching in the 2000s (McKenna & Walpole, 2008; Walpole & McKenna, 2012). Emerging out of this rich history, virtual coaching work only began to appear in dribs and drabs in the research and practice literature over the past two decades, starting around the late-2000s and gaining more prominence in the past several years.

Across these decades, however, three major areas have remained the primary foci of research into literacy coaching: the shifting roles and responsibilities of coaches; the relationships and structures needed to support coaching work (e.g., coach–teacher relationships, coach–principal relationships, social networks in schools); and the efficacy of coaching in terms of improving teaching and learning outcomes. Research in each of these areas has broadly shaped how we have come to understand coaching today. Moreover, this body of work is now also forming the basis for what we are beginning to understand about the possibilities and pitfalls of virtual coaching work. Therefore, we review each area briefly.

Three Intertwined Bodies of Coaching Literature

Roles and responsibilities have been a perennial area of interest and investigation in part because what "coaching" means to educators has traditionally varied according to context. Researchers and practitioners have spent more than two decades attempting to describe and understand the essential underlying roles that coaches and specialized literacy professionals play in schools (Deussen et al., 2007; Galloway & Lesaux, 2014; Killion, 2009; Pletcher et al., 2019; Toll, 2007). Coaches' work has been described as sometimes tilting toward different audiences (e.g., "teacher-oriented," "student-oriented," or "data-oriented" [Deussen et al., 2007, p. 4]); focusing on identities the coach may shift between as they go about their work (e.g., operating as a "data coach," a "resource provider," a "mentor," or even a "catalyst for change" [Killion, 2009, pp. 10–13]); and balancing many and varied responsibilities within a single day or week (e.g., "stick[ing] to a schedule while remaining flexible," "hold[ing] brief but effective coaching conversations," "seek[ing] support from administration . . . " and more [Pletcher et al., 2019]).

The roles and responsibilities literature has been incredibly helpful in providing researchers, policymakers, and educators insight into the wide array of roles and responsibilities that coaches undertake. In practice, it helps district and school administrators support coaches as they don different caps across their days and weeks, shifting roles and responsibilities in response to teacher and school needs. This literature has also helped us collectively understand some of the reasons why coaching may not always be as effective as we might like, in part because coaches can sometimes be nudged by external forces into playing administrative or clerical roles that are less effective in supporting teachers' shifts in practice (Smith, 2007). As we turned our attention to virtual coaching, we were curious to understand if and how coaching through primarily virtual modalities solidified or shifted coaches' roles and responsibilities.

The second body of literature critical to understanding elementary literacy coaching centers around the relational nature of coaching and how important it is for coaches to forge and maintain strong relationships with teachers, principals, and other community members such as specialists and parents. This body of literature is characterized by studies of how coaches negotiate their relationships with teachers (Ippolito, 2010; Rainville & Jones, 2008; Robertson et al., 2020). Most recently, Robertson et al. reviewed a great deal of this relational literature and neatly concluded that the power of coaching work is to be found in the co-construction of knowledge and expertise, in the "dialogic flow between coach and teacher that assumes equity in knowledge, experience, and emotional exchange" (Robertson et al., 2020, p. 64). This relational literature suggests that coaching is a complex social endeavor and that the improvement of teaching and learning rests in part on coaches' relational skills and abilities to forge strong partnerships with teachers. Moreover, this literature extends to coaches' relationships with principals and other school community members (Bean et al., 2018; Ippolito, 2009; Kral, 2007; Matsumura et al., 2009; Shanklin, 2007). The stronger the coach–principal relationship, and the more support that principals offer coaches in terms of fostering a schoolwide culture of coaching and collaboration (Ippolito & Bean, 2019), the more likely that coaching work will take root and flourish. Again, as we began to make sense of virtual coaching's possibilities and pitfalls, we were very curious to understand how coaching relationships were strengthened or stretched thin when communications shifted from classroom and hallway conversations to email, text, Zoom, Skype, or FaceTime interactions.

Which leads to the third and perhaps most important body of literature—research on the efficacy of coaching. One of the most important perennial questions about coaching is both the simplest to ask and the most difficult to answer: "Does coaching work?" Researchers have spent decades trying to answer the question of whether and to what extent coaching work delivers on its promise to shift teachers' practices and improve literacy outcomes for students. While some large-scale studies have found modest gains for students and teachers as the result of coaching work (Biancarosa et al., 2010; Marsh et al., 2008), a recent meta-analysis of the efficacy literature paints a dramatic and complex picture. Kraft et al. (2018) suggest that small-scale coaching work can indeed have a positive effect for teachers and students; however, when scaled up, the effects of coaching seem to diminish. This raises important questions about the complex, relational nature of coaching and scalability: Should we continue to invest in coaching models within large districts or even at the state level? Is it better to let each school district determine its own coaching model, within certain parameters? These and more questions were raised as we began to consider the possible efficacy of coaching in virtual modalities, and the number of schools and teachers whom coaches could reasonably reach via virtual work.

These three bodies of literature—respectively focused on coaching roles and responsibilities, relationships, and efficacy—became critical anchors for our thinking as we turned our attention to the nature of virtual coaching and the innovative work that has emerged over the past decade and now most recently in response to the COVID-19 pandemic.

Questions about coaches' shifting roles and responsibilities, the nature and strength of their relationships with teachers and administrators, and the efficacy and outcomes of their work were all thrown into sharp relief when we considered them in the context of virtual coaching.

Early Understandings of Virtual Coaching

Upon the foundation of coaching literature built over the previous decades, research and practice articles and books detailing virtual coaching began to emerge around 2010. The virtual coaching research and practice literature has been limited, but the work that has emerged falls into roughly three categories: accounts of the use of video reflection and coaching as a professional development and teacher preparation tool; accounts of real-time coaching via technology (e.g., Skype, FaceTime, Bluetooth headsets); and studies comparing the efficacy of in-person to virtual coaching, especially as shifts to virtual coaching have become necessary due to geographical, budget, or (most recently) epidemiological constraints.

Research focusing primarily on the use of video as a reflection tool for coaching suggests that teachers' and coaches' joint attention on video footage of teachers' work helps teachers better understand their own practice and the shifts that may need to be made (Ortlieb et al., 2015; O'Shell, 2019). This body of literature has evolved most recently to also focus on the role that video reflection and virtual teaching and coaching opportunities can play in preparing preservice teachers for classroom work, especially during the 2020 pandemic (Keefe, 2020). Short practice-focused articles sharing tips and tricks for how coaches and teachers might use software such as Sibme to record, annotate, and analyze teaching lessons together also began to appear mid-pandemic in 2020 and 2021 (Blumke, 2021).

Meanwhile, other research has focused on the use of Skype, FaceTime, and other video communication software (Leighton et al., 2018; Rock, Gregg, et al., 2009; Rock, Schoenfeld, et al., 2013), as well as a wide variety of internet audio/visual tools and Bluetooth headsets, for coaches to provide real-time as well as asynchronous feedback to teachers about their instructional work. These studies often focus on case studies of coaches and teachers navigating virtual coaching work (Leighton et al., 2018) or on coaching in specific geographical regions (e.g., Eastern Caribbean countries) where the possibility of coaches traveling between schools is often limited (MacKinnon et al., 2019). A subset of these studies has begun to focus on the efficacy of such models. A notable example comes from South Africa, where findings suggest that virtual coaching was just as effective as in-person coaching after a 1-year study of a modified virtual coaching intervention (Kotze et al., 2019).

Most recently, as the year 2020 approached, literature on virtual coaching began to shift attention toward how coaches spend their time and their perceptions of efficacy within virtual coaching work (Oller, 2019). Relatedly, practice-related writing has simultaneously focused on ways in which teachers and coaches might utilize various digital tools to effectively communicate and facilitate deeper conversations about practice (Affinito, 2018; O'Shell, 2019). In many ways, the small but growing body of research and practice literature on virtual coaching is reminiscent of the three foundational areas of research in the larger body of coaching literature, alternately focusing on describing coaches' work (i.e., roles and responsibilities), relationships, and efficacy—with a large initial focus, understandably, on describing the work.

While the body of virtual coaching literature is small (especially compared to the larger body of coaching literature, which itself is quite small compared to other domains of literacy research such as vocabulary or comprehension instruction and intervention), the literature does raise important questions that relate to the three overarching categories of coaching research.

- How have virtual coaching innovations shaped coaches' roles and responsibilities in schools?
- What do coaches' relationships with teachers, administrators, and other community members look like in light of widespread virtual coaching innovations?
- Finally, and most importantly, in what ways is virtual coaching effective in shaping teachers' practices and improving outcomes for students?

These questions were at the forefront of our minds as we began our own investigation into the innovations, successes, and challenges in virtual coaching work across states that arose during the 2020–2021 COVID-19 pandemic.

Lessons Learned about Elementary Virtual Coaching during the COVID-19 Pandemic

Sources of Data and Learning

In order to investigate innovations, successes, and challenges related to pandemic-era elementary virtual coaching, we drew primarily on two sources of data. The first source was an extended case study of virtual coaching across Akron, Ohio. Akron is a large district serving over 21,000 students across 47 schools PreK–12. At the time of our investigation, the district employed over 36 instructional coaches with preparation in all curriculum areas, supported in the content areas by six district coaches who were specialists in English language arts, math, or science. Additionally, the school-based coaches were supported by Kristine (Kristi) Sacha who served as the district's Instructional Coach Liaison for over 5 years, both supporting the learning and development of the coaches and strengthening the district's coaching model. Akron is an example of a district that has invested heavily in coaching over time, and in virtual coaching work specifically, both before the pandemic (to a small extent) and during the pandemic (to a great extent). Thus, the Akron coaches, and Kristi as their district Coach Liaison, were able to reflect on their own lessons learned from their large-scale shift to virtual coaching—much of which is shared in the following sections.

Simultaneously, we launched a small cross-state virtual survey and focus group study in December 2020 to better understand elementary coaches' experiences of virtual coaching in states that have historically invested heavily in elementary coaching work. We reached out to key literacy leaders in districts and technical support units across Florida, Massachusetts, Ohio, and Pennsylvania for recommendations of elementary literacy coaches and invited those coaches to respond to a 21-question survey that gathered brief narrative written responses about their coaching experiences before the pandemic, during the early months of the pandemic (March–June 2020), and mid-pandemic (December 2020–January 2021). Twenty-seven coaches responded to the survey with narrative responses and were then invited to participate in one of three follow-up 90-minute virtual focus groups conducted via Zoom. The three groups were crafted such that coaches from across all four states were able to participate in each group, allowing for a cross-state and cross-district conversation about virtual coaching in each group. In total, 23 of the original 27 coaches were able to participate in the focus groups.

The following "lessons learned" reflect the combined discoveries we have made by talking with and collecting qualitative data from the aforementioned coaches and from our co-author, Kristi, as a former leader of the coaching program in Akron. While surely many more lessons have been learned than the ones shared here, we focus on those that were shared and salient across all participants.

Successes and Opportunities in Virtual Coaching

Lesson 1: Opportunity and Access in Coaching Can Increase with Virtual Coaching

During the 2020–2021 COVID-19 pandemic, elementary literacy coaches (out of necessity) began offering many more and varied ways for teachers and administrators to connect than ever before. Case studies (Leighton et al., 2018) and other small-scale studies previously described innovations in virtual coaching using FaceTime or asynchronous digital communication. However, the pandemic ushered in a new era of widescale usage of digital tools to foster coaching conversations. Although this may have been overwhelming and exhausting for coaches at first, it may have also increased teacher opportunities to access coaches, with possible increased equal participation in coaching work across a wider swath of teachers.

One example comes directly from Akron, Ohio, in which the 36 coaches began to offer a wider variety of modalities and opportunities for teachers to connect. As teachers became comfortable with using new virtual platforms (e.g., Google Classroom), coaches began sharing different virtual teaching tools and strategies that could increase student engagement and strengthen online teaching practices. Coaches were suddenly able to collaborate easily with different teams of teachers and even connect teachers across schools in ways that were previously quite challenging in-person. Coaches developed and offered various communication structures for new collaborations to take place. Some of these structures included [via Google Meet or Zoom] "Coffee with the Coach," "Sip and Shares," "Lunch and Learns," "Tech Time," and "Pop-up Professional Development" (see Table 10.1 for expanded descriptions of these services in Akron).

By decoupling coaching conversations from in-person planning time or hallway conversations, and offering a more flexible menu of virtual meeting opportunities, coaches were suddenly able to meet with teachers at many different points throughout the week (one-on-one or small-group; formally or informally). By offering sessions based on teacher needs, coaches found ways to connect, build credibility in the virtual world, and provide a hook for future coaching work.

Whereas opportunities existed prior to the pandemic to connect in virtual spaces, the pandemic compelled coaches to find new times and spaces in which to reach out to teachers (e.g., via Zoom, FaceTime, Google Meet, text messaging), particularly to offer the just-in-time support teachers needed around learning digital tools and platforms (see Table 10.1 and Figure 10.1 for examples). In Akron, Ohio, the intimacy and just-in-time nature of the resulting coaching conversations proved to be crucial. Kristi described virtual coaching meetings in Akron as "more immediate" during the pandemic. A coaching Google Meet or Zoom meeting could take place within a shorter timeframe—as opposed to lengthier in-person engagements. This allowed for more flexibility and collaboration across classrooms, schools, and days/times of the week. Virtual meetings could suddenly happen with groups of teachers not needing to come to the same physical space, and travel time was eliminated completely. Virtual coaching allowed for the connection of teachers across schools within the same district, teachers who were teaching the same grade levels or same content, but who traditionally struggled to connect in person. The initial

TABLE 10.1. Virtual PL and Coaching Opportunities in Akron, Ohio

PL coaching offering	Description
Coffee with the Coach	"Coffee with the Coach" became an informal way for coaches to build relationships and trust with teachers in virtual environments. During the pandemic, many educators felt challenged and overwhelmed, and they needed time to decompress, share frustrations, and ask questions in a safe space. This coaching space gave both teachers and coaches regular, as-needed opportunities to connect.
Sip and Share/ Lunch and Learn	More than ever, during the 2020–2021 school year, educators needed time to collaborate and share ideas. Teachers who were sometimes hesitant to collaborate, or who were previously viewed as expert teachers, were now forced to learn new ways to engage and help students achieve online. The "Sip and Share" and "Lunch and Learn" informal collaboration and learning opportunities were set up by the coaches, but often teachers (in addition to the coaches) would use this time to share ideas about what was working in online teaching environments. By offering these informal coaching opportunities during meal times, it became a safe and informal way to grow and learn.
Tech Time	For years coaches have shared technology tools and resources, but the pandemic created an urgency for their use. Coaches would offer various "Technology Help Camps" or "Tech Times" throughout the week to provide quick support and practice in using tech tools that helped teachers reach students in more impactful and engaging ways. Sometimes the Tech Times were differentiated by 101 and 201 sessions, to distinguish between introductory sessions for novices and refining sessions for more experienced tech users. Sometimes coaches would offer an "introduction to the tool" during tech time at the start of the week, and then they would offer a "practice session" later on in the week. Coaches also offered to follow up with teachers one-on-one in their online classrooms, to model or co-teach using the tools and resources highlighted during Tech Times.
Pop-up PD	During PLCs and staff meetings, educators would ask questions or share frustrations about virtual learning. Coaches would listen to needs and offer "Pop-up PD" (virtually) based on those questions and comments, often directly after the meeting in which the teacher concern was raised. This kind of virtual PD would include a quick "show and tell" as part of a partner or small-group problem-solving conversation. Coaches might also ask teachers to share a tool or strategy they were using to help solve an instructional challenge. Impromptu collaboration and sharing was more possible in this low-stakes virtual coaching opportunity.

(continued)

TABLE 10.1. *(continued)*

PL coaching offering	Description
Coach Camps	Coaches held weekly virtual PDs for other coaches in the district, often focusing on various tech tools and resources (e.g., Google Docs, Google Forms, Google Arts and Culture, Flipgrid, Screencastify, Hyperdocs, Edpuzzle) to help everyone stay current and share what was supporting online learning. Coaches frequently took the ideas from these coach camps and offered similar coach camps with their own teachers on the same topic in the following weeks. These coach camps were optional, and they allowed coaches and teachers to participate in ways that prioritized individual learning needs. All camps were recorded and shared via a Google Doc resource across the coaching network so that everyone could access the resources when it was convenient, or participants could watch them again for more support.

increased demand for coach support was so great and varied that coaches needed to find new ways and times to connect with teachers. While that initial demand for coach support tapered off a bit across the year of pandemic schooling, the new and varied coaching connections remained.

Lesson 2: Relationships Can Grow and Flourish with Just-in-Time Virtual Coaching

With more and varied virtual ways of connecting with coaches, teachers had additional opportunities during 2020–2021 to receive exactly the support they needed when they needed it. As a result of both the immediacy and intimacy of a one-on-one Zoom or Google Meet call, coach–teacher relationships may have actually grown stronger. In response to the question, "What are the critical factors in successful virtual coaching?" one K–12 Pennsylvania coach told us:

> "I think it's relationships . . . having relationships with teachers so that they feel comfortable coming for help. Even our teachers who don't normally come to the coaches are coming now because they're learning new things. . . . So, I think relationships."

A Massachusetts K–4 coach agreed that the critical factor was responsive relationships:

> "I agree . . . it's being responsive to teachers and also what the district is asking of us. And I will say in terms of critical factors this year, I think it's just time with teachers and whatever that looks like."

Google Arts and Culture Integration

LINK to doc with Objectives, Standards, and Curriculum Connections

	Engage	
	***Is Art important to society?*** Warm up group activity. Shared document.	LINK to Live DOC LINK to student sample work

	Explore/ Challenge	
	*WHAT IS ART?* As you think about the answer to what is art, work through the questions in the video. Please answer in complete sentences and use reasons to support your opinion.	Link to EdPuzzle
	Bonus Challenge: Follow → this link to explore a piece of interactive artwork. Use the Jamboard to give your opinion about the art.	LINK to *'The Peak'* LINK to Opinion Jam

	Explain/ ELA Connections	
	**1. Review Fact and Opinion** Kahoot! Kahoot! Link	**3. Learn the benefits of practicing art analysis**. Open this Form, watch the video and complete the questions. *How Art Can Help You Analyze* FORM
	2. Read about the artist Frida Kahlo in this BL book pages 14-20 only. LINK to BOOK. Make a text to self-connection and add it to this shared document. LINK to Shared Doc	**4. Study this Format for Art Critique Writing:** Four Step Art Critique (Elements of art could be explored here also)

Google Arts and Culture Integration Resources assembled by:
Janet Hazlett, Instructional Coach, Akron Public Schools.

FIGURE 10.1. Example of a coach camp document focused on Google Arts and Culture.

<table>
<tr><th></th><th colspan="2">Apply</th></tr>
<tr><td>Google Arts & Culture</td><td>For Teachers:

Go to:
Google Arts and Culture
Use your templates to capture ideas for a lesson or take notes the old-fashioned way! Visit or find:<ul><li>At least three museums</li><li>360° videos/stills</li><li>Search a work of art by name, movement, color</li><li>Visit a cultural site</li><li>Search a historical event or era</li><li>Find the National Park link and the 4 360° tours</li><li>Wow! What else??</li></ul>Ohio EdTech Video GAC from 3/16/20</td><td>For Students:
Use this graphic organizer to analyze a selected work of art from Google Arts and Culture. (Add List here—or let them find their own art.) Attach this document to the Google Classroom assignment. We will use this organizer as the research and notes for our opinion writing essay.
Graphic Organizer

Directions for Opinion Essay
(More activities here? Writing Process, Writer's Workshop Lessons, Google Classroom Assignments)</td></tr>
</table>

<table>
<tr><th></th><th>Share and Reflect</th></tr>
<tr><td>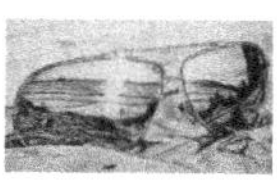</td><td>Take a Breath:<ul><li>How could you guide your teachers to effectively use this tool?</li><li>What are some limitations?</li><li>Cautions?</li></ul>Final thoughts . . .
"One of the things this moment is teaching us is that anything is possible. It will be imagination and innovation that gets us all to the other side." Steven Spielberg SGN 5/20

Amanda Gorman: Miracle of the Morning Graduation Poem minute 23:16</td></tr>
</table>

Google Arts and Culture Integration Resources assembled by:
Janet Hazlett, Instructional Coach, Akron Public Schools.

FIGURE 10.1. *(continued)*

Given that teachers had a definite need for coaching support in 2020–2021, where they did not feel threatened because of their lack of understanding of how to teach virtually, they felt comfortable reaching out to seek support from the coach. This need for coach support was perhaps most intense in the early days of the pandemic, as one Florida K–5 reading coach explained: "When the pandemic first struck, teachers were in panic mode. So instead of 'coaching,' I was now a life-saving device. Teachers came to us for resources, materials, and basically the answers of how to make e-learning work." As one Ohio coach wrote to us early in the pandemic:

> "The trust that was evident during this [virtual coaching] work will stay with me forever. I never felt more needed as a coach than during the past few months."

In some ways, coach–teacher relationships blossomed in newly profound ways during the 2020–2021 year. For many coaches and teachers, small-group and one-on-one Zoom and Google Meet conversations provided new and rich opportunities to develop trusting relationships. Pre-pandemic, some teachers may have been unwilling to talk with coaches about their instructional challenges. Given the widespread and relatively swift shift to full-time online teaching in 2020–2021, coaches reported teachers describing themselves feeling like first-year teachers again. This created an environment in which it was more acceptable to be vulnerable, ask questions, and receive help from coaches. Although this vulnerability and relational work with coaches was positively reported by the coaches, and coaches were able to connect with seasoned teachers in some new and exciting ways, it also highlighted that work was still needed in developing a culture where coaching is viewed as needed by all, not just by new or struggling teachers.

One of the important lessons related to virtual coaching relationships during the pandemic was that often teachers just needed someone who would listen to them with an open mind, as they (teachers) struggled to master the complexities of teaching online. While the notion of virtual coaching relationship-building clearly needs further study, early reports from the coaches in our studies suggest that strong, responsive coach–teacher relationships can be forged in virtual environments.

Lesson 3: Modeling Lessons with Video Can Be Powerful

Whereas traditional coaching cycles are characterized by in-person coach–teacher planning, observation, and debrief sessions (each of which takes significant time and scheduling); virtual coaching work in our studies focused in part on coaches capturing digital footage of themselves modeling instruction, or of model instruction from others' classrooms, and using that footage to support coaching work across a wide swath of teachers. The use of video footage gathered via Zoom, Screencastify, Sibme, iPhone, and other online communication and video recording tools allowed teachers and coaches to collaboratively review and debrief teaching moves at both a granular level and at scale across a greater number of teachers than coaches previously reported reaching. As one Massachusetts K–5 literacy coach illustrated:

> "I [work] across five elementary buildings and it was impossible [pre-pandemic]. The job was too big. And the pandemic made it acceptable for me to record one 10-minute model lesson that can now reach 56 different teachers. Whereas before I was stuck in that 10 minutes [of modeling, individually] and then the debrief . . . all involved with just one teacher, if I was lucky. So now we have a situation where I can reach more people in a much more efficient way."

This same coach later elaborated that:

> "I create and/or adapt the reading and writing lessons from our newly adopted ELA curriculum into virtual slides. I then make model videos of the lessons using these slides. I also create interactive, asynchronous model read aloud lessons that incorporate writing in response to reading and make videos of those. These lessons are not written into our current curriculum. Lastly, I create interactive vocabulary slides that I have developed from the words in the read aloud texts. These, too, are not a part of the current curriculum materials. These model lessons and curriculum resources are entered into a shared calendar for grades 3–5 teachers to access and use. I am available, when requested, to meet with teachers individually and troubleshoot problems they might be having."

Across the coaches, districts, and states represented in our studies, we frequently heard about this type of time-intensive creation of video demonstration lessons and virtual instructional materials that teachers could immediately use. This certainly was the case in Akron, Ohio, where it was reported to be easier to record instruction, lessons, and PL opportunities and share the resulting resources with teachers and coaches, once both teachers and coaches were immersed in the virtual learning environment.

Not every coach we spoke with employed these strategies, yet those who did reported being able to reach more teachers and focus attention on nuanced instructional practices in ways that previously felt confined to only the few teachers that the coach could meet with in-person in any given day or week. Suddenly, these same coaches were now reaching dozens or more teachers instantaneously. One additional advantage of this method is that coaches can document teacher engagement by tallying views and usage of coach-created digital documents (such as Figure 10.1), tracking document views and usage through Google's Activity Dashboard.[1] Looking for coach-generated materials appearing in teachers' virtual shared classroom spaces (e.g., in Google Classrooms) can also be a way to document impact.

Although some of the existing virtual coaching literature has focused on the video capture of teachers' work and review by coach–teacher pairs, this relatively new practice of widespread sharing of coach-generated video and digital materials as models and inspiration for teacher work allowed for different (and sometimes more directive) coaching conversations. The dissemination of model footage and materials allowed for the possibility of both a high degree of teacher reflection as coaches talked with teachers in small groups and one-on-one about the materials. However, it also allowed for a mechanism that aligned coach-introduced instructional practices and materials across a much larger number of classrooms. As researchers continue to understand the effects of coaching on teaching and learning at scale (Kraft et al., 2018), future research must examine the efficacy of virtual coaching work when delivered via video/virtual materials to large numbers of teachers.

Challenges and Tensions in Virtual Coaching

Lesson 1: Balancing Teachers' Needs with Setting Boundaries around Coaching Work

The shift in 2020–2021 to a more varied and frequent menu of coaching opportunities across virtual mediums has been exciting, but it has also meant that many coaches were suddenly working 24/7. For many of the coaches we spoke with, the increase in forms and times of communication were mostly viewed as a positive element, but there was also widespread agreement about the exhaustion and dissolution of work/life boundaries that accompanied this shift. One Massachusetts grade 3–8 coach admitted:

> "It's a constant conversation . . . there's no boundaries to it. I'm literally [working through] weekends . . . because many of the people are my friends."

---

[1] For more details about tracking document use, see *support.google.com/docs/answer/7378739* and *www.youtube.com/watch?v=eeQuWHHAbao*.

A Pennsylvania K–2 coach echoed this experience:

> "My entire building never used, let alone heard of Google Classroom [before the pandemic]. I became responsible for teaching/modeling/showing teachers how to create, build, utilize Google classroom. I would say that the entire months of March and April [2020] I was busy and supporting teachers 100% of my day from waking until bedtime. I found myself needing to 'power down' for my own sanity."

This level of intensity in virtual coaching work was not always sustained across the pandemic, yet coaches did agree that their pandemic work hours expanded as a result of the shift to virtual coaching. In the case of one Ohio K–5 coach—when comparing her fall 2019, spring 2020, and fall 2020 calendars (spanning pre-, early-, and midpandemic coaching and the shift to virtual coaching)—it was easy to see how the timing and very nature of her coaching interactions shifted. In the fall of 2019, she spent longer chunks of time in classrooms and in attending or delivering PL, all during normal school hours; notably, she might only have recorded three or four longer in-person commitments per day separated by breaks (e.g., minimum of 45 minutes and maximum of 4 hours per commitment). Meanwhile, in the spring of 2020 (in the early days of the pandemic), it was more common to see eight or nine shorter engagements per day (30- to 45-minute commitments) stacked one on top of another, every day, from sunrise to sunset, without breaks. Finally, looking at her fall 2020 calendar, we found more lunch breaks and planning times built back into her calendar, and more intensive coaching work included (e.g., coaching cycles) as opposed to the less intensive resource sharing of her early pandemic work. Moreover, her fall 2020 calendar showed a clearer return to regular school hours. All of this helped us to understand the ways in which coaches' work expanded and shifted dramatically during the pandemic and as virtual coaching schedules allowed for the elimination of lengthy travel time between coaching commitments.

Our review of coaches' schedules during the pandemic suggests that coaches and administrators may need to continue setting boundaries around synchronous and asynchronous communication long after the pandemic fades. As virtual coaching continues and as teachers' online instructional needs expand, coaches may need principal support in continuing to establish and protect work/life boundaries. For example, if a coach invites teachers to send emails, text messages, meeting requests, and so on, then coaches and principals might simultaneously convey the idea that teachers should continue to reach out whenever they have a moment (including late at night or on the weekends), but that coaches may only respond on certain days or within certain windows of time (e.g., establishing clear day, evening, and weekend response-time guidelines). Without setting clear boundaries up front, coaches run the risk of exhaustion and potentially frustrating teachers and administrators who have differing expectations.

An additional, if perhaps pandemic-specific, element of this lesson learned about how coaches spent their time was that coaches reported spending equal amounts of time supporting teachers' social-emotional needs as they did supporting teachers' curricular and instructional needs. One Ohio K–5 coach said of this pandemic coaching work that she hadn't participated in many coaching cycles, which was more typical prepandemic; instead, she "felt more like tech and emotional support" for teachers. This emotional support role, together with simply listening to teachers' concerns, was reported as a critical role across coaches, especially during the unusually stressful and isolating times of 2020–2021. However, as the pandemic recedes, coaches will need to be careful to balance meeting teachers' social-emotional needs with their teaching and learning needs.

Continued coach learning will need to take place around how virtual and hybrid (part in-person and part online) learning can be executed most effectively, particularly as many U.S. elementary school leaders continue to think creatively about learning modalities and the opportunities virtual learning affords for differentiation and supporting equitable learning outcomes for all. Coming out of the pandemic, a readjustment period may need to take place in which coaches continue their own PL while simultaneously providing a bit less social-emotional support and tilting back toward more teaching and learning conversations with teachers.

Lesson 2: Virtual Relationship Building Can Be Awkward

Many complications of virtual teaching emerged during the pandemic: the issue of time, given teachers' many and new responsibilities (e.g., content creation; learning new tools); the stress they may feel as they attempt to use unfamiliar technologies to provide both asynchronous and synchronous instruction; and even their struggles in engaging students new to virtual instruction. In a virtual classroom, it can be challenging to find evidence of student thinking and understanding. In many classrooms, cameras are off, students are muted, and teachers are teaching to photos, icons, or blank screens. Even as teachers ask questions or give assignments, it can be difficult to tell if students have mastered concepts. Teachers are left with questions of whether they should move forward or adjust instruction.

Coaches also face many complications, including their inexperience with virtual coaching and teaching. In Akron, Ohio, coaches had to find ways to make student learning visible in the virtual setting. They had to push their own learning by finding and trying out digital formative assessment tools, designing engaging and relevant assignments, and adapting classroom discussion techniques for the online space, all to ensure that even the most resistant students were engaged and learning. The best approach in those situations was for coaches to truly partner with teachers in trying out different strategies and ways of engaging students in meaningful ways. Coaches engaged in cycles and partnerships with teachers individually, but they also reported that the "team approach" often helped remedy tough situations by harnessing the power of the "teaching group" (with fellow teachers offering suggestions and brainstorming alongside the coach). This allowed the teachers to feel a bit more supported in this new uncharted territory.

But forging strong virtual coach–teacher relationships wasn't always smooth sailing. Although the *importance* of developing relationships and trust in coaching remained the same, it could at times be challenging in the virtual setting. In the past, often the spark of a coaching partnership happened in the unforeseen moments (e.g., the coach passing a teacher in the hall, talking by the copy machine, or even stopping in a classroom after school to ask a teacher a question). These natural moments of connection simply didn't happen organically in entirely virtual environments. Instead, connections needed planning. Coming together on a Google Meet is a planned and usually scheduled event. Both parties must agree to the time and be ready to connect. Thus coaches reported having to find different, and sometimes spontaneous ways, to connect with teachers. Texting, phone calls, offering optional help camps or support sessions, or emailing teachers to check in were helpful ways to make connections and build trust. Coaches offered optional connection times for teachers to come together for a virtual informal brainstorm session or to try a new tech tool. These casual online connections were reported to help build relationships, but they still weren't as authentic and natural as being in the same physical space.

Finally, although coaches were eager to support teachers and make an impact in virtual and hybrid classrooms, they had to tread lightly in their requests of teachers, or in their laser focus on coaching cycles, as sometimes overwhelmed or stressed teachers would view coaches as "one more thing." Some coaches reported a few teachers insinuating that coaches had it "easy" during the pandemic because they were not necessarily teaching students directly. This suggests the need for coaches to continue to find ways to involve themselves deeply in the teaching and learning work of schools, and even to offer more virtual co-planning and co-teaching opportunities. For many of the coaches we talked with, it was difficult to balance the need to continually focus on systemwide rigorous teaching standards and foster student growth while also ensuring that teachers felt supported and as if coaches were true partners (and not just bystanders) in the challenging work of teaching online.

Lesson 3: We Still Need to Guard against Coaches Being Pulled into Noncoaching Work

During the pandemic, a number of coaches were (understandably) asked to support classroom instruction by teaching classes of students directly, meeting with small groups of students for intervention work, or tackling district-level curricular design tasks. Some were even asked to take on work for which they hadn't been prepared. As one Massachusetts 3–8 coach indicated, "I've never done intervention work in small groups, and now I am." One Florida K–5 coach reported, "As of right now I am pulling small groups [of students] and attending [teacher] planning sessions." A Massachusetts 3–8 coach reported, "I am spending much less time with individual teachers [this year]. I am writing a lot of curriculum." Another Massachusetts K–4 coach reported, "We are primarily functioning as curriculum coordinators in the way we are supporting teachers. We are creating curriculum maps and pacing guides, facilitating district-level curriculum planning meetings, and working more closely with the elementary principals to align instruction." Another Florida K–5 coach reported, "Coaching (at my particular site) is almost nonexistent. I believe that this is due to our administration and their personal fears of the pandemic." Even in Akron, Ohio, where the coaching model continued and flourished for most of the 2020–2021 school year, coaches were pulled to teach in March 2021 when the number of classrooms multiplied as families were given an option to have their children return to full-time in-person learning or to continue learning online for the remainder of the year.

All these roles and responsibilities have served important purposes during the pandemic, yet we also need to carefully guard against the dissolution and diffusion of coaching work as the pandemic recedes. Coaches being pulled for instructional or administrative tasks is one of the traditional ways that the coaching literature identifies as potentially subverting the effect of coaching on instructional improvements. One thing we have learned from past research is that working exclusively with one teacher at a time (Mangin & Dunsmore, 2015), or being pulled into too many administrative or clerical tasks, can diffuse coaching work and limit the opportunity for system growth and improvement.

Implications and Suggestions for Schools Considering or Continuing Virtual Coaching

Given the many benefits and challenges of virtual coaching shared by the coaches and coaching leaders across the four states at the center of this work (captured in Table 10.2, from across our data sources), we now share a few key suggestions for schools introducing virtual coaching as part of their ongoing coaching program, or for those schools planning to continue the virtual coaching work that began during the 2020–2021 pandemic.

Invest in Flexible Relationship-Building Time and Structures

For decades, the coaching literature has documented the critical importance of coaches forging strong relationships with teachers and principals alike. This imperative seems even more important in virtual coaching work. It seems important to establish and communicate multiple different days/times, types of connection opportunities (e.g., formal, informal, one-on-one, small-group), and different modalities (e.g., Zoom, phone, text, FaceTime, asynchronous shared Google Docs or Jamboards). This simple innovation allows teachers and principals to connect with coaches when it is most convenient and when support is most needed.

While some of the new times and formats for coach communication arose specifically in response to the rapid shift to virtual work prompted by the COVID-19 pandemic, there are elements that may linger long after the pandemic has faded. For example, offering weekly virtual coach check-ins for individuals, as well as small and large groups, makes great sense—particularly for coaches working across buildings. Scheduling different types of virtual hangouts could also be quite productive (e.g., a mixture of informal "Coffee with the Coach" sessions followed by more formal modeling or demonstration sessions). Whereas those who are exclusively coaching in-person might be limited by time and geographic constraints, offering a variety of virtual connection opportunities could greatly accelerate coaching work and strengthen relationships.

Invest in Infrastructure, Administrative Support, and Coaching Networks

As critical as district and principal support as well as an active coaching network are for traditional in-person coaching, they may be even more essential for virtual coaching, given the potential for coach isolation and

TABLE 10.2. Potential Benefits and Challenges of Virtual Coaching

Benefits of virtual coaching	Challenges of virtual coaching
Virtual coaching offers immediacy of support	Interactions are potentially awkward
Virtual coaching promotes ease of collaboration at scale across grade levels, content areas, and schools	It can be difficult to make deeper, personal connections
Virtual coaching produces excitement about learning new skills, topics, and technology	Some teachers and coaches may lack confidence and knowledge, and feel anxiety about working in a new digital environment
Virtual coaching easily provides brief, personalized support	Bite-sized virtual, on-demand coaching may not be as strategic or systematic
Coaches can work with teachers at almost any time of day or night, when it works best for both educators	Coaches and teachers may struggle to set boundaries and preserve a work/life balance
Recording of lessons and professional learning can easily be shared at scale; teaching can become public	It is sometimes difficult to see evidence of teacher understanding and implementation of new practices
Virtual coaching can provide new and more varied ways for coaches to connect with teachers	The focus may shift from reflective coaching cycles (e.g., co-teaching, modeling, observation and debrief) to primarily providing resources and quick check-ins
Coaches are able to position themselves more easily as partners in learning (e.g., tackling new technology)	Coaches may feel less knowledgeable (e.g., with technology)
Engaging in virtual coaching can support instructional innovation and creativity (e.g., use of new technology)	Understanding and using new technology can create anxiety on all fronts
Some teachers and coaches thrive in virtual environments	Some teachers and coaches experience great frustration and stress in virtual environments

role shift. Coaches in our focus groups reported varied decision-making authority and experiences, with some indicating that they alone made the decisions about who, what, and when to coach. Others explained that their partnerships with principals and administrators were helpful in several ways. First, by sharing and gaining approval from administration, they were more comfortable moving ahead with their coaching agendas. Second, discussions with administrators gave them a better sense of the broader picture as related to district goals—for example, what to prioritize in terms of curricular emphases. Finally, providing regular opportunities for school- and district-based (homegrown) coach PL is important—particularly around technology and facilitating adult learning virtually. In Akron, Kristi and the coaches met on a regular basis, sharing ideas, brainstorming ways they might support teachers, and even learning about new technological tools. This network of coaches, guided by a coaching leader, provided a safe place for sharing successes and challenges, and for raising questions about future directions and efforts.

Invest in Video Models to Keep a Laser-Like Focus on Teaching and Learning

The opportunity to record instruction, annotate it, and collectively reflect on it is an opportunity that shouldn't be missed—particularly when that instruction can be used as a model for a large number of teachers across a school or district. Even more so than coaches observing teachers' in-person work, the opportunity for shared reflection (teachers and coaches looking at teaching videos together) can become a cornerstone of coaching cycles now and well beyond the pandemic. We have seen the power of this kind of joint reflection in our own PL work with coaches and school leaders time and time again, and perhaps the pandemic will generate more comfort and familiarity with these strategies.

Moreover, using recorded lessons for coach PL also has potential. For example, a network of coaches can observe a recorded lesson to hone their observation skills (e.g., What are they seeing? What are teachers and students doing? What are the strengths of this lesson?) (Ippolito & Pomerantz, 2013/2014). They can look at a series of lessons to identify instructional patterns among teachers in their buildings. Further, coaches can think about what questions to ask and what feedback they might want to provide as they engage in coaching conversations with teachers whose lessons they observed. Perhaps the pandemic, which prompted virtual instruction at scale and resulted in a bevy of video-recorded lessons, can lead the field to think more seriously about the power of making one's teaching public.

Looking to the Future

Although the world of education has faced a challenging task during the pandemic, the crisis has generated opportunities that schools and districts might use to facilitate effective virtual literacy coaching. Coaches can meet more easily and efficiently with teachers and with other coaches, using virtual tools such as Zoom and Google Meet. At the same time, once the pandemic has ended, coaches can return to face-to-face meetings with individuals and groups to establish working partnerships and to better prepare teachers for using virtual tools for upcoming meetings.

In other words, PL in the form of literacy coaching must rely on the *best of both worlds*. Schools can build on what has been learned with these early, toddler-like steps into the world of virtual coaching to develop more effective coaching practices moving forward. We are just beginning our journey to learn more about what works with virtual coaching. Not yet, but soon, we will need to address the following question: When might coaching be more effective face-to-face, and when might we be better off using virtual tools to facilitate coaching? For now, in the world of coaching, we must collectively exhale—these have been trying and exciting times. There is plenty of room for continued innovation alongside the need for additional study of virtual coaching, when and how it can be used, and to what effect.

REFERENCES

Affinito, S. (2018). *Literacy coaching: Transforming teaching and learning with digital tools and technology.* Heinemann.

Bean, R. M., Draper, J. A., Hall, V., Vandermolen, J., & Zigmond, N. (2010). Coaches and coaching in reading first schools. *Elementary School Journal, 111*(1), 87–114.

Bean, R. M., Swan Dagen, A., Ippolito, J., & Kern, D. (2018). Principals' perspectives on the roles of specialized literacy professionals. *The Elementary School Journal, 119*(2), 327–350.

Biancarosa, G., Bryk, A. S., & Dexter, E. R. (2010). Assessing the value-added effects of literacy collaborative professional development on student learning. *Elementary School Journal, 111*(1), 7–34.

Blumke, K. (2021, February). Virtual coaching takes off. *Edutopia.* Retrieved April 10, 2021, from *www.edutopia.org/article/virtual-coaching-takes.*

Costa, A., & Garmston, R. (2002). *Cognitive coaching: A foundation for Renaissance schools* (2nd ed.). Christopher-Gordon.

Darling-Hammond, L., Hyler, M. E., & Gardner, M. (2017). *Effective teacher professional development.* Learning Policy Institute.

Darling-Hammond, L., Wei, R. C., Andree, A., Richardson, N., & Orphanos, S. (2009). *Professional learning in the learning profession: A status report on teacher development in the United States and abroad.* National Staff Development Council and The School Redesign Network, Stanford University.

Deussen, T., Coskie, T., Robinson, L., & Autio, E. (2007). *"Coach" can mean many things: Five categories of literacy coaches in reading first* (Issues & Answers Report, REL 2007-No. 005). United States Department of Education, Institute of Education Sciences, National Center for Education Evaluation and Regional Assistance, Regional Educational Laboratory Northwest.

Galloway, E. P., & Lesaux, N. K. (2014). Leader, teacher, diagnostician, colleague, and change agent: A synthesis of the research on the role of the reading specialist in this era of RTI-based literacy reform. *The Reading Teacher, 67*(7), 517–526.

Garmston, R., Linder, C., & Whitaker, J. (1993). Reflections on cognitive coaching. *Educational Leadership, 51*(2), 57–61.

International Literacy Association. (2018). *Standards for the preparation of literacy professionals 2017.* Author.

Ippolito, J. (2009). Principals as partners with literacy coaches: Striking a balance between neglect and interference. Literacy Coaching Clearinghouse. Retrieved October 14, 2018, from *https://eric.ed.gov/?id=ED530261.*

Ippolito, J. (2010). Three ways that literacy coaches balance responsive and directive relationships with teachers. *Elementary School Journal, 111*(1). 164–190.

Ippolito, J., & Bean, R. M. (2019). A principal's guide to supporting instructional coaching. *Educational Leadership, 77*(3), 68–73.

Ippolito, J., & Pomerantz, F. (2013/2014). Protocols as essential tools for literacy professional learning communities in the common core era. *Massachusetts Reading Association Primer, 42*(2), 44–55.

Joyce, B., & Showers, B. (1996). The evolution of peer coaching. *Educational Leadership, 53*(6), 12–16.

Keefe, E. S. (2020). Learning to practice digitally: Advancing preservice teachers' preparation via virtual teaching and coaching. *Journal of Technology and Teacher Education, 28*(2), 223–232.

Killion, J. (2009). Coaches' roles, responsibilities, and reach. In J. Knight (Ed.), *Coaching: Approaches and perspectives* (pp. 7–28). Corwin Press.

Kotze, J., Fleisch, B., & Taylor, S. (2019). Alternative forms of early grade instructional coaching: Emerging evidence from field experiments in South Africa. International *Journal of Educational Development, 66,* 203–213.

Kraft, M. A., Blazar, D., & Hogan, D. (2018). The effect of teacher coaching on instruction and achievement: A meta-analysis of the causal evidence. *Review of Educational Research, 88*(4), 547–588.

Kral, C. (2007). Principal support for literacy coaches. *Literacy Coaching Clearinghouse.* Retrieved April 9, 2021, from *https://eric.ed.gov/?id=ED530296.*

Leighton, C. M., Ford-Connors, E., Robertson, D. A., Wyatt, J., Wagner, C. J., Proctor, C. P., & Paratore, J. R. (2018). "Let's FaceTime tonight": Using digital tools to enhance coaching. *The Reading Teacher, 72*(1), 39–49.

MacKinnon, G., Marsh-Roberts, T. A., Jones, Y., Williams, D., Hamilton-Dopwell, A., & King, C. (2019). Factors That Impact the Implementation of Virtual Literacy Coaching in the Eastern Caribbean. In K. Graziano (Ed.), *Proceedings of Society for Information Technology & Teacher Education International Conference* (pp. 1950–1958). Association for the Advancement of Computing in Education (AACE). Retrieved April 9, 2021, from *www.learntechlib.org/primary/p/207913.*

Mangin, M. M., & Dunsmore, K. (2015). How the framing of instructional coaching as a lever for systemic or individual reform influences the enactment of coaching. *Educational Administration Quarterly, 51*(2), 179–213.

Marsh, J. A., McCombs, J. S., Lockwood, J. R., Martorell, F., Gershwin, D., Naftel, S., . . . Crego, A. (2008). *Supporting literacy across the sunshine state: A study of Florida middle school reading coaches.* Prepared for Carnegie Corporation of New York. RAND Corporation.

Matsumura, L. C., Sartoris, M., Bickel, D. D., & Garnier, H. (2009). Leadership for literacy coaching: The principal's role in launching a new coaching program. *Educational Administration Quarterly, 45*(5), 655–693.

McKenna, M. C., & Walpole, S. (2008). *The literacy coaching challenge: Models and methods for grades K–8.* Guilford Press.

Oller, T. J. (2019). *Virtual school literacy coaches in Florida: A study of perceptions of efficacy and time invested in literacy coaching activities.* Dissertation.

Ortlieb, E., McVee, M. B., & Shanahan, L. E. (Eds.). (2015). *Video reflection in literacy teacher education and development: Lessons from research and practice.* Emerald.

O'Shell, D. (2019). Using video to showcase great teaching. *Educational Leadership, 77*(3), 50–52.

Pletcher, B. C., Hudson, A. K., John, L., & Scott, A. (2019). Coaching on borrowed time: Balancing the roles of the literacy professional. *The Reading Teacher, 72*(6), 689–699.

Rainville, K. N., & Jones, S. (2008). Situated identities: Power and positioning in the work of a literacy coach. *The Reading Teacher, 61*(6), 440–448.

Robertson, D. A., Padesky, L. B., Ford-Connors, E., & Paratore, J. R. (2020). What does it mean to say coaching is relational? *Journal of Literacy Research, 52*(1), 55–78.

Rock, M. L., Gregg, M., Howard, P. W., Ploessl, D. M., Maughn, S., Gable, R. A., & Zigmond, N. P. (2009). See me, hear me, coach me: Virtual bug-in-ear technology brings immediacy to professional development. *Journal of Staff Development, 30*(3), 24–32.

Rock, M. L., Schoenfeld, N., Zigmond, N., Gable, R. A., Gregg, M., Ploessl, D. M., & Salter, A. (2013). Can you Skype me now?: Developing teachers' classroom management practices through virtual coaching. *Beyond Behavior, 22*(3), 15–23.

Shanklin, N. (2007). What supports do literacy coaches need from administrators in order to succeed? Literacy Coaching Clearinghouse. Retrieved April 9, 2021, from *https://eric.ed.gov/?id=ED530330.*

Smith, A. T. (2007). The middle school literacy coach: Considering roles in context. In D. W. Rowe, R. T. Jiménez, D. L. Compton, D. K. Dickinson, Y. Kim, K. M. Leander, & V. J. Risko (Eds.), *56th Yearbook of the National Reading Conference* (pp. 53–67). National Reading Conference.

Toll, C. A. (2007). *Lenses on literacy coaching: Conceptualizations, functions, and outcomes.* Christopher-Gordon.

Walpole, S., & McKenna, M. C. (2012). *The literacy coach's handbook: A guide to research-based practice* (2nd ed.). Guilford Press.

CHAPTER 11

How Micro-Courses Shape Teachers' Perceptions, Engagement, and Learning in Professional Development

Leigh A. Hall

Watch a related video from the author at this link.

"I can't even begin to tell you how much I have enjoyed this."

I was talking with Roxanne, a high school teacher, about her experiences in participating in online professional learning (PL) centered on literacy instruction.

"What have you enjoyed?" I asked.

"I've never had access to this level of information before, and it's really pushing me to try new things. . . . I'm just a teacher who lives out in the middle of nowhere in this very tiny rural town. The PD [professional development] we get here is very limited. But now, finally, I am able to get access to PD that is going to help me teach reading better. . . . A lot of my students have significant difficulties with reading, and for most of my career I have felt like I just couldn't help them as well as I should. . . . So now I'm just happy that I'm getting access to so much information that will really help my students."

Roxanne's challenge—developing her pedagogical knowledge so that she could design reading instruction to support her students—is a common one, particularly among teachers of adolescents. Most middle and high school teachers have received little, if any, preparation to support adolescents' literacy development (Hardin & Koppenhaver, 2016). However, most adolescents will struggle to do more than extract basic facts from texts (National Assessment of Educational Progress [NAEP], 2019). Although students with reading difficulties may be common in middle and high school classrooms, they sit alongside students who meet or exceed grade-level expectations in reading and writing. Therefore, teachers need to be able to provide instruction that responds to students with a diverse range of academic needs (Spires et al., 2016).

In this chapter, I examine how online PL (OPL) can be designed so that it engages teachers while improving their pedagogical knowledge. I begin by examining the benefits of OPL and the theories that support it. Next, I discuss how I designed an OPL experience for middle and high school teachers to improve their knowledge of literacy instruction. I then share the lessons learned from this effort regarding what teachers did and did not like and how their learning was impacted. Finally, I conclude with recommendations and a challenge for going forward with OPL.

The Advantages to OPL

PL plays a critical role in helping teachers understand how to design literacy instruction that can serve the needs of diverse learners. However, in order for it to be effective, it must be designed so that it is active, engaging, and responsive to the needs of educators (Darling-Hammond et al., 2009). One-shot workshops are often unsuccessful at improving teachers' knowledge of pedagogy or improving their instructional practices (Kragler et al., 2014). For PL to be successful, it needs to be sustained over time, allow teachers repeated opportunities to collaborate and receive feedback, and support teachers in connecting new ideas to their specific context (Desimone, 2009; Duffy, 2004).

While PL can take a variety of approaches, OPL is emerging as a way to help teachers gain access to the latest research and instructional practices regardless of where they live. OPL can give teachers access to a wider range of content, resources, and experts than may be possible in a face-to-face context (Stoetzel & Shedrow, 2020). OPL can also be structured so that teachers have greater choice in what they learn and can identify content that will support their immediate needs.

On the surface, OPL may seem more isolating than traditional face-to-face learning where teachers would be surrounded by their colleagues. However, fostering well-developed, interactive social networks can allow teachers to engage in collaborative learning with colleagues who have a range of knowledge and experiences (LaPointe-McEwan et al., 2017). These interactions can result in teachers feeling socially connected and less isolated (Cho & Tobias, 2016). It is these interpersonal relationships, which emerge from within the online space, that may be most important to learning (Oztok & Kehrwald, 2017).

Additionally, OPL can allow teachers greater convenience and choice in their learning (Collins & Liang, 2015; Dede et al., 2009; Fishman et al., 2013). As a result, OPL can give teachers the freedom to tailor PL to their needs (Powell & Bodur, 2019). When teachers are able to decide what to learn, and when to learn it, they often view the experience as meaningful, engaging, and useful to their instruction (Knight, 2007; Sailors & Price, 2015). Being in control of their PL and able to engage with content that aligns with their instructional goals can foster positive emotions (Osman & Warner, 2020). When teachers experience positive emotions, they may engage more deeply with PL and be more likely to apply what they have learned (Hunt, 2016).

Theoretical Framework

My approach to OPL is grounded in theories of mobile, on-demand learning (McQuiggan et al., 2015) and constructivism, while also viewing PL as a culturally and socially situated practice (Lave & Wenger, 1991). Because of the internet, more opportunities exist now for information to be shared. We can access knowledge faster, and easier, than ever before. Learning does not need to occur at predefined times or within a set context (Sharples et al., 2016). Instead, learning can happen anywhere, at any time. Individuals have greater control over what, how, and when they learn as well as who they learn from.

When designing OPL that is influenced by mobile learning, it is important to remember that the learner, and not the technology, is viewed as portable. While some devices can easily be moved from place to place, and accessed when needed, it is the learner who dips in and out of content as it best suits them (Shuler, 2009). Mobile learning then allows learners to break free of the space and time constraints that have accompanied traditional face-to-face approaches by giving them more freedom and choice in what and how they learn (Alrasheedi et al., 2015).

PL as a Constructivist and Socially Situated Practice

When PL is viewed as a constructivist practice, learners are seen as being actively involved in their own learning process (Vygotsky, 1980). Rather than receive information passively, they work to formulate their understandings and to incorporate it into their existing knowledge (Huang et al., 2019). How they understand the information they are presented with is further shaped by their prior experiences and background knowledge (von Glasersfeld, 1995).

However, teachers do not work or learn, in isolation; rather, they are situated within one or more professional communities that they interact with in myriad ways. PL can be shaped, and reshaped, by these communities and the experiences within them can influence teacher learning (Korthagen, 2010; Pella, 2011). The learning that can happen within these contexts is a dynamic process where teachers interact with content and each other to support their professional goals.

Although online learning may seem isolating, it can be constructed so that teachers have the opportunities to discuss their work, including the challenges, questions, and problems they have in relation to it, with a larger community working on similar things (Borup & Evmonova, 2019). Learning in an online environment can be strengthened when teachers can interact with peers and instructors in relation to content (Paquette, 2016). Researchers have argued that the interpersonal relationships that are fostered within an online space may be one of the most critical factors in supporting learning (Oztok & Kehrwald, 2017).

Teachers need space to share their thoughts and questions, but it must be done within an environment that is trusting and supportive. Their interactions within their communities allow them to acquire new professional knowledge, while also having the potential to transform their professional identities (Fox & Bird, 2017; Rensfeldt et al., 2018). As educators learn new information, it can redefine who they are, what they do/do not value in their instruction, and the kinds of experiences they provide for their students. Ultimately, PL should help educators create new knowledge, develop new ways of teaching, and provide support as they work toward learning and implementing new ideas.

Designing an OPL Experience

In the fall of 2017, my colleague and I traveled 5 hours across the state to meet with a principal and teachers at a high school located in a rural town with a population of 527. The staff was concerned about the students' test scores on the state reading exam and wanted to meet with us to discuss professional development opportunities. We spent two days at the high school meeting with teachers and students to discuss their goals and concerns as it related to reading instruction.

We learned that many teachers had questions about how to incorporate reading instruction into their content area, and they were worried if their current practices were effective. From engaging with students, we learned that many saw themselves as poor readers and a little more than half claimed they did not engage with reading outside of school. However, nearly all students said they wanted to improve their reading abilities and would welcome receiving instruction that would allow them to access texts more easily.

In speaking with the principal, we agreed that teachers would benefit most from a long-term approach where they could get regular, ongoing support as they learned and applied new pedagogical techniques. However, the distance prevented me and my colleague from being able to travel to the school as often as we would have liked. Therefore, we proposed that the PL take place in a primarily online environment where teachers could receive ongoing support as they engaged with, and applied, the content. This would give them unlimited access to content and support regardless of the distance that separated us.

Background on the OPL Experience

The first step in getting the OPL launched required developing courses for teachers to take. I decided that the courses should be asynchronous and on-demand, giving teachers the opportunity to engage in the OPL when and how it best suited them. Courses were focused on learning one to three objectives. Examples of courses teachers could take included (1) What Is Disciplinary Literacy?, (2) Developing Academic Vocabulary, and (3) Understanding Reading Skills and Strategies. All courses were housed on Thinkific, a platform that allows for creating and sharing online courses. Course creators were practicing classroom teachers and/or doctoral students who specialized in literacy education. All course creators had a minimum of a master's degree in education and were current or former classroom teachers.

Teachers had access to 43 courses that covered a range of topics, including reading comprehension, writing instruction, vocabulary instruction, and use of technology to support reading and writing. Fifty-four percent of the courses (n = 23) took 5 hours to complete, and 46% (n = 20) took 15 hours to complete.

Teachers decided what course or courses they wanted to take and when. There were no prerequisites enforced. They could move as quickly or as slowly as they liked, and no deadlines were imposed. Teachers were not required to complete a course once they began it, and they could stop for any reason and/or switch to a different one. Once enrolled in a course, they had unlimited access to its content and could return to it even after it was completed.

The structure for each course was the same. Teachers were first provided with the objectives they would learn and an overview of the course. Next, they completed a pretest to determine how well they understood the objectives. After participants completed the pretest, they gained access to course content. All course content was unavailable until the pretest had been completed.

Course content was presented as videos and divided up into chapters. Each chapter focused on teaching one objective. At the end of each chapter there was a challenge where teachers demonstrated what they had learned by either (1) explaining their understanding of the concepts presented in the course and/or (2) applying concepts to their instruction and discussing what happened. Completing challenges was optional, and teachers could decide if they wanted to complete all, some, or none within a course. However, the majority of teachers (92%) chose to complete all of the challenges, with 6% choosing to do some and 2% choosing to do none. At the end of each course teachers completed a posttest. After completing the posttest, they received a certificate of completion for the course.

Launching the Experience

This study was conducted over a 2-year period. Participants were initially recruited within the PI's state through existing listservs of teachers and administrators. Participants were also recruited through the project website and social media. Any middle and high school teacher was welcome to participate. A total of 74 middle school and 116 high school teachers participated (total $n = 190$). Teachers had an average of 14 years of experience. The majority of teachers, 79%, had a master's degree ($n = 151$) followed those with a bachelor's degree, 20% ($n = 38$). One participant held a doctorate. Fifty-four percent ($n = 103$) taught English/language arts, 33% ($n = 63$) mathematics, 7% ($n = 13$) social studies, and 6% ($n = 11$) science.

Understanding the Experience

I drew on four data sources in order to understand both how teachers did/did not learn from the OPL and their perceptions of it. These data sources included (1) pre- and posttests for each course taken, (2) two surveys administered each year to understand their overall perceptions, (3) interviews focused on what information was retained over time, and (4) interviews that focused on understanding teachers' thoughts about OPL.

Understanding Teachers' Learning and Retention

The pre- and posttests embedded in each course allowed me to understand how teachers had improved their knowledge as it related to a specific course at that moment in time. However, the scores did not tell me how well teachers retained information over time. In order to understand retention, I interviewed 23 teachers for an average of 45 minutes each. I used a mix of random and purposeful selection to identify participants to be interviewed.

I first grouped teachers into one of the three categories based on how many courses they completed. Teachers were categorized as being either low-use, average-use, or super-users. The majority of teachers (*n* = 177, or 93%) engaged in an average of three courses per year and were considered to be average users. From this group, I randomly selected 15 teachers to interview and 13 agreed.

Super-users were individuals who engaged in 20 or more courses during the study. They often went straight from one course to the next with little to no break and/or engaged in multiple courses at one time. Super-users accounted for 5% of the participants, or 10 total users. Given that this group was so small, I invited all 10 to be interviewed and seven agreed. Finally, three participants (2%) were considered to be low-use users and completed one to two courses per year. I invited all three to be interviewed, and each agreed.

During the interviews, I focused on the extent to which teachers were able to retain content over time. I identified a course each teacher had completed within the last (1) year, (2) 6 months, (3) 3 months, and (4) during the month of the interview. During the interview, I asked the same questions they had been given on the posttest for the course at each timepoint. In instances where teachers had taken multiple courses within a given timeframe, I randomly selected which one would be discussed. When a teacher had not taken a course within a particular timeframe (i.e., the last 3 and/or 6 months) I focused on discussing the courses that fit into the other timeframes.

Understanding Teachers' Experiences and Perceptions

I used surveys and interviews to understand teachers' experiences and perceptions of participating in the OPL. Surveys were administered to all participants in the third and ninth month, during years 1 and 2. The purpose of each survey was to better understand (1) how and why teachers engaged with the online PD experience and (2) the factors they believed supported or hindered their use of the platform and their learning from it. Each survey asked the same set of questions.

The purpose of the interviews was to have in-depth discussions with teachers about their experiences and to better understand the survey responses. Fifteen teachers were randomly selected to discuss what they thought about their OPL experience. Interviews lasted 20–30 minutes each and took place on Zoom.

Lessons from OPL: What Teachers Thought and What They Learned

Greater Access to Information

The majority of teachers (93%) who participated in the OPL believed that having unlimited access to content allowed them to get the information they wanted, when they needed it, so they could improve their practice and be more responsive to their students. Teachers believed that being able to take courses when they wanted was the factor that most supported their learning. Andy explained:

> "I really appreciate that I can start a course whenever I want and that there are no deadlines . . . because sometimes I start a course with the intention of finishing it in a week or two but then something comes up that delays me, but I don't have to worry about that because I know I can just go right back to it when things calm down."

Having unrestricted access to content allowed participants to revisit and review it as needed. They were able to rewatch videos to help them design instruction or work through a confusion, whenever they needed to. It did not matter if they had finished the course one week, one month, or one year ago. Surveys indicated that 24% went back into at least one course each month to review the content and apply it to their instruction. Additionally, another 42% said they rewatched videos on an as-needed basis. The extent to which they rewatched videos fluctuated based on what they needed to know and when they needed a refresher. Kathleen explained:

> "I love, love, love that I can go back to the videos whenever I need to. Sometimes I am not ready to apply what I have learned. I often choose a course that I know will help me and that I will eventually use, but sometimes I might not be ready to use the information for a month or two . . . when I go to apply something new, I sometimes forget what I learned or I have a question about how to do something. Being able to go back and take a look at something again is extremely helpful to my practice."

Thirty-four percent of the teachers had previous experience with OPL. These teachers noted that, in their prior experiences, it was common for OPL to not provide unlimited access to content.

Randy shared with me his previous experiences with OPL and his belief that the way in which they were structured limited his ability to learn:

> "This isn't my first time taking courses online . . . but I think the biggest problem with what I did before was that it ran like a university course. . . . Once you purchased the PD you had so many weeks to take it and then that was it. You also couldn't move around in the course. I had to watch the first video before the second and so on which means sometimes I had to sit through things I already knew. You could go back and review content, but when your time was up, your time was up. You couldn't go back to the course to review anything once you hit that deadline."

Randy's concern was shared by others. After 2 years, an average of 78% expressed concern with OPL that did not allow them to retain access to the content. In my interview with Lea, she noted how having unrestricted access to content was critical for her long-term development:

> "I think of it like a book you buy for a course, only these are mostly videos. When a course is over, I still have the book and materials, and I can look at them again when I need to. . . . Being able to go back and watch videos again when I need to is very important, and sometimes I don't do it right away. I might take a course but then later forget something from it. That's why being able to rewatch what I want, when I want, is important to me. . . . I think it really helps with my teaching and just my overall learning."

Focused Choice

The courses available to teachers were centered on narrow topics that could be completed in a relatively short amount of time. For example, the course *The Power of Picture Books* focused on helping teachers (1) understand how picture books could help adolescents improve their reading/writing abilities and (2) create a lesson that incorporated the use of picture books for teaching a reading/writing skill or strategy. Teachers believed that having short, focused courses allowed them to identify the topics they needed to learn more about in order to address an instructional issue in a timely manner. Eighty-two percent said they preferred to engage in their PL in this format.

For example, Jennifer explained how she honed in on courses that would allow her to improve her writing instruction:

> "I've really been working on my writing instruction the last couple of years. I don't need to take all of the writing courses that you have, but I looked through the list to see what might be helpful. . . . I saw a course on how to teach grammar and thought I could use that! I

have been teaching grammar, obviously, but I think the way I do it is so bad—just super dry and boring. And so I thought that maybe a course on grammar would be helpful to me, help me motivate my students, and I loved that I could just make use of it right away!"

Jennifer's comment shows the importance of providing choice in PL—regardless of whether it is offered online or face-to-face. Providing Jennifer with PL on writing instruction, without any knowledge of what she already knew or needed to learn, could potentially be a waste of time. Rather than providing Jennifer with information she already knew, or was not ready for, the approach used here allowed her to evaluate the offerings and decide what worked best for her. If Jennifer had begun the course and had not found it helpful, she was free to leave it and try another.

Ninety-two percent of teachers indicated they believed having extensive choices allowed them to improve their overall learning. Melanie explained:

> "I appreciate that I get to pick what I want to learn and that there is a lot to choose from. . . . My experience with professional development has been that I either have to attend a workshop, and they tell me what the topic is, or I have a very limited number of options to choose from . . . and that's not what's always best for my learning or I imagine anyone else's. Sometimes what is being offered isn't what I need to be learning."

Teachers also noted that having a wide range of choices allowed them to tailor what they learned to the needs of their students. Dawn said:

> "I am very selective about what I take. I think about what my students are struggling with. Are they having problems with writing? If so, I look through the writing courses to see what might be of help. Then I take that course and apply it to how I work with my students."

In surveying participants, I learned that an average of 74% approached identifying what courses to take in similar ways. Most teachers were not concerned with how many courses they were taking. Instead, they used the available options to target their learning so that they could better support their students. Teachers identified the struggles their students were having, identified the gaps in their professional knowledge, and sought out courses that would resolve this issue. Barry explained:

> "When I'm looking at taking a course, I really think about the needs of my students. I consider where they are having difficulties but also

how I am falling short in helping them. . . . I then look for something that falls in line with that. Sometimes I start applying the information before I have even finished the course. . . . It's really exciting to be able to get access to research-based practices right when I need it, and I think it's really improved my instruction."

No Interest in Interacting

During Year 1, a central component of the OPL experience allowed teachers to share their work and receive feedback and support. Teachers were encouraged to share their work, ask questions, and respond to the work of their peers. Teachers who opted to complete a challenge were asked to share their responses within the platform. Course creators were available to provide feedback. However, the expectation was that teachers would talk about their work primarily with each other. However, at the end of Year 1 only 1% of the participants had engaged in any dialogue.

During the first year, I sent teachers four emails, one each quarter, reminding them how social interaction around their work could improve their learning. Surveys sent out during Year 1 asked teachers how and why they did/did not participate in discussions about their work or the work of others. Across all surveys from Year 1, 89% of respondents indicated they understood that participating in discussions around their work, and the work of others, would likely result in them learning more.

However, teachers claimed they had no interest in participating in discussions about their work or anyone else's. In the Year 1 surveys, 94% of teachers indicated that they were "highly unlikely" to engage in discussions around their work or the work of others. When asked why they chose not to engage in discussions around this work, teachers cited (1) lack of interest (74%), (2) limited time to participate in further discussion (93%), and/or (3) the belief that doing the challenges was enough (88%). Kimberly explained, "I don't really feel the need to talk about my work or what other people are doing. . . . I'm very busy. . . . I get a lot out of these courses, and I think what I get is enough."

Kimberly's statement that she was too busy and that what she learned was enough was a belief held by many of the teachers I spoke with. In my discussions with James, he explained that he rarely read any feedback that was provided to him about his work. However, like Kimberly, he believed that what he learned from doing the work was enough:

> "I have read some of the feedback, but I would say not most of it . . . and even if I do read it it's usually several months later and I've forgotten some of what I wrote in the first place. . . . I'm not really concerned about receiving feedback on my work or reading it because

I just don't have the time . . . but I do find the challenges to be very helpful. I like being able to put the ideas into practice, and I do think writing up what I did helps me process things and just, you know, refine my learning even more. . . . I think that between taking the courses, doing the work, and writing it all up that I learn a great deal, and I'm happy with that—even without the feedback."

While teachers may not have engaged in discussions around their work, many of them did read the feedback that was provided to them and said they found it useful. At the end of Year 1, 85% claimed they applied the feedback they received to their instruction. Mandy explained:

> "I read a lot of the feedback I'm given. . . . I don't think I've read all of it, but I'm pretty sure I have read most of it. . . . I feel like I don't have time to really read it and engage with it, but I wish I did! It [the feedback] is very useful to me, and I do think it's enhanced my learning."

The remaining 15% said they never read the feedback and had no plans to do so. Debbie said:

> "I know the feedback is there, but I've never read it. . . . I guess I just don't think about it. Like I'm doing a course to learn something, and once I've gotten through the course I feel like I learned what I came for. So, no, I'm not going back to read the feedback once I'm done. . . . I'm sure it's great. It's not a question of if it will help me. I imagine it would. . . . It's just that my brain has moved on to something else."

Where the Learning Happens

As noted earlier, teachers varied as to how many courses they took. Because there were no requirements, they could take courses when they wanted to and sign up for as many as they wanted. This resulted in teachers engaging in a range of courses for varying amounts of time. However, the majority of teachers (n = 177, or 93%) engaged in an average of three courses per year and were considered to be average users.

Pre- and posttests suggested that all participants, regardless of how many courses they took, improved their learning. The scores also suggest that the frequency of the teachers' engagement with the OPL did not matter in terms of their learning. Table 11.1 shows the average score each group obtained.

While pre- and posttest scores provide insight into how teachers improved their knowledge about literacy instruction, they do not tell us

TABLE 11.1. Pretest and Posttest Scores for Different Types of Users

Type of user	Average pretest score	Average posttest score
Low-use user	36%	81%
Average user	36%	83%
Super-user	34%	84%

how well teachers retained information over time. However, the interviews showed that average- and low-use users were able to retain an average of 75% of what they had learned from courses taken up to 1 year prior. In my interview with Nathan, an average user, we discussed his understanding of the concept of disciplinary literacy approximately 1 year after he had completed the course. On his pretest, Nathan had provided the following statement when asked to define disciplinary literacy, "This refers to the different ways we help students read and write in history, science, etc. . . . It's about things like how we teach students to read charts and graphs or use comprehension strategies."

By the time he completed the course, however, Nathan had a much different understanding of the term as evidenced by what he wrote on his posttest, "I realize now that disciplinary literacy is about specialized ways for teaching reading and writing in the different subject areas. . . . Students in my science classes need to learn how to read and write in ways that are age-appropriate but are moving them toward understanding what reading and writing looks like in the scientific community."

By comparison, interviews with super-users showed that they retained little of what they learned. For courses taken within 1 month of their interview, super-users retained an average of 75% of the content. At 3 months, their retention dropped to an average of 60%. After 6 months, it had dropped to 48%. Finally, for courses taken a year before the interview, super-users averaged 35% in terms of content retention. During our interviews, super-users were initially confident about how much they had learned. For example, Jessica stated:

> "I have taken so many courses! I really have just taken advantage of every possible opportunity to increase my knowledge about my literacy instruction. . . . It has absolutely paid off, and I have learned so much!"

An example of super-users' ability to retain information can be seen in my interview with Alexis. We began the interview by discussing a course she had completed a month before called *Introduction to*

Metacognition. I asked Alexis to start by defining the term *metacognition*, and she answered:

> "Yes, I remember this. This is the ability to be aware of your thinking . . . when students read we want them to pay attention to how well they are understanding what they have read and recognize where that understanding may fall short or they are confused. Rather than move on, we want them to have tools at their disposal they can then use to fix-up any difficulties or confusions they are having."

Alexis's response showed she understood the basic concept of metacognition and how it applied to reading. However, when we began to discuss the course *Supporting Students' Reading of Digital Texts*, which she had completed six months earlier, her retention dropped. Alexis had difficulty discussing basic concepts from the course, including how reading digital texts differed from print-based ones and how she might adjust her instruction to help students better comprehend digital texts:

> "All I can remember at this point is that there are some important differences between reading digitally versus not [print-based texts] . . . and I do know that I should give focused instruction on each. But how these types are different, besides the obvious, I can't tell you much there. . . . I remember there are some differing features, but I couldn't name them . . . and I can't tell you how I might teach each one so my students could read them both equally well. . . . I really thought I had learned this, and I remember enjoying the course because it helped me to understand the differences in print and digital texts and how to teach students to read them better. I'm pretty surprised I can't remember the details at all."

Each super-user I interviewed was confident that they had learned and retained a great deal of information. While no one believed they had perfect retention, overall, they thought they had a solid understanding of the concepts covered in the courses they had completed. When I asked Elaine how well she thought she understood content from 6 or more months ago she said:

> "I have learned just so, so much, and I have taken a lot of courses! I am sure there are things I don't remember 100% perfectly, but overall, I think I remember a lot of it very well. . . . I think I still know the big takeaways and how to apply what I learned to my teaching—stuff like that . . . I may need a reminder here and there to set me on the right path, but then I'm pretty sure I'd be good to go!"

However, as we got into our interview Elaine had difficulty recalling concepts correctly from 6 or more months earlier, even when given gentle reminders. For example, in discussing the disciplinary literacy course, I asked Elaine to explain the difference between disciplinary literacy and content area literacy. She responded, "Oh shoot! I know this. I know I know this. I do remember that they are different, but I cannot remember how."

I next asked her if she could define either term thinking that doing so might illuminate the difference. She responded:

> "Ugh. This is frustrating. I feel like it's on the tip of my tongue, and I can't get it out. They are different. I know that. One is more focused on teaching strategies, right? But aren't they both focused on teaching strategies? I know it's about teaching reading in the different subject areas, and I know they are different, but I can't remember how they are different. . . . I guess I didn't remember some of this stuff as well as I thought!"

"Well," I said, "content-area literacy is typically thought of as a more generic approach to helping students learn to read and write within the content areas. Does that help?" Elaine shook her head and responded:

> "I wish it did, but it doesn't. It's just not coming back to me the way I thought it would. . . . You know I really didn't understand a lot of what the courses were about when I began them, and I thought I learned so much from them! I know I did learn from them, but why am I having problems with some of it? It seems like the further back we go the less I remember."

Conclusion

PL is critical in helping middle and high school teachers build their knowledge in providing effective literacy instruction for diverse learners. OPL has shown the potential to reach and engage teachers in ways that traditional face-to-face learning has not (Collins & Liang, 2015; Fishman et al., 2013). However, to date, the research base for OPL is limited. This study was able to identify critical factors that can be used to help engage and support teachers in their learning in online contexts.

First, teachers want to have choice in what they take and when they take it. When given the opportunity to choose freely, teachers often selected content that would be of the most immediate use. Providing such access requires PL, in general, to be structured differently than it has been in the past. Rather than have set dates and times for engaging in their learning, teachers prefer to start their learning when it best aligns with their instructional needs. Although some teachers will take courses out of pure interest and may not have plans to implement what they learned, the majority identify topics they plan to use in the near future.

In order to accommodate teachers in identifying and starting courses when it makes sense to them, OPL must be structured so that they can start at any time and have unlimited access even after they have finished. Most PL, be it face-to-face or online, comes with imposed deadlines. Even when teachers have control over when they can start learning, there is often a time limit as to when they must be finished. Once this limit is reached, they no longer have access to the content. However, teachers will go back to content as needed as they begin to implement what they learned. Having ongoing access allows them to review areas where they have questions or may be struggling.

Although teachers preferred being able to choose what they learned and when they learned it, this study found two important factors to consider when engaging teachers in OPL. First, there may be a limit on how much information can be retained over time. Researchers have varied in their recommendations for how much time is required to make a difference in teachers' PL (Parsons et al., 2019). For in-person PL, researchers have argued that 14 contact hours may buy an optimal amount of time, coupled with a blend of in-person workshops, time to apply what was learned, and focused coaching sessions and/or additional workshops that are sustained over time (Darling-Hammond et al., 2017; Desimone & Stuckey, 2014).

In OPL, such as this, teachers did not have to focus their learning on one topic (i.e., improving comprehension instruction). They were able to choose what they learned and when; this gave them the freedom to take courses on a number of topics. Super-users then did not engage in sustained, focused learning on a single topic but rather exposed themselves to a broad range of ideas. This lack of focus, in addition to consistently taking in larger amounts of information, may be what created issues with their retention.

Finally, this study identified an important challenge that we must address in OPL going forward. The teachers in this study were given the opportunity to participate in an interactive community around their work, and they were provided with information about how such information could support their learning. While teachers understood that participating in the community should strengthen their learning, they had no interest in participating. In order to optimize the potential that OPL offers, we should consider how we can structure such communities so that they provide teachers with focused opportunities to examine and discuss their work.

REFERENCES

Alrasheedi, M., Capretz, L. F., & Raza, A. (2015). A systematic review of the critical factors for success of mobile learning in higher education (University students' perspective). *Journal of Educational Computing Research, 52,* 257–276.

Borup, J., & Evmenova, A. S. (2019). The effectiveness of professional development in overcoming obstacles to effective online instruction in a college of education. *Online Learning, 23,* 1–20.

Cho, M.-H., & Tobias, S. (2016). Should instructors require discussion in online courses? Effects of online discussion on community of inquiry, learner time, satisfaction, and achievement. *The International Review of Research in Open and Distributed Learning, 17*(2), 123–140.

Collins, L. J., & Liang, X. (2015). Examining high-quality online teacher professional development: Teachers' voices. *International Journal of Teacher Leadership, 6*(1), 1–17.

Darling-Hammond, L., Hyler, M. E., & Gardner, M. (2017). *Effective teacher professional development.* Learning Policy Institute.

Darling-Hammond, L. Wei, R. C., Andree, A., Richardson, N., & Orphanos, S. (2009). *Professional learning in the learning profession: A status report on teacher development in the United States and abroad.* National Staff Development Council.

Dede, C., Ketelhut, D. J., Whitehouse, P., Breit, L., & McCloskey, E. M. (2009). A research agenda for online teacher professional development. *Journal of Teacher Education, 60,* 8–9.

Desimone, L. (2009). Improving impact studies of teachers' professional development: Toward better conceptualizations and measures. *Educational Researcher, 38,* 181–199.

Desimone, L., & Stuckey, D. (2014). Sustaining professional development. In. L. Martin, S. Kragler, D. Quatroche, & K. Bauserman (Eds.), *Handbook of professional development in education: Successful models and practices, PreK–12* (pp. 467–482). Guilford Press.

Duffy, G. G. (2004). Teachers who improve reading achievement: What research says about what they do and how to develop them. In D. Strickland & M. L. Kamil (Eds.), *Improving reading achievement through professional development* (pp. 3–22). Christopher-Gordon.

Fishman, B. J., Konstantopoulos, S., Kubitskey, B. W., Vath, R., Park, G., Johnson, H., & Edelson, D. C. (2013). Comparing the impact of online and face-to-face professional development in the context of curriculum implementation. *Journal of Teacher Education, 64,* 426–438.

Fox, S., & Bird, T. (2017). The challenges to professionals of using social media: Teachers in England negotiating personal-professional identities. *Education and Information Technologies, 22,* 647–675.

Hardin, B. L., & Koppenhaver, D. A. (2016). Flipped professional development: An innovation in response to teacher insights. *Journal of Adolescent and Adult Literacy, 60,* 45–54.

Huang, R. Yang, W., & Li, H. (2019). On the road to participatory pedagogy: A mixed-methods study of pedagogical interaction in Chinese kindergartens. *Teaching and Teacher Education, 85,* 81–91.

Hunt, C. S. (2016). Getting to the heart of the matter: Discursive negotiations of emotions within literacy coaching interactions. *Teaching and Teacher Education, 60,* 331–343.

Knight, J. (2007). *Instructional coaching: A partnership approach to improving instruction.* Corwin Press.

Korthagen, F. A. J. (2010). How teacher education can make a difference. *Journal of Education for Teaching, 36,* 407–423.

Kragler, S., Martin, L. E., & Sylvester, R. (2014). Lessons learned: What our history and research tell us about teachers' professional learning. In L. E. Martin, S. Kragler, D. J. Quatroche, & K. L. Bauserman (Eds.), *Handbook of professional development in education: Successful models and practices, PreK–12* (pp. 483–505). Guilford Press.

LaPointe-McEwan, D. Deluca, C., & Klinger, D. A. (2017). Supporting evidence use in networked professional learning: the role of the middle leader. *Educational Research, 59,* 136–153.

Lave, J., & Wenger, E. (1991). *Situated learning: Legitimate peripheral participation.* Cambridge University Press.

McQuiggan, S., Kosturko, L., McQuiggan, J., & Sabourin, J. (2015). *Mobile learning: A handbook for developers, educators, and learners.* Wiley.

National Assessment of Educational Progress. (2019). 2019 reading assessment results. Retrieved from *www.nationsreportcard.gov.*

Osman, D. J., & Warner, J. R. (2020). Measuring teacher motivation: The missing link between professional development and practice. *Teaching and Teacher Education, 92,* 1–12.

Oztok, M., & Kehrwald, B. A. (2017). Social presence reconsidered: Moving beyond, going back, or killing social presence. *Distance Education, 38,* 259–266.

Paquette, P. (2016). Instructing the instructors: Training instructors to use social presence cues in online courses. *Journal of Educators Online, 13,* 80–108.

Parsons, S., Hutchinson, A., Hall, L., Ward-Parsons, A., Ives, S., & Leggett, A. (2019). U.S. teachers' perceptions of online professional development. *Teaching and Teacher Education, 82,* 33–42.

Pella, S. (2011). A situative perspective on developing writing pedagogy in a teacher professional learning community. *Teacher Education Quarterly, 38,* 107–125.

Powell, C. G., & Bodur, Y. (2019). Teachers' perceptions of an online professional development experience: Implications for a design and implementation framework. *Teaching and Teacher Education, 77,* 19–30.

Rensfeldt, A., Hillman, T., & Selywn, N. (2018). Teachers 'liking' their work?: Exploring the realities of teacher Facebook groups. *British Educational Research Journal, 44,* 230–250.

Sailors, M., & Price, L. (2015). Support for the Improvement of Practices through Intensive Coaching (SIPIC): A model of coaching for improving reading instruction and reading achievement. *Teaching and Teacher Education, 45,* 115–127.

Sharples, M., Taylor, J., & Vavoula, G. (2016). A theory of learning for the mobile age. In C. Haythornthwaite, R. Andrews, J. Fransman, & E. M. Meyers (Eds.), *The SAGE handbook of e-learning research* (2nd ed., pp. 63–81). SAGE.

Shuler, C. (2009). *Pockets of potential: Using mobile technologies to promote children's learning.* Joan Ganz Cooney Center at Sesame Workshop.

Spires, H. A., Kerkhoff, S. N., & Graham, A. (2016). Disciplinary literacy and inquiry: Teaching for deeper content learning. *Journal of Adolescent and Adult Literacy, 60,* 151–161.

Stoetzel, L., & Shedrow, S. (2020). Coaching our coaches: How online learning can address the gap in preparing K–12 instructional coaches. *Teaching and Teacher Education, 88,* 1–11.

von Glasersfeld, E. (1995). *Radical constructivism. A way of knowing and learning.* Falmer Press.

Vygotsky, L. S. (1980). *Mind in society: The development of higher psychological processes.* Harvard University Press.

EPILOGUE

Creating Professional Learning That Works

Lessons for Going Forward

Leigh A. Hall

Professional learning (PL) is an important component of equitable, high-quality classroom instruction for all students. Through PL educators can enhance their instructional knowledge and learn a range of strategies and techniques to support student learning. As the authors of this volume have noted, effective PL must consider a range of factors about the teachers they serve as well as the social and cultural contexts of their learning. In this epilogue, we conclude by examining the themes that have emerged from this book regarding best practices in PL and the research that we need to ensure its continued success.

Designing PL

PL must be designed so that it is continuous, systematic, and intentional (see Greenleaf et al., Chapter 3; Amendum et al., Chapter 5). Teachers need PL that is designed to support deep pedagogical and content knowledge related to how students learn to read and write. However, the gaps that teachers have in their knowledge about designing literacy instruction will vary across grades, content areas, and the needs of the students they serve. PL should therefore be designed so that it identifies these gaps and works with teachers over time to both learn and apply new instructional strategies.

Designing PL so that it is responsive to teachers' needs means moving away from a one-size-fits-all approach. Even when teachers have similar gaps in their knowledge of literacy instruction, that does not mean they need to learn the same things at the same time. The knowledge teachers need to develop should align with the needs of their students and the goals they have in place for them. This means that for PL to be truly responsive, it should be a collaborative effort between teachers and teacher educators that results in a more customized approach.

Multiple authors in this volume have considered how PL might be made more customizable and how teachers can be supported in their application of new pedagogical techniques. For example, Amendum and colleagues (Chapter 5) designed a PL model where teachers received real-time virtual coaching tailored to not only building their knowledge about reading instruction but also to helping them understand how to adapt instructions for students with reading difficulties. A key component of Amendum's model was that it engaged teachers in situated learning where their coaching experiences were grounded in the everyday work of their daily instruction and the successes and challenges that arose within it. Situated learning theory posits that the PL that teachers receive will be more effective when it occurs within the context that the new knowledge is being applied (Korthagen, 2010; Langer, 2009). Because teachers received feedback specific to their context, their learning became both situated and customized in ways that could allow them to provide instruction equitable for each student.

Whereas Amendum and colleagues used digital tools to design PL that was situated, Padesky et al. showed how the tools can be used to support teachers' agency in their own learning. In Chapter 9, Padesky et al. examined how a digital repository and a communication link, in combination with in-person coaching, can be used to engage teachers in sustained interactions, on their time, with colleagues and teacher educators. Through co-creating structures and processes around their PL, Padesky et al. sought to place teachers' voices front and center, giving them extensive agency in their PL experience. While the school they worked in identified a shared goal, teachers were able to design a path for how they would reach it, allowing their PL to be situated within their classroom contexts.

Research on the importance of teacher agency in PL has increased over the last decade (Imants & Van der Wal, 2020). Professional agency occurs when teachers are given the structures and opportunities to make choices that impact their learning and their work (Eteläpelto et al., 2013). When teachers have some degree of autonomy in shaping their learning, it can result in increased motivation to learn and changes in their instruction (Goller & Paloniemi, 2017; Vähäsantanen & Eteläpelto, 2011).

Despite the benefits of agency, it is not without its pitfalls. Giving teachers agency over the problems that need to be addressed, and how they should approach understanding and respond to them, can limit teachers' access to expertise (Horn, 2016). While teachers can learn when given agency in their PL, how they frame the problems plaguing them and how they go about designing a PL plan can vary based on their experience and degree of understanding (Horn, 2016). Teachers who have a greater depth and more nuanced understanding of a given problem are more likely to understand the complexity of it and engage in more sophisticated approaches for addressing them.

In Chapter 11, Hall shows the challenges that teacher agency can bring to bear on their PL. In Hall's study, teachers were able to choose what they wanted to learn and were able to participate in a community where their learning was shared and discussed. The majority of teachers reported that they selected topics that aligned with their most immediate professional needs. However, teachers were largely uninterested in sharing and discussing their work with others. They cited a lack of time and interest as their reasons for not in these discussions. The teachers who were interviewed fully recognized that their decisions to not participate in discussions likely limited their learning. However, they were all happy with what they did learn from engaging with the content and applying it to their instruction. This suggests that although teacher agency is critical to PL, it can also limit if, when, and how teachers choose to learn as well as the relationships they form.

While teacher agency can be important in PL, limited research suggests that access to an expert coach may have the strongest influence on changes in teachers' instructional practices (Sun et al., 2014). Interactions with colleagues can and does support teacher learning (Lave & Wenger, 1991). However, coaches who are viewed as experts in their field can influence and shape those interactions and potentially strengthen them so that they are more effective even when the coaches are not present (Coburn & Russell, 2008).

PL and Relationships

The relationships created over time between teachers and the teacher educators who work with them are a critical component of PL (Thompson et al., 2020). It is through these relationships that teachers gain confidence to try out new pedagogical approaches, become open to hearing feedback, and provide support for others. Strong relationships can also support collaborations and provide space for teachers to openly reflect on, and critique, their practices.

Nearly every chapter in this book has touched on the importance of relationship building in face-to-face, hybrid, and purely virtual contexts both in terms of the positive benefits of what relationship building can do and what happens when it falls short or is missing. As Le Fevre notes in Chapter 1, PL is an incredibly complex endeavor that requires a range of interactions within and across different groups of people. Even when groups want to use PL to tackle the same problem, their expertise, understanding, and approaches to doing so will vary. How PL is then structured, and the stances stakeholders take and engage in, can then set the tone for how relationships are created and enacted.

Le Fevre stresses the importance of fostering an evaluative inquiry stance that emphasizes the impact of PL on students. Such a stance is shared by Reichenberg (Chapter 6) who argues for framing PL around the concerns and challenges teachers are experiencing so that the learning becomes powerful, meaningful, and authentic. As a result, PL can become collaborative, with everyone involved sharing expertise, reflecting on what is/is not working, and building relationships where success is created together.

How such relationships get formed and the impact they can have on PL can shift and even become tricky to navigate, when PL morphs into hybrid and purely online forms. For example, three chapters—Brock et al. (Chapter 2), Padesky et al. (Chapter 9), and Ippolito et al. (Chapter 10)—discuss the importance of relationship building in hybrid environments. Hybrid environments offer multiple benefits for PL. First, they can allow teacher educators to work with teachers who may live a significant distance away—limiting how often they can interact in person. Second, they offer teachers opportunities to engage with learning when it best suits their schedule.

In virtual spaces, relationships can be more challenging to form, as informal, unplanned interactions do not naturally occur and are instead replaced with synchronous and asynchronous discussions and events. This can limit or restrict interactions and the ability to form strong relationships. However, as Ippolito noted, while creating relationships becomes more challenging in a digital space, they are just as critical, if not more so, to work toward developing. Ippolito argues that, in virtual spaces, we need to be flexible about how we form relationships and provide teachers with multiple, and sometimes optional, opportunities for interactions that will allow them to connect in ways that best suit their needs.

The environments that PL takes place in play an important role in building relationships and fostering the different stances researchers have discussed. The greater our connection with each person in a group is, the higher our interactions will be with each other, allowing interpersonal relationships to form. Strong interpersonal relationships result in greater connections between individuals and influence how motivated teachers are both in their own learning and in supporting the learning of their colleagues (Armellini & De Stefani, 2016). In purely online contexts the formation of these relationships is critical for creating a sense of belonging and reducing isolation.

For example, in many of the chapters (e.g., Amendum et al., Chapter 5; Brock et al., Chapter 2; Padesky et al., Chapter 9; Ippolito et al., Chapter 10), regular structured engagements with teachers allowed for relationships to form over time through in-person meetings and conversations where connections could be further developed. However, Hall's chapter (Chapter 11) shows the challenges of fostering relationships in a purely asynchronous environment. Discussion boards can foster relationships and support learning even in purely asynchronous environments where the participants have never met (Wenting et al., 2021). However, in this case teachers enacted their agency in ways they believed supported their own learning and not the community as a whole. As a result, no relationships were formed, and the community did not flourish. This suggests that giving teachers options in how they engage with purely asynchronous learning can result in compromising relationship and community development as well as overall learning.

Future Research in PL

Throughout this book, we have examined how we can design literacy PL that is sustainable, equitable, and responsive to educators and the students they serve. The researchers featured within have shown that forming relationships, understanding cultural and social contexts, and providing flexible opportunities for learning are critical if we want to construct learning experiences that are supportive. While all the chapters have highlighted what has worked, they also have stressed the areas that we need to continue to examine if we want to refine our PL models and make the most of them.

First, multiple authors stressed the importance of creating relationships and fostering a community within PL environments. Creating strong relationships allows for all participants to be comfortable in sharing their goals, providing feedback, and sharing where they need help. The role of relationships is critical in creating a sustainable culture of PL. Studies that examine how relationships are formed within and among teachers of varying backgrounds and experiences can help us get at more nuanced approaches and identify factors that constrain and support a culture of PL.

However, relationships exist inside cultural contexts. Future research will want to consider how cultures of PL are created within and across contexts. Educators have many options for how they engage with their PL, and the researchers in this book showed a range including face-to-face, hybrid, and online. Although not examined in this book, it is important to note that educators also have the opportunity to engage in private, online groups that exchange ideas, information, and feedback. Understanding how teachers carve these paths for themselves and how their networks influence their learning can help us identify the characteristics of both hybrid and online models that provide for more personalized learning as well as understand how teachers engage in more independent PL practices.

Several chapters focused on using virtual spaces to facilitate PL. The research on how virtual spaces can be used for PL is relatively new and still emerging. However, virtual spaces provide critical ways for teacher educators to engage with teachers in ways that support flexibility in learning and that can be customized to their most immediate needs. Future research will want to consider a number of questions such as (1) what kinds of designs best support PL in online environments, (2) should online learning be a mix of synchronous and asynchronous opportunities and what role might in-person learning have within it, and (3) when might PL be more beneficial face-to-face and when might it serve a better purpose within a virtual space?

Additionally, future research will want to examine how we can foster communities and relationships within these virtual environments in ways that support learning. Given the importance of community and relationship development in teacher learning, it is critical that we consider how to foster it within virtual environments and the factors that support and inhibit its development. While asynchronous learning has a lot to offer in terms of access, it may be limited to the extent that it can foster relationships that support learning. Future research may wish to consider the degree to which learning is limited, when communities and relationships are not fostered, and if that trade-off is relatively acceptable.

REFERENCES

Armellini, A., & De Stefani, M. (2016). Social presence in the 21st century: An adjustment to the community of inquiry framework. *British Journal of Educational Technology, 47,* 1202–1216.

Coburn, C. E., & Russell, J. L. (2008). District policy and teachers' social networks. *Educational Evaluation and Policy Analysis, 30,* 203–235.

Eteläpelto, A., Vähäsantanen, K., Hökkä, P., & Paloniemi, S. (2013). What is agency?: Conceptualizing professional agency at work. *Educational Research Review, 10,* 45–65.

Goller, M., & Paloniemi, S. (2017). Agency at work, learning, and professional development: An introduction. In M. Goller & S. Paloniemi (Eds.), *Agency at work: An agentic perspective on professional learning and development* (pp. 1–14). Springer.

Horn, I. (2016). Professional development is broken, but be careful how we fix it. Retrieved from *https://teachingmathculture.wordpress.com/2016/03/07/professional-development-is-broken-but-be-careful-how-we-fix-it.*

Imants, J., & Van der Wal, M. M. (2020) A model of teacher agency in professional development and school reform. *Journal of Curriculum Studies, 52*(1), 1–14.

Korthagen, F. A. J. (2010). Situated learning theory and the pedagogy of teacher education: Towards an integrative view of teacher behavior and teacher learning. *Teaching and Teacher Education, 26,* 98–106.

Langer, P. (2009). Situated learning: What ever happened to educational psychology? *Educational Psychology Review, 21,* 181–192.

Lave, J., & Wenger, E. (1991). *Situated learning: Legitimate peripheral participation.* Cambridge University Press.

Sun, M., Wilhelm, A. G., Larson, C. J., & Frank, K. A. (2014). Exploring colleagues' professional influence on mathematics teachers' learning. *Teachers College Record, 116*(6), 305–335.

Thompson, P. W., Kriewaldt, J. A., & Redman, C. (2020). Elaborating a model for teacher professional learning to sustain improvement in teaching practice. *Australian Journal of Teacher Education, 45*(2), 81–103.

Vähäsantanen, K., & Eteläpelto, A. (2011). Vocational teachers' pathways in the course of a curriculum reform. *Journal of Curriculum Studies, 43*(3), 291–312.

Wenting, Z., Xiao, H., Zilong, P., Chenglu, L., Ying, C., & Min, L. (2021). Exploring the relationship between social presence and learners' prestige in MOOC discussion forums using automated content analysis and social network analysis. *Computers in Human Behavior, 115,* 1–17.

Index

Note. *f* or *t* following a page number indicates a figure or a table.